Bingeworthy British Television

Bingeworthy British Television

The Best Brit TV
You Can't
Stop Watching

Sarah Cords and Jackie Bailey

Published in 2019 by Citizen Reader Books
Madison, WI
www.citizenreader.com

ISBN-13: 978-0-9600487-0-0
ISBN: 0-9600487-0-7

Library of Congress Control Number: 2019902243

Cover designed by Rob Williams, Fiverr.com/cal5086
Cover photograph courtesy of Ashlan Bishop

Contents

Historical Dramas

Crime Dramas

Introduction

I have always loved television. I didn't get to watch a whole lot of it when I was little, but when I did, I was just happy to watch anything: *Family Ties*, *The Muppet Show*, *Cheers*, *Northern Exposure*, *The X-Files*; these shows and many more comprised my favorites, and I was forever blowing off chores and homework to sneak in a little more time with my beloved TV (or, I should say, my brother's beloved TV—in the days before screens were everywhere my family had one television in the living room, and the one my oldest brother had saved up to buy in his bedroom, where I could watch while my mother thought I was doing my algebra in *my* bedroom).

And then one day, when I was in my twenties, I stumbled across an episode of the drama *Ballykissangel* on my local PBS station. It was on at eight o'clock on Saturday nights, and even though at that age I was supposed to be out with my peers, increasingly I found myself staying in to find out what happened in the doomed love affair between Father Peter Clifford (a celibate Roman Catholic priest) and Assumpta Fitzgerald (the feisty local pub owner).

The story of my life since then has been one of moving ever more steadily away from American television (I couldn't even tell you what's on these days. *Modern Family*? Are they still making new episodes of *Modern Family*?) and towards British television. For a long time I had to rely on PBS and DVDs from my library, but now…it's everywhere, available through several screening services and online.

It's heaven.

What I'm missing, though, is someone to bingewatch Brit TV with. The mister enjoys an episode here and there of *Death in Paradise* and *Doc Martin*, but he, silly man, seems to want to make a living, exercise periodically, read, raise the children and do other things that seriously get in the way of our television-viewing time.

So the first thing I did was go and find myself a British friend, who actually lives in Great Britain, to talk with me about all the great programmes (that's the way she spells "programs"! I love her so much!) and to let me know how she and her nation are feeling about extremely important subjects like Meghan Markle, Doctor Who finally being a woman, and all the plot twists in *Bodyguard*. And this has really made my life better. But once you've got one friend to watch telly with, you find yourself wanting to share it with even more friends.

So I wrote this book, to share some of the best and most widely available British and Irish (and even some Canadian and Australian) television series around, in the hopes that you will find them and watch them with me.

A Word about the Format of the Book

The book is divided into six main genres of television: Comedies, Dramas, Historical Dramas (also known as "Period Dramas"), Crime Dramas, Historical Crime Dramas, and Literary Adaptations. For each series included, we have provided information about how long the series ran (and how long it will take you to bingewatch it), who wrote it, what it's about, why it's bingeworthy, main cast members, trivia, and what other similar programs you might want to bingewatch next.

In sidebars throughout the book you will find insight from Jackie, our resident Great Britain resident, who provides us with all the "need to know" insider info we could want, like: What makes British television unique? Why are their series so short? Why are there so few guns in British police dramas?

And yes, I am well aware that I have left out a massive amount of wonderful programs. If I'd included every British program I've watched a thousand times (I'm looking at you, *The Ice House*), this book would have been 500 pages long. Jackie and I tried our hardest to choose representative shows in each genre, shows that were very popular when they first ran in the UK, and shows that are still easily available (either on DVD or any number of streaming services) today. We also chose to think optimistically and leave some series for our next book!

At the end of the book you will find thematic lists of programs and a comprehensive index so you can find your favorite title right away.

Now, go get a cuppa, put your feet up, and get ready to watch some of Great Britain's—make that, the world's—best television. Are you sitting comfortably? Then let's begin.

Comedies

Absolutely Fabulous

Run Time

The first three series of half-hour episodes aired from 1992 to 1995, and were capped with a two-part finale episode. Two more series aired from 2001 to 2005, and included three special one-off episodes. A small series of three episodes aired from 2011 to 2012, and a feature film was released in 2016. Total run time? About twenty-four hours, give or take a couple of Comic Relief Sketches, and including the ninety minutes of the feature film.

Creator and Writers

The show began as a sketch on the comedy variety show *French and Saunders*, with Jennifer Saunders as the whiny Baby Boomer mother and Dawn French playing the straight-laced daughter who was doing the actual parenting in the duo. French and Saunders continued as the primary writers, with assistance on eight episodes from comedian Sue Perkins.

What It's About

Ah, the worlds of fashion and beauty magazines and eternal youth. These are the worlds that Edina ("Eddie") Monsoon and her best mate, Patsy Stone, inhabit and seek to rule. Of course, they are mortal women just like the rest of us, but they refuse to bow to that reality and simply try harder to know more faces, ingest more alcoholic and pharmaceutical concoctions, and wear more expensive and exclusive designers than anyone else.

Interfering with their mojo, but only slightly, are Eddie's prim teenaged daughter, Saffron ("Saffy"), whose hatred for her mother's best friend Patsy lies under the thinnest of veils; Eddie's stream of ex-husbands and their new partners, who frequently pop in to visit; and Eddie's mother June, who often joins with Saffy to point out the more ridiculous aspects of Eddie's and Patsy's lifestyles and obsessions (a source, it must be said, of much rich material).

Why It's Bingeworthy

The beating heart of *Ab Fab* (as it's known by its most dedicated fans) is the codependent best-friendship between Eddie and Patsy. Heading into middle age, fighting it every step of the way, the two do have careers (Eddie as the head of her own PR firm and Patsy as a fashion magazine editor), but the thing that really keeps them going is their shared desire to stay forever

4

young, reliving their 1960s glory days, and their talent for completely ignoring everyone else's opinions. They are very much a closed unit, and they like it that way. Everyone who's been lucky enough to have had a best friend who will back them up no matter what they do will recognize themselves in these women.

Over the course of the show's five series and two decades, Edina and Patsy traveled to France and New York City, Saffy had a baby of her own (with an accompanying love relationship arguably even more complicated than any her mother ever had), and their house went through a number of disasters and accompanying makeovers, but at the heart of the show was the fact that its four tough leading women refused to soften, evolve, or age into quiet obscurity.

Never has caustic codependency been so much fun. This is one of the best-known Britcoms around, and any Anglophile worthy of that title will want to watch this program.

Main Cast

Jennifer Saunders…Edina Monsoon
Joanna Lumley…Patsy Stone
Julia Sawalha…Saffron Monsoon
June Whitfield…Mother (Edina's)

Trivia

Roseanne Barr bought the rights to adapt the series for America in the 1990s, but never followed through on the project.

Although she played her daughter on the program, Julia Sawalha is only ten years younger than Jennifer Saunders.

What to Binge on Next

Diehard fans of *Ab Fab* might also go to the comedy well from which the program sprang: the original run of the sketch show *French and Saunders*, starring Dawn French and Jennifer Saunders.

Caustic put-downs fly constantly between all the characters on *Absolutely Fabulous*; they also do so on the comedy *Vicious*, starring Ian McKellen and Derek Jacobi as partners who show their love for each other (and their friends) with incessant (and completely hilarious) insults.

As Time Goes By

Run Time

This program first aired between 1992 and 2002, and concluded with two reunion specials in 2005. The program's regular episodes were thirty minutes long, while the specials were an hour long, making for a total run time of roughly thirty-five hours.

Creator and Writers

The original concept was TV writer's Colin Bostock-Smith's, but Bob Larbey, who is also well known for such Britcoms as *The Good Life* and *Brush Strokes* (co-written with John Esmonde), wrote all of the episodes.

What It's About

Is it possible to rekindle your first love affair?

Jean Pargetter and Lionel Hardcastle first fell in love in London during the Korean War, while Jean was working as a nurse and Lionel was about to be posted to Korea. They lost contact (Jean's letter to Lionel went astray and he was too proud to write her first), only to run into each other again decades later. When they meet for the second time, Jean is a widow with an adult daughter, and Lionel is divorced and newly back from Kenya, where he ran a coffee plantation for many years.

Even though they are both, ahem, advanced in years, Jean's and Lionel's second courtship has all the angst of a relationship among teenagers–will they or won't they? Luckily for the viewer, it takes an enjoyably long time and many wrong turns to find out if they can pick up where they left off.

Why It's Bingeworthy

If you ask me what one show perfectly captures the British spirit of humor and romance perfectly...this is the show. But I am, perhaps, biased; this is the one show above all others that I could watch on an infinite loop.

The romance is there; once they get over an extremely rocky start to their new relationship, hardly an episode goes by without Lionel or Jean saying something suitably understated (and therefore British) but also very loving to one another. The comedy is there too; not only in the situations, but particularly in the characters and their lively dialogue with one another.

Dame Judi Dench and Geoffrey Palmer seem perfectly cast and the chemistry is just as lively between them as it is between any number of younger couples in film or on television. The supporting cast is also strong; a particular stand-out is Philip Bretherton as the dashing Alistair Deacon, who annoys both his love interest Judith (and the viewer) with his fear of commitment, but who also never fails to be charming.

Main Cast

Judi Dench... Jean Pargetter
Geoffrey Palmer...Lionel Hardcastle
Moira Brooker...Judith Hanson
Jenny Funnell...Sandy Edwards
Philip Bretherton...Alistair Deacon

Trivia

The program placed twenty-ninth on the "Britain's Best Sitcom" poll list created in 2004 by the BBC.

Many scenes in the show were filmed at a real house in Holland Park. Midway through the series, the first owners of the home moved, and the BBC had to "woo the new owners" to get them to continue to allow filming at the home.

What to Binge on Next

Judi Dench was no stranger to playing a wry older woman who's still up for romance when she starred in *As Time Goes By*. In the earlier sitcom *A Fine Romance*, also penned by Bob Larbey, she played a similar role opposite her real-life husband Michael Williams.

Another classic series, this one from the 1980s, also highlights a couple who manage to make fumbling toward their romantic entanglement last for several seasons was the similarly gentle and very funny series *To the Manor Born*.

Blackadder

Run Time

Everywhere I've looked, each of the four seasons of *Blackadder* are titled and described as four discrete productions: *The Black Adder*, *Blackadder II*, *Blackadder the Third*, and *Blackadder Goes Forth*. Each of these four series (which aired in 1983, 1986, 1987, and 1989, respectively) included six thirty-minute episodes, making for a series run time of twelve hours, while multiple specials (*Blackadder: The Cavalier Years*, *Blackadder's Christmas Carol*, and *Blackadder: Back & Forth*) would add another nearly two hours to your viewing time, if you can find them.

Creator and Writers

Richard Curtis and Rowan Atkinson created the show, with Atkinson helping Curtis to write the first season. The subsequent seasons were written by Curtis and Ben Elton.

What It's About

Ever wanted to learn British history in a completely mean-spirited, hilarious, and inaccurate way? Then the classic comedy series *Black Adder* is for you! In each of the four different seasons of this comedy classic, the creators tackled a different period in British history: the fifteenth century (during the reign of a fictional king, Richard IV); the Elizabethan era, starring Queen Bess, of course; the late nineteenth century during the reign of George III; and during 1917 and the Great War (World War I).

Each series featured the main character Edmund Blackadder, who started the series as a scheming bastard and whose descendants, all named Edmund Blackadder, became increasingly smarter as their family fortunes and class status fell (don't feel too badly—all of the Edmunds were unpleasant and cynical beasts). Edmund's comic foil throughout is his servant Baldrick, whose descendants also appear in each subsequent series as a general "dogsbody" to each Blackadder, and who become progressively dumber and more slovenly. Also present in every series is at least one dim-witted aristocratic friend, whose connections Blackadder both disparages and seeks to exploit at any turn.

Why It's Bingeworthy

Public opinion seems to agree that the program got much better after its uneven first season, so be sure to watch beyond series one (or just skip to series two and go onward from there). Once the show ironed out its rough humor and characterization parts, it went on to become one of the most-loved and iconic sitcoms ever produced in the U.K., and as such, is important viewing for those of us who consider ourselves English at heart (if not birth).

Many of its writers and stars would go on to become comic icons in their own rights: Richard Curtis wrote the popular series *The Vicar of Dibley* and the films *Four Weddings and a Funeral* and *Love Actually*; Ben Elton, already well-known for co-writing *The Young Ones*, also wrote the series *The Thin Blue Line* (starring Rowan Atkinson). Rowan Atkinson, of course, found superstardom as Mr. Bean, and Hugh Laurie, who starred in the third and fourth series, went on to star in the American TV drama *House* and a ton of other programs. These are important people to know!

Main Cast

Rowan Atkinson...Edmund Blackadder
Tony Robinson...Baldrick
Tim McInnerney...Lord Percy Percy/Captain Kevin Darling
Hugh Laurie...The Prince Regent/Lieutenant George
Miranda Richardson...Queen Elizabeth I/Amy Hardwood/Mary Fletcher-Brown
Stephen Fry...Melchett

Trivia

In a 2004 poll to determine Britain's best sitcom of all time, this show placed second (*Only Fools and Horses* took the top spot).

In the original series, Edmund Blackadder was based on a character in Shakespeare's play *King Lear*, also named Edmund, who schemed to steal the throne from his father.

What to Binge on Next

Although Rowan Atkinson only wrote for the first series of *Blackadder*, if you're a fan of his you might also want to watch the hugely popular program in which he starred, *Mr. Bean*, or the movies that were spun off from it (he also starred in the underrated comedy *The Thin Blue Line*, which was also written by Elton).

Comedians Hugh Laurie and Stephen Fry both play important parts in this series; you might want to seek out another historical comedy in which they co-starred, *Jeeves and Wooster*, or track down their variety comedy program *A Bit of Fry and Laurie*.

Viewers interested in tracking down all the classic British TV programs they can find might also consider other "top five" sitcoms from the 2004 BBC poll list mentioned above: *Only Fools and Horses*, *Fawlty Towers*, *The Vicar of Dibley*, and *Dad's Army*.

Jackie on...
How to Know You're
Watching TV in the UK

The Watershed

In the UK, children are protected from watching unsuitable content by 'the watershed'. This is a set of rules that governs when programmes with adult material are allowed to be shown. Generally, this means that nothing unsuitable for children is allowed to be broadcast before 9pm.

Sexual content, violence, offensive language and drug taking are all banned from appearing before 9pm and 18-rated content mustn't be shown before 10pm. In recent years programmes have tried to push theses boundaries and the watershed isn't as strong as it used to be, but if you're in the UK be prepared for a sudden change of tone in programming at 9pm!

The TV Licence

Every household in the UK that watches or records television is required, by law, to purchase a TV licence. This currently costs £150.50 (about $200) per year. This money is used to fund the BBC and means that all BBC channels (on television and radio) are broadcast without any adverts. This enables the BBC to produce content which isn't commercially viable. It can create documentaries on niche subjects without having to worry about viewing figures; educating the British public in a way that isn't possible for channels relying on the mass-market audience.

The BBC also spends a large amount of TV licence revenue on radio broadcasts.

- BBC Radio 1 (music and entertainment for the teen audience)
- BBC Radio 2 (music and entertainment for those over the age of 35)

Watching TV in the UK (continued)

- BBC Radio 3 (classical music)
- BBC Radio 4 (news, informative discussions, comedy and drama)
- BBC Radio 5 (sports coverage)

These advert-free radio stations are listened to by the majority of the UK population, with many people enjoying the quality content over the commercial music stations.

Adverts

There are far more commercials on US television than on British. The average hour of British television contains just 8 minutes of adverts, compared to 20 minutes in America. Programmes broadcast by the BBC contain no adverts at all, due to the TV licence.

The content of adverts is also different. There are no pharmaceutical adverts on British television, due to the fact that all drugs are purchased through the National Health Service. There is also little direct comparison between rival products -the British prefer to hear about the positive aspects of an item, rather than hear about the flaws of the market leader.

Short Series

In the UK, television series tend to be much shorter than those in the US - many UK programmes are only 6 - 8 episodes long. This is because most TV programmes in the UK are written by a single author; whilst those in the states have an entire team of writers. This means the US writing teams are capable of producing far more content than their UK counterparts.

Black Books

Run Time

Three series ran between 2000 and 2004, each containing six twenty-five-minute episodes, for a run time of roughly nine hours.

Creator and Writers

Created by Irish comic Dylan Moran, with writer Graham Linehan brought in to sand down Moran's rough edges a bit. Moran is credited as the writer on all eighteen episodes, with Kevin Cecil, Andy Riley, and Graham Linehan as co-writers on several episodes.

What It's About

He's the least friendly, most uncouth, completely-useless-at-business store owner ever: Bernard Black, proprietor of Black Books. What he really wants you to do, as a matter of fact, is bugger off and stop bothering him by shopping at his store. Then he'd have more time to berate his good-natured and co-dependent bookshop assistant and roommate Manny, as well as more time for lunchtime drinkies with his friend Fran, who runs (also poorly) the gift shop next door.

Creator Dylan Moran noted that his aim with the series was largely to "cram as much elaborate stupidity into a half-hour that could make it be coherent and that you would believe," and he largely nailed that desire. Various episodes feature Bernard's ever more desperate attempts to get out of filing his taxes, Manny's and Fran's almost always unsuccessful ploys to get Bernard to run a successful shop or persuade any woman to go on a date with him, and Manny's obsessions with *The Little Book of Calm* and appearing in magazines like *Big and Beardy*, among many other surreal storylines.

Why It's Bingeworthy

As with any series in which Graham Linehan is involved, you're going to have to watch this show with a friend, because it's endlessly quotable and you'll want someone to be able to recite it back and forth with you. ("Are these books genuine leather?" "They're genuine Dickens.")

It's quick, it's hilarious, it pokes fun at wine snobs and skinheads alike, and it features one of the best three-way friendships in all of television. It also features no shortage of physical and sight gags, as when Bernard, while on the telephone, tries to put off a customer who is asking him a question by writing "on phone" on a post-it note and sticking it to his own forehead. The series also includes cameo appearances by such Brit acting luminaries as Martin Freeman, Nick Frost, Simon Pegg, and creator Graham Linehan.

Main Cast

Dylan Moran...Bernard Black
Tamsin Greig...Fran Katzenjammer
Bill Bailey...Manny Bianco

Trivia

The exterior scenes of the bookshop were filmed outside a real bookshop in Bloomsbury, London, called Collinge & Clark.

A 1998 pilot episode of the show shown at the Channel 4 sitcom festival featured a plot in which both Bernard and Manny planned to commit suicide.

What to Binge on Next

If you're a fan of *Black Books* you'll definitely want to track down Dylan Moran's comedy specials *Monster*, *Monster II*, and *Like, Totally*; his humor is Irish and dark and surreal and hilarious.

Once you've watched *Black Books*, you should also watch two other classics created by Graham Linehan, *Father Ted* and *The I.T. Crowd*.

Another cult classic sitcom you might enjoy is *Spaced*, created and written by Simon Pegg and Jessica Stevenson, about two roommates nearly totally consumed by their own pop culture interests and individual fantasy lives.

Coupling

Run Time

Coupling aired for four series and a total of twenty-eight half-hour episodes from 2000 to 2004, making its run time fourteen hours.

Creator and Writers

The show was created by Steven Moffat, who had earlier used the break-up of his first marriage as inspiration for his sitcom *Joking Apart. Coupling* is based on his return to dating and his relationship with Sue Vertue, who co-produced this show with him.

What It's About

Steve and Susan face the same challenges that every new couple faces: each other's past relationship baggage, communication problems, and sometimes widely differing expectations for a romantic partnership. Their past relationship baggage, however, is a bit more present in their lives than it is for most: Steve was formerly in a long-term relationship with Jane, who becomes friends with Susan and her friend Sally, while Susan previously dated both her co-worker (and Steve's friend) Jeff, and Patrick, who becomes good friends with Steve and Jeff.

Having problems keeping everyone straight? Well, so do the characters, sometimes, but they each have their own hallmark: Steve is Everyman, prone to at least one outburst per episode about the many ways in which men and women will never understand one another, although he usually ends by finding a new way to tell Susan he loves her. Steve's love interest Susan is easily annoyed but still appreciative of his charm and is a warm "live and let live" type. Patrick is the playboy of the group, reputedly well-endowed and perpetually popular with the opposite sex, while Jeff is the hapless Welsh underdog with a million theories (wait until you hear him explain the "giggle loop") that the viewer loves to love. Susan's friend Sally is obsessed with reversing the signs of aging, none of which she has, and Jane has a surplus of neuroses and fantasy lives that would keep any therapist employed for life.

There's very little these six won't do, and even less they won't talk about. At times the show will make you despair about the chances of people ever having mutually satisfying partnerships, but it's still got some of the most postmodern but still lovely declarations of love ever, as when one character declares his love for another while his two friends perform a routine to the couple's song…the theme music from the TV comic *Spider-Man*. Don't ask. Just watch.

Why It's Bingeworthy

Over the course of four seasons the six friends in this sitcom managed to tackle a number of pressing relationship issues: Why do women want small decorative pillows on their furniture? Why won't men stay the night? When confronted with your boyfriend's "cupboard of love" (read: his closet full of recordings of previous trysts), are you upset, or do you mainly just look for the tape with you on it? And, of course, the biggie: Will men and women ever truly be happy in monogamous relationships?

The storytelling conventions and filming techniques used throughout the series (split screens detailing the different break-up behaviors of the genders; an episode telling the story of a break-up in reverse chronological order, ending with the couple getting back together) make the show a little something special.

There's no denying that in the #MeToo era the show is somewhat dated in its handling of gender stereotypes. But there's also no denying that the show is very funny, and if the individual performances are well acted, the chemistry between the characters is better than anything seen on such American sitcoms as *Friends* or *Parks and Recreation*. Even when fan-favorite Jeff left the show after the third series, the character brought in to replace him, Oliver (played by Richard Mylan), the show's storylines and chemistry between the characters continued without missing many beats.

As long as people try to find their perfect partner, they'll find something to appreciate in *Coupling*.

Main Cast

Sarah Alexander…Susan Walker
Jack Davenport…Steve Taylor
Katie Isitt…Sally Harper
Ben Miles…Patrick Maitland
Gina Bellman…Jane Christie
Richard Coyle…Jeff Murdock

Trivia

Show creator and producer Moffat and Vertue would go on to produce the 2010 incarnation of *Sherlock* together.

Actor Richard Coyle, who played the very Welsh Jeff Murdock, is not actually from Wales. His series four replacement, Richard Mylan, is from Wales, but played his character Oliver as an Englishman.

What to Binge on Next

If you like *Coupling*'s forthright and mature dialogue, you might also enjoy the sitcom *Lovesick* (which first aired under the perhaps less tasteful but arguably more accurate title *Scrotal Recall*) featuring Johnny Flynn as Dylan Witter, a man who is diagnosed with chlamydia and embarks on perhaps the strangest two-fold mission in all of television: to inform his former lovers of their possible infection, and also to find true love.

Steven Moffat has a history of mining his relationships past for his art: an earlier sitcom that he created and wrote, *Joking Apart*, is based on the break-up of his first marriage and features actors Robert Bathurst and Fiona Gillies as a couple who fall in love, marry, and divorce, all in the course of twelve episodes.

Another comedy that may appeal to fans of *Coupling* is the Amazon Prime program *Catastrophe*, in which Sharon Horgan and American comedian Rob Delaney play Sharon Morris and Rob Norris, a couple who share a brief fling while Rob is in London for work, and then marry after Sharon reveals that she has become pregnant after their encounters. Although a drama, not a comedy, the classic British series *Cold Feet* also follows the dating, marrying, parenting, divorcing, and dating exploits of a group of six friends.

Detectorists

Run Time

This series aired between 2014 and 2017, and consisted of eighteen half-hour episodes in three series (along with one Christmas special), making this one a nine-hour bingewatch.

Creator and Writers

Mackenzie Crook, well known for his roles in *The Office* and the *Pirates of the Caribbean* movies, created the show and wrote all nineteen of its episodes.

What It's About

Please don't call Andy and Lance metal detectors—that term is reserved for the tool they use to perform their detecting. They are detectorists, and serious ones at that: members of the Danebury Metal Detecting Club, engaged in rivalries with other detectorists, and fiercely protective of the areas around their village (the fictional town of Danebury, in northern Essex) for which they have received permission to go detecting.

Both men spend most of their time and energy on "finding their gold," although Andy has a serious girlfriend and Lance can't stop doing favors for his ex-wife (even though she has a new boyfriend).

I'm not going to say any more, because this is a series you just have to watch and you should watch it fresh. Suffice to say that plenty of life and friendships and fierce metal detecting rivalries go on in this show, but the characters' quiet dedication to their chosen loves in life (including metal detecting) is what makes it beautiful to watch.

Why It's Bingeworthy

This show is the exact opposite of suspense-filled, on the edge of your seat television programming, and yet, from the very first moment you start watching it (starting with the gorgeous Johnny Flynn-performed theme song), you will find yourself skipping sleep and calling in sick to work just so you can continue to watch it. And no matter what you miss during the nine or so hours it takes you to watch the series in its entirety, you will feel completely sated and happy when you are done. I promise. It's wonderful.

Main Cast

Mackenzie Crook…Andy Stone
Toby Jones…Lance Stater
Rachael Stirling…Becky
Aimee-Ffion Edwards…Sophie

Trivia

Creator and writer Mackenzie Crook actually found his gold (which the British Museum thought was a Roman-era pendant or earring) while metal detecting during the filming of the show.

Actor Rachael Stirling is the daughter of the incomparable Dame Diana Rigg (who also plays Stirling's character Becky's mother on the show).

What to Binge on Next

Honestly, *Detectorists* is so great that it will give you a warm glow about life itself; when you're done watching, turn off the TV and go live a little bit.

Then, when you're exhausted by all that living, come back to the television and head for other feel-good sitcoms that don't shy away from dark humor but which still have a light comedic touch: these include *Moone Boy*, *The Vicar of Dibley*, and *Only Fools and Horses*. Also of interest might be the drama *The Durrells in Corfu*; another comedy classic featuring a pair of very different friends who nonetheless occupy the same wavelength is *Jeeves & Wooster* (starring Stephen Fry and Hugh Laurie).

Father Ted

Run Time

Father Ted aired three series between 1995 and 1998, for a total of twenty-four twenty-five-minute episodes, with one hour-long Christmas special between the second and third series, for a run time of nearly thirteen hours.

Creator and Writers

Graham Linehan and Arthur Mathews created and wrote the series. Linehan is the deranged genius who gave us *The I.T. Crowd* and *Black Books*; Mathews contributed to *Black Books* and would go on to co-create and write the surreal Britcom *Toast of London* (in conjunction with its star, Matt Berry).

What It's About

Three Irish priests, all with issues that make them vaguely (or totally) unsuitable to interact with the public, are exiled to Craggy Island, where their parishioners include the criminally insane; the angrily unhappily married; and the generally aged and batty (like their tea-obsessed housekeeper, Mrs. Doyle). Father Ted Crilly is sometimes driven to distraction by his colleagues, the exceptionally dim Father Dougal Maguire and the profanity-spewing and drink-addled Father Jack Hackett. Then again, Ted also got into his own trouble, appropriating funds from his last parish; he may also have kicked his supervising bishop up the arse, so he's not really in a position to question his exile.

Somewhere there are probably Catholics who are offended by *Father Ted*, but I am not one of them. Insider knowledge of the religion's quirks (and all religions have their own) simply makes the jokes that much funnier.

Father Ted also makes extensive use of some of the best sight gags ever, as when Dougal calmly snips off the corner of a puzzle piece to make it fit (that description doesn't do the moment justice; you've just got to watch it), or when Ted tries to explain to Dougal the difference between toy cows that are "small" and real cows that are "far away" (just trust me on this).

Why It's Bingeworthy

Perhaps the most surreal and quotable comedy ever, every episode of *Father Ted* is a masterpiece of hilarious weirdness and no-holds-barred action.

From an episode that was a spoof on the popular movie *Speed* (with Father Dougal the one being trapped on the milk truck that was rigged to explode if it went under four kilometers per hour) to several featuring popular talk show host Graham Norton as a hyperactive youth pastor, every single episode of this lamentably not-long series yields a gold mine of existential moments, like Father Dougal asserting that, "Oh Ted, you're not meant to take it seriously, heaven and hell and everlasting life."

Main Cast

Dermot Morgan...Father Ted Crilly
Ardal O'Hanlon...Father Dougal McGuire
Frank Kelly...Father Jack Hackett
Pauline McLynn...Mrs. Doyle

Trivia

Tragically, the show's star, Dermot Morgan, died of a heart attack in 1998, after completing filming for the third season. He was forty-eight years old.

Thirty years after this show's initial run, you can still book "Father Ted" tours in Ireland, and a stage play of the same name is being developed.

What to Binge on Next

Any surreal comedy featuring character trios and foursomes might appeal to you after you've finished your run of *Father Ted*, and there's a surprising amount of those available: there's *Black Books* and *The I.T. Crowd*, also created by Linehan (and featuring Irish actors Dylan Moran and Chris O'Dowd, respectively); *The Young Ones*, a classic comedy from the early 1980s featuring four university roommates with varying degrees of antisocial behavior problems; and *Spaced*, a sitcom created and written by Simon Pegg and Jessica Stevenson, about a group of housemates with their own obsessions and weirdnesses.

Another very frank and hilarious Irish comedy is *Mrs. Brown's Boys*, starring comedian Brendan O'Carroll as matriarch Agnes Brown, whose love for her family and friends is as big as the family itself (even if she does express it with all the subtlety of a sledgehammer, sometimes).

Fawlty Towers

Run Time

The entire series consists of twelve episodes in two series, first broadcast in 1975 and 1979. All the episodes were thirty minutes long, so the run time is six hours.

Creator and Writers

John Cleese and his then-wife Connie Booth created, wrote, and co-starred in the series.

What It's About

Basil Fawlty, proprietor of the hotel Fawlty Towers, is everything you don't want in your hospitality staff: excitable, eccentric, violent, and violently snobbish. He's hell on his long-suffering employees, most notably his bellman Manny (an immigrant from Spain) and his chambermaid and waitress Polly; he's also derisive towards and terrified of his domineering wife, Sybil. Trust me: Fawlty Towers is not a place where you want to schedule a relaxing vacation.

Basil's scheming nature and obsequious desire to serve a higher class of clientele drops him in any number of compromising situations, as when he imitates Hitler in front of a German couple or mistakes a common thief for an aristocrat. Luckily each episode ends with Basil failing to achieve his class-centered goals, and with his employees and wife running the hotel much more successfully without him when he retreats to lick his wounds.

Why It's Bingeworthy

Well, it's a classic, innit?

Fawlty Towers is somewhat problematic in that it is from a different age (although it should be noted that the BBC, even back in 1974, thought it had some problems: one of their script editors thought it "full of clichéd situations and stereotypical characters"), with the racial and classist attitudes to boot. The broad humor of the series—Basil's Nazi march among them—will emphatically not be for everyone. But it's funny and high-energy and there are few more satisfying viewing experiences than watching Basil get his comeuppance in each episode. It was also created by one of the founders of Monty Python (Booth starred in several Python films as well) and is still hailed as a British television must-watch.

Main Cast

John Cleese...Basil Fawlty
Prunella Scales...Sybil Fawlty
Connie Booth...Polly Sherman
Andrew Sachs...Manuel

Trivia

Creators, writers, and co-stars Cleese and Booth divorced in 1978, a year before the second and final series aired in 1979.

The character of Basil Fawlty was based on a real hotelier who terrorized the Monty Python team when they stayed in his Torquay hotel in 1971.

British comedians, comedy writers, and actors still love the show: in 2017, in a survey done by the TV network Gold, they named it the "Best British sitcom of all time."

What to Binge on Next

Well, it's the chicken-or-the-egg question: if you're viewing *Fawlty Towers*, have you already seen all of the Monty Python movies and specials you can? Because if not, you might want to track them down, starting with *Monty Python's Flying Circus* (the comedy sketch show) or the movies *Monty Python and the Holy Grail* or *Monty Python's Life of Brian*.

If you're quite into classic British telly (don't be afraid to admit it), you might want to check out some other beloved shows like *Dad's Army*, *Only Fools and Horses*, and *One Foot in the Grave*.

Gavin & Stacey

Run Time

The series consists of nineteen half-hour episodes and one hour-long Christmas special in three seasons, and ran from 2007 to 2010. The total run time is nearly eleven hours.

Creator and Writers

James Corden (yes, *The Late Late Show*'s James Corden) and Ruth Jones created and wrote the show, and also starred in it. They're triple threats!

What It's About

At its heart this sitcom is about two couples: one perfectly in love, with only geography separating them, and another whose magnetism is more of the repellant than the attractive kind.

The gushier twosome are the show's namesakes, Gavin and Stacey, who first "meet" over long work-related phone calls, and who eventually decide that Gavin will travel from Essex (in the east) and Stacey will travel from Wales (in the west) to meet in person in London. Each brings a friend for support: Gavin brings Smithy, a loud and opinionated man who loves life and loves his meals even more, and Stacey brings Nessa, her street-smart friend who contains hidden depths of both world-weariness and sentimentality. Sparks fly—for both couples—and the rest of the series finds Gavin and Stacey trying to find a way to marry and deciding where to settle down, while Nessa and Smithy mostly try to avoid each other, until one little surprise gives them a reason to try and make it together.

Why It's Bingeworthy

Before James Corden was the hottest thing to hit American late-night TV and Carpool Karaoke, he was one of the main players in this sitcom about two couples; it's fun to watch him here in a role he wrote.

The four principal actors do a wonderful job, but this sitcom also boasts strong peripheral characters, most notably Stacey's protective (and very Welsh) Uncle Brynn, and Gavin's protective and loving (and very Essexian) parents Mick and Pam. It's also full of hilarious and unexpected, completely-unrelated-to-the-plot side moments that you will simply have to re-watch, like the conversation between Nessa and Stacey's mom's elderly neighbor regarding their respective investments in the Tokyo stock market.

It's like your favorite American rom-com movies from the nineties, only a bit longer and with a sometimes crass but always very forthright British sense of humor. The first episode in particular includes some naughty bits that are definitely NSFW.

Main Cast

Mathew Horne...Gavin Shipman
Joanna Page...Stacey West
James Corden...Neil ("Smithy") Smith
Ruth Jones...Vanessa ("Nessa") Jenkins

Trivia

The surnames of the main characters, Shipman and West, match the names of two of the U.K.'s most infamous serial killers. They chose the names on purpose; Jones has said, "I suppose we were hoping that people wouldn't realize and then when it does come to light, it's even more delicious."

Although large parts of the show were set in Gavin's Essex hometown, none of the series was filmed there; it was filmed in London and Wales.

What to Binge on Next

If you like Corden's extremely offbeat brand of humor, you might also enjoy his sitcom *The Wrong Mans*, co-starring Mathew Baynton and featuring a pair of office workers who get caught up in kidnapping and larceny.

Although slightly less sweet in tone, modern romantic sitcoms such as *Him & Her*, about a twenty-something couple, and *Lovesick*, about a man working through his romantic history one partner at a time (prompted by the diagnosis of an STD that he feels duty-bound to report to former lovers), might also be a good follow-up to *Gavin & Stacey*. Fans of Horne's turn here as Gavin might also enjoy him in the campy mystery series *Agatha Raisin*, where he more than holds his own against Ashley Jensen's wonderful title character.

Although it's much more sedate in tone and dialogue, the romantic sitcom *As Time Goes By*, starring Dame Judi Dench and Geoffrey Palmer also highlights an at-times prickly love relationship (but don't worry, it all comes right in the end).

The Good Life

Run Time

The show consists of thirty half-hour episodes over the course of four series (including both a Christmas special that aired in 1977 and a "command performance" that aired in 1978, after the fourth series concluded). It aired between 1975 and 1978, and its total run time is fifteen hours.

Creator and Writers

The show was created by the comedy writing team of John Esmonde and Bob Larbey; they also wrote all the episodes.

What It's About

Successful plastics engineer Tom Good is fed up to his back teeth with the modern rat race: get up, go to work, go home, go to sleep, go back to work. He's looking for something more as he turns forty…and that something more turns out to be Tom himself, at home, as he quits his job and pledges to live, along with his wife Barbara, solely "off the land" of their suburban home's backyard.

Barbara takes his decision with good grace and throws herself into the enterprise with him, looking for ways to live off the grid and planting and growing their own food (as well as introducing a variety of livestock to their neighborhood). Two people who do not take as well to this unorthodox back-to-the-land set-up are his neighbors, Jerry and Margo Leadbetter. Jerry, an easygoing sort, understands Tom's ennui and is willing to help out when possible, but Margo, who believes strongly in social class and the niceties of suburban living, is less apt to turn a blind eye (or ear) to the various sights, smells, and sounds emanating from her neighbors' newly productive backyard.

Why It's Bingeworthy

Esmonde and Larbey wrote the role of Tom Good especially for veteran actor Richard Briers, and it shows: he tears into the part with gusto, investing Tom with a second wind for life that infects everyone in a positive way. It's widely regarded as a true comedy classic in Great Britain, came in ninth on the BBC's 2004 list of Best Sitcoms, and is still widely mentioned in pop culture and television history circles.

More than all of that, it's just a lot of fun. This series is from the 1970s and showcases some of the freewheeling attitudes of the time; you'll enjoy watching the flirtations between the various neighbor spouses here (even Margo can't really resist Tom Good's charms)! It's also comforting to know that people seeking to re-connect with the earth and live off the grid is not a new phenomenon; corporate life has been getting everyone down for a while now!

Main Cast

Richard Briers…Tom Good
Felicity Kendal…Barbara Good
Paul Eddington…Jerry Leadbetter
Penelope Keith…Margo Leadbetter

Trivia

In the United States the program was broadcast and known under the title *Good Neighbors*.

Outdoor filming took place at a pair of real houses in the North London suburb of Northwood. After filming the rather well-used lawn and yard of the house that filled in for the Goods' were repaired and returned to their original state; all animals used in filming were removed at the end of each working day.

Twenty-one million viewers watched the program's Christmas special in 1977.

What to Binge on Next

The Good Life is still fondly remembered by many viewers in the U.K. Other classic series that have stood the test of time might provide fun viewing as well, including *Waiting for God*, about residents of a retirement home who find comfort in one another (and in making caustic comments about their respective family members and the home's staff); *Dad's Army*, about Home Guard volunteers during World War II who take their charge to keep their seaside village safe from Nazi invaders *very* seriously; and *Open All Hours*, set in a small grocer's shop in Yorkshire and featuring the proprietor's knack for selling (and avoiding matrimony).

This program also helped launch the careers of its main actors, so viewers might also enjoy the sitcom *To the Manor Born* (starring Penelope Keith), *Yes,*

Minister (starring Paul Eddington), and the cozy mystery series *Rosemary & Thyme* (starring Felicity Kendall). The show was written to showcase the talents of Richard Briers, who has also been in many notable TV productions, including the drama series *Monarch of the Glen*.

Another classic sitcom about the soul-killing nature of the corporate work world is *The Fall and Rise of Reginald Perrin*.

Jackie on...
TV Seasons in the UK

Question: Jackie, in the U.S. we used to have definite seasons of TV. New programs would debut in the spring and fall and reruns would run all summer. Does that happen in the UK?

Answer: The pattern for new TV shows in the UK is very similar to the US. Most new series begin in line with the start of a new school term—September, January and April. Important programmes (apart from one-off specials) won't air over the Easter or Summer holidays, as too many people are away.

We don't have sweeps week over here. TV ratings are measured continually by monitoring a carefully selected panel of approximately 5000 households. These households have a device fitted to their television which continually monitors their viewing habits. This means that viewing figures can be estimated every day and if a programme has an unusually large number of viewers we'll often hear about it on the news.

A lot of programmes are repeated, but peak times (7pm-10pm) will normally contain original content. There are more repeats on Sundays and over the summer.

The Inbetweeners

Run Time

The Inbetweeners consists of three series and a total of eighteen twenty-five-minute episodes, which aired between 2008 and 2010. The total run time is a little under eight hours.

Creator and Writers

Damon Beesley and Iain Morris created the show, and wrote all eighteen of its episodes.

What It's About

It's the start of a new school year, and Will's mother, in an attempt to save him from bullying, has him start at a new school. Although most students don't want anything to do with him, his posh accent, or his obvious nerdiness, he nonetheless does find his own small group of compatriots, including Simon, perpetually high-strung and helplessly in love with his gorgeous (and oblivious) classmate who lives next door; Jay, a blowhard with an easily crushed soul; and Neil, the dim but cheerful doofus. The four go on to become an unlikely and sometimes contentious group of friends.

Throughout this series the boys manage to get into a number of shocking situations, most of which include miscommunication mishaps with parents; both defiance and fear of their sadistic school teacher Mr. Gilbert; and physically and emotionally embarrassing moments with members of the opposite sex.

Why It's Bingeworthy

Any mother of boys, girlfriend of boys, friend of boys, anyone who has ever dealt with teenage boys full stop, will recognize all four of these kids. Of course they're obnoxious. Of course they are overly fascinated by their bodies, girls' bodies, bodily functions, etc. But they're also so clueless and so helpless that you almost just want to hug them. And then slap them upside the head. Hard.

The show can be very, very gross, make no mistakes about it. Think "camping tent full of vomit" or "car full of, ahem, the product of masturbation" gross. But if you've got a strong stomach, an appreciation for the absurd, and a willingness to pity these boys in a motherly kind of way, you might get more than a few laughs out of this program.

Main Cast

Simon Bird…Will McKenzie
Joe Thomas…Simon Cooper
James Buckley…Jay Cartwright
Blake Harrison…Neil Sutherland
Greg Davies…Mr. Gilbert

Trivia

After the series ended, two popular and lucrative feature films were released: *The Inbetweeners Movie* (2011) and *The Inbetweeners 2* (2014).

A short-lived American version was filmed for MTV in 2012, and flopped.

What to Binge on Next

A similar program featuring the exploits of a slightly older group of young adults in college is *Fresh Meat* (which also stars Joe Thomas, who plays Simon in *The Inbetweeners*).

A classic sitcom that might appeal to you if you enjoy *The Inbetweeners* is *Men Behaving Badly* (starring Martin Clunes and Neil Morrissey), which shows two grown men acting like teenagers (basically), still engaged in sophomoric humor and in general trying the patience of the more mature women around them. There is also the HBO sitcom *Flight of the Conchords*, about two friends from New Zealand who try to break into the music business in New York City but who largely exist in their own clueless bubble.

Skins is a drama featuring teenaged characters, but is much more dramatic and dark in tone and situations.

The I.T. Crowd

Run Time

This show ran for four seasons and total of twenty-four episodes between 2006 and 2010; a stand-alone special aired in 2013. Each episode ran for approximately twenty-four minutes, while the special was forty-seven minutes long, making for a run time of nearly ten and a half hours.

Creator and Writers

Graham Linehan created and wrote the series.

What It's About

Is your computer not working? Have you tried turning it off and on again?

Roy Trenneman and Maurice Moss are employees in the I.T. department of Reynholm Industries, and if any employees call them for technical assistance, that's the first question they're going to be asked. They are quite happy in their insular department, located, of course, in the basement of corporate headquarters (and which includes a server room that is inhabited by an even more contact-shy worker and goth named Richmond Avenal).

Their cozy den is upset somewhat with the arrival of management: supervisor Jen Barber, who takes charge of the disregarded I.T. department (the work of which she doesn't understand, like not knowing what "I.T." stands for) as a form of career advancement. Although she regularly tries to interact with the company's founder and chief executive, Denholm Reynholm, and later, his even more eccentric son Douglas Reynholm, to prove the importance of their department, she never gets anywhere and the trio continues to be consigned to oblivion in their basement offices.

Why It's Bingeworthy

As in any series Linehan creates, the friendships between the odd but harmless members of the I.T. department make the show worth watching. Roy seeks to avoid work at all costs; Moss is utterly clueless on how to interact normally with other humans; and Jen is reluctant to admit that she's just as happy hanging out with her co-workers as she is trying to rise through the ranks of Reynholm Industries. The supporting cast is also strong; Noel Fielding's appearances as the goth inhabitant of the server room are brief but memorable, and both of the Reynholm bosses are recognizable executive caricatures, although Matt Berry brings a little something special to the entirely unsympathetic role of Douglas Reynholm.

The show also provides a lot of physical humor and surreal comedy, as when Moss inadvertently signs up for a cookery class taught by a German cannibal who is actually advertising for someone to eat, not for someone to whom he can teach cookery. And that's about as normal as the storylines get. In all it's a just a completely strange and hilarious viewing experience.

Main Cast

Chris O'Dowd...Roy Trenneman
Richard Ayoade...Maurice Moss
Katherine Parkinson...Jen Barber
Noel Fielding...Richmond Avenal
Matt Berry...Douglas Reynholm

Trivia

A fifth series was planned, but Linehan's and the actors' scheduling conflicts made it impossible to do an entire series, so a stand-alone episode was filmed and aired in 2013.

Numerous attempts have been made to adapt this program for American TV, and although a pilot was filmed starring Richard Ayoade, Joel McHale, and Jessica St. Clair, it was never picked up for a full season.

What to Binge on Next

If you've not already seen Graham Linehan's other surreal comedies, among them *Father Ted*, *Black Books*, and *Count Arthur Strong*, you're going to want to go do that, right away.

Chris O'Dowd also created and starred in another delightful sitcom titled *Moone Boy*; if you enjoy Matt Berry you might also really enjoy the sitcom he created, *Toast of London*, about an underemployed London stage actor who nonetheless has a healthy ego.

Although focusing on a pair of roommates (rather than a trio of workmates), the comedy program *Peep Show* (starring David Mitchell and Robert Webb) is also very strange—in the best possible way—and therefore might be perfect watching for you if you enjoyed *The I.T. Crowd*.

Jeeves & Wooster

Run Time

Jeeves & Wooster aired from 1990 to 1993, and is comprised of twenty-three episodes in four seasons. Each episode's run time is fifty minutes, so you can get through this entire series in just a little over nineteen hours.

Creator and Writers

The program is based on the Jeeves novels by P.G. Wodehouse, and was adapted for the screen by Clive Exton (who also wrote all of the episodes).

What It's About

Bertie Wooster lives in a rarefied world of British aristocratic life in the 1920s: he belongs to a gentleman's club, enjoys the finest dining and drinks that London has to offer, gets up late, and, when he needs just a bit of variety, pops round to any fellow aristocrats' homes in the country for more wining, dining, and generally just taking it easy. His only two problems are his seeming inability to find a good and loyal manservant, and to avoid becoming inadvertently engaged to any of the daughters of the country homes in which he spends a lot of his loafing time.

For Bertie, it's a wonderful day when his first problem is solved, and a gentleman's gentleman named Jeeves shows up to accept his employment and generally take over most aspects of his schedule and life. Jeeves of course performs all the functions that a valet must: he knows how to brew up a secret-recipe hangover cure; he himself dresses impeccably and knows what his master should wear for all occasions as well; and he's aces at helping Wooster get out of any number of various scrapes and hijinks in which he somehow manages to become involved. Sure, Jeeves is also sometimes responsible for getting Bertie into those scrapes, but somehow both of them always manage to escape uncomfortable situations, expectations from Bertie's very demanding aunts, and any semblance of matrimonial promises.

Why It's Bingeworthy

There is absolutely no way I can describe for you how fun, how rollicking, how lighthearted this program is. You simply HAVE to watch it.

Main Cast

Hugh Laurie…Bertie Wooster
Stephen Fry…Jeeves
Robert Daws…Tuppy Glossop
Mary Wimbush…Aunt Agatha
Brenda Bruce…Aunt Dahlia
Liz Kettle…Honoria Glossop

Trivia

The main theme for the program perfectly sets the mood and was written by composer Anne Dudley (who has also worked on soundtracks for *Kavanagh QC* and *Poldark*).

Many of the supporting characters were played by multiple actors during the show's run. Gussie Finknottle was played by Richard Braine and Richard Garnett, and Barmy by Adam Blackwood and Martin Clunes. The role of Bertie's Aunt Dahlia was played by a different actress in each of the four series (and they were all perfect in their own ways)!

Bertie Wooster was not particularly musical in the original novels, but that aspect of his character was added to take advantage of the fact that Hugh Laurie is an accomplished musician and could play all his own piano songs.

What to Binge on Next

If you can't get enough of Stephen Fry and Hugh Laurie here, you're also going to want to catch them in their comedy variety program *A Bit of Fry and Laurie*, as well as the classic comedy series *Blackadder*, in which they both play key historical roles.

Screenwriter Clive Exton has a real touch with this particular era; he also wrote screenplays for *Poirot*, the adaptation of Agatha Christie's cozy mysteries featuring detective Hercule Poirot. He also wrote scripts for the more modern-day but still somewhat gentle mystery series *Rosemary & Thyme*.

If you're a Fan of Wooster's affable leading man and his more intellectually gifted counterpart Jeeves you might also enjoy the mystery series *Campion*, in which lead actor Peter Davison combines affability and intellect in his gentleman sleuth Albert Campion.

Keeping Up Appearances

Run Time

The show aired from 1990 to 1995. It consisted of forty-two half-hour episodes and two longer specials, for a total run time of nearly twenty-three hours. Purists may also want to track down two hour-long retroactive specials that aired in 1997 and 2008, as well as a thirty-minute "prequel" titled *Young Hyacinth* that aired in 2016, and which starred Kerry Howard as young Hyacinth Walton (later Bucket), in the early 1950s.

Creator and Writers

The show was created and written by Roy Clarke, who was also responsible for the hugely popular sitcoms *Open All Hours* and *Last of the Summer Wine*.

What It's About

Middle-aged matron Hyacinth Bucket (pronounced "Bouquet") has one aim in life: genteel respectability in the form of an upper-crust existence. Make that two aims: to achieve gentility, and to be noticed achieving it.

There are a few stumbling blocks on Hyacinth's road to respectability, and most of them take the form of her downwardly mobile family: sister Daisy and Daisy's unemployed husband Onslow, whose embrace of a slobby lifestyle scandalizes Hyacinth; her sister Rose, who lives with Daisy and Onslow and who never met a gentleman she didn't like (including the married vicar of Hyacinth's church); and her Daddy, who also lives with Rose and Onslow but who often manages to escape and wreak havoc while reliving his war missions.

But Hyacinth isn't about to let anything, even family, get in her social-climbing way. She will continue to host candlelight suppers and riparian entertainments for all the right people, and if you're her family, her long-suffering husband, or her neighbors, you probably just want to go along with her plans sooner rather than later. It's just easier that way.

Why It's Bingeworthy

My husband rolls his eyes slightly whenever I sit down to enjoy any episode of *Keeping Up Appearances* (as I've seen them all multiple times). What he doesn't understand about this program is its perfectly calibrated British mix of all-out physical comedy and sometimes crass innuendo with the essential harmlessness of Hyacinth and her social class pretensions. Everyone in the program goes out of their way to avoid Hyacinth, but when she's completely unavoidable (and she often is: Hyacinth Bucket as played by the wonderful Patricia Routledge is a force of nature), they submit with the stiff upper lip and resigned good humor that is the mark of the true Brit.

I love the characters, including Hyacinth's long-suffering husband Richard, and her terrorized neighbor Liz. The show also boasts a classic Christmas episode that I have to re-watch every holiday season.

Main Cast

Patricia Routledge…Hyacinth Bucket
Clive Swift…Richard Bucket
Josephine Tewson…Elizabeth ("Liz") Warden
David Griffin…Emmet Hawksworth
Judy Cornwell…Daisy
Geoffrey Hughes…Onslow
Shirley Stelfox…Rose

Trivia

In 2010 a theater play based on the program was created and toured in the U.K.

Geoffrey Hughes, who played the beer-swilling Onslow, was appointed Deputy Lord Lieutenant for the Isle of Wight in 2009, making him "the official link between the island and royalty at formal engagements."

What to Binge on Next

Fans of Patricia Routledge might also want to check out the cozy mystery series *Hetty Wainthropp Investigates*, in which she plays a character who is less interested in fitting in with the neighborhood than she is in solving its crimes.

My PBS affiliate has shown episodes of *Keeping Up Appearances* alongside episodes of another classic sitcom, *As Time Goes By*, for seemingly dozens of years now. Whenever I watch one program I feel like I must watch the other as well; they're both from the same era and, although they are very different in tone, are both funny and touching in their own ways.

League of Gentlemen

Run Time

This dark comedy originally aired for three series from 1999 to 2002, and returned for a "three-part revival miniseries" in 2017. A feature film, *The League of Gentlemen's Apocalypse*, was released in 2005. Counting all eighteen original episodes (at thirty minutes per), a Christmas special in 2000 (sixty minutes), the three revival episodes (thirty minutes), and the movie (ninety minutes), and you're looking at a time investment of thirteen hours.

Creator and Writers

The show was created and written by the comedy troupe League of Gentlemen, consisting of Mark Gatiss, Steve Pemberton, Reece Shearsmith, and Jeremy Dyson, who originally started working together in 1994 and were given their own BBC Radio 4 program in 1997.

What It's About

Welcome to Royston Vasey, in the heart of northern England, home of many of the strangest characters you'll ever meet in British sketch comedy. And that takes some doing! (See: *Little Britain* or *The Mighty Boosh* or the classic program *The Goodies*.) The show is meant to be a mashup of horror and bizarre, dark comedy, and showcases a number of characters that the main actors and writers actually grew up around in their respective hometowns: the "local shop" owners, a local boy returned home to stay with his uncle and aunt, and a jobs counselor who is not actually very interested in helping any of her class attendees to obtain jobs.

Why It's Bingeworthy

I'm calling Jackie in on this one, as I don't actually understand the show or its appeal. But she does:

"*The League of Gentlemen* is as dark and surreal as television gets. It isn't for those who are easily offended, but if you want to watch something totally different from anything else you'll be rewarded with comedy scenes as surprising as they are strange. There's a family obsessed with toads, a drunken vicar who doesn't believe in God, and Legsakimbo, the homosexual school theatre group.

On the surface it looks as though *The League of Gentlemen* is deliberately being as provocative as possible, but underneath there is a tenderness to the grotesque characters. This programme shows that it is possible to care about anyone, despite their flaws. There's nothing else on television anywhere in the world that's as weird as this!"

Main Cast

All four of these cast members play various characters.
Mark Gatiss
Steve Pemberton
Reece Shearsmith
Jeremy Dyson

Trivia

A stage play based on the program, *The League of Gentlemen Are Behind You!*, was developed in 2005.

The town name of Royston Vasey is the real name of one of the actors who appears in the show (a comedian known by the name Roy "Chubby" Brown).

The show was filmed in many different locations around Derbyshire and has no laugh track.

What to Binge on Next

The members of this comedy troupe have been involved in many other British TV projects (and very surreal ones at that): Steve Pemberton in particular has played a large role in writing and starring in the dark comedy series *Psychoville* and the anthology program *Inside No. 9* (both of which he co-writes with Reece Shearsmith). Pemberton is a true chameleon: he is also known for his roles as a low-class resort vacationer in the more sitcom-ish comedy *Benidorm*; the Ripperologist who sincerely wants to help Rupert Penry-Jones solve modern East End murders in *Whitechapel*; and the accountant with a nasty plan in *Happy Valley*.

Another sketch comedy show you might like is *Little Britain*, in which Matt Lucas and David Walliams play a multitude of British characters as caricatures, while another strange comedy which is hailed as a classic (and which I also don't get at all) is *The Young Ones*, starring Adrian Edmondson and Rik Mayall.

Jackie on...
Game Shows in the UK

The Generation Game is a classic British gameshow. It was first broadcast in 1971, but has returned to screens many times since then. The show consists of families competing against each other in set tasks, often demonstrated by professionals, and that the contestants try to copy. This normally ends in hilarious failures to make sausages, ice a cake, or plaster a wall!

The original host, Bruce Forsythe (who, sadly, died in 2017), is the most iconic. Several of his catchphrases have entered British culture; in fact, a British citizenship test could probably involve ensuring you know to shout "NICE!" in response to Bruce's opening line: "Nice to see you, to see you..."

Pointless was first shown in 2009, but has quickly become one of the most popular game shows on British television. One hundred members of the public are asked a series of questions; the number of points that the contestants get is gauged by the percentage of the public who knew the answer. This means the scoring system is reverse that of most game shows - the contestant with the lowest score wins. Its popularity is due to the fact that most people watching the show are able to answer almost all of the questions – it's thinking up obscure answers that wins the game.

University Challenge is the hardest gameshow on television. It pits teams from the UK's top universities against each other, asking a barrage of questions that most viewers don't even understand, let alone know the answer to! The show began in 1962 and the format has changed little since then - there have only been two different hosts (Bamber Gascoigne and Jeremy Paxman). Each series starts with 28 teams of 4 and in every episode two teams compete against each other, with the loser being knocked out.

University Challenge is especially famous for the split screen, showing one team on top of the other. It's probably one of the most mocked programmes on British television, with comedians frequently including parodies in their performances.

Little Britain

Run Time

In its first and most popular appearance from 2003 to 2005 (on TV; it was a radio program first) *Little Britain* consisted of twenty episodes in three seasons. After the third season, in 2006, a two-part Christmas special titled *Little Britain, Abroad*, about the show's characters' travels, aired, and, in 2008, creators Lucas and Walliams wrote a "fourth season" of six episodes for the American market, titled *Little Britain USA*. At thirty minutes per episode, that all adds up to about fourteen hours of total viewing time.

Creator and Writers

The show was created and written by David Walliams and Matt Lucas, who also played a wide variety of characters in the show's sketches.

What It's About

With its deep-toned and serious announcer informing you during the opening credits that Britain has "had running water for over ten years" and also "invented the cat," how can you expect anything other than greatness from this sketch comedy program that undertakes to introduce you to Britain's people?

In each episode Walliams and Lucas offer you rapid-fire and satirical vignettes of those people, almost all played by Walliams and Lucas. There's Lucas's vapid schoolgirl Vicky Pollard, every authority figure's worst nightmare; Walliams's secretary with a wicked crush on the Prime Minister (played by Anthony Stewart Head with the same erudite appeal that made so many *Buffy* viewers fall in love with him as Giles); and Lucas's Daffyd Thomas, the "only gay in the village." I've listed just a few here; there's actually an entire Wikipedia page (nicely alphabetized) available that lists all of Walliams's and Lucas's characters.

Why It's Bingeworthy

Little Britain does just what it says it will and introduces you to its creators' ideas of the character types who make up British society. It's satirical and it can be harsh, but it's also very, very funny, and it is firmly lodged in the subconscious of many Brits as one of their favorite comedy programs (although many television critics hated it, and said so in print). There's a lot to be learned about British culture and pop culture here, especially for some of the sketches that have not aged particularly well (but which are easily explained with a quick look around the Internet). You'll have the absolute inside track on the great British skill of self-mockery if you can see the humor in this program.

Although the show first aired in the late 1990s and early 2000s, both Lucas and Walliams freely admit that doing such a show might prove difficult today. But their energy, as manic as it is, keeps the show from feeling cruel towards the characters it lampoons. To call it a love letter to the British personality (or personalities) would probably be taking things a bit too far, but what can I say? Two ways in which I'm American are my enthusiasm and my love of exaggeration.

Main Cast

David Walliams...various characters
Matt Lucas...various characters

Trivia

Co-creator David Walliams went on to have an even more successful and lucrative subsequent career as a children's book author.

In 2011 Matt Lucas and David Walliams dissolved their comedy partnership after several years of "being at loggerheads" with one another. They did not speak or meet again until they met at the funeral of a mutual friend in 2018.

What to Binge on Next

Little Britain is among the stranger British comedies you'll find; other comedy and sketch shows which fall into this "might be too weird for even the most Anglophile of American viewers" camp include *League of Gentlemen* (a horror/dark comedy hybrid from the 1990s, written by and starring Mark Gatiss and Steve Pemberton, among others); *The Mighty Boosh*; and *The Catherine Tate Show* (although this last show, starring comedian Catherine Tate, is a bit less surreal).

At the end of 2010, a one-series program that was again co-created by Lucas and Walliams, *Come Fly with Me*, aired on BBC One. It's a mockumentary set in an airport, with Walliams and Lucas playing various characters, both employees of various airlines and passengers.

Miranda

Run Time

The show, which aired from 2009 to 2015, is comprised of three series containing eighteen episodes, and a Christmas special in two parts that doubled as the series finale. Regular episodes were thirty minutes long and the two specials were thirty-five minutes long, making for a run time of just a touch over ten hours.

Creator and Writers

The show's creator, comedian Miranda Hart, also wrote all its episodes; other writers include Richard Hurst and James Cary.

What It's About

Miranda's friends from her posh former school and her demanding mother spend most of their time underestimating her, which is ironic, considering that she stands a bit over six feet tall. Luckily Miranda seems mostly intent on living and enjoying her own life, as well as engaging in a rich fantasy life in which she is much more debonair. After receiving a small inheritance from an uncle, she uses it to buy and run a joke shop, along with her diminutive (and more business-minded) friend Stevie, and spends her days working in her shop and harboring a crush on another friend, Gary, who is a chef in the restaurant next door.

That relationship endures many ups and downs throughout the run of the show, but what never changes is Miranda's essential kindness and her *joie de vivre*, as often shown when she breaks into spontaneous song, or when engaging in some ridiculous lies to try and escape whatever horrible (and more "suitable") dates or work situations into which her mother is trying to force her.

Why It's Bingeworthy

It's just so fun! It's quick and lighthearted and romantic and basically everything you're looking for when you'd rather not face reality on a dreary rainy Sunday afternoon.

Hart has stated she is a fan of many classic British television stars, and the physical humor in the show is top-notch (with many jokes revolving around her height and awkwardness). The dialogue is also lively and all of the characters are genuine—and the actors all really look like they're having fun on the show. It's infectious; I guarantee you'll feel cheerier after watching even one episode.

Main Cast

Miranda Hart…Miranda
Tom Ellis…Gary Preston
Sarah Hadland…Stevie Sutton
Patricia Hodge…Penny (Miranda's mother)

Trivia

Creator Miranda Hart is 6' 1" tall. This series is based on an earlier semi-autobiographical program that Hart performed on BBC Radio 2.

Miranda Hart cites as her comedy influences Morecambe and Wise, Tony Hancock, Joyce Grenfell, and Tommy Cooper.

What to Binge on Next

Hart has stated many times that she is a fan of classic British comedies such as *Some Mothers Do 'Ave 'Em* and *Hi-de-Hi!* These programs and other classics like *Dad's Army* and *Are You Being Served?* might all be fun viewing if you like the gentler comedy stylings of *Miranda*.

Other programs in which characters seem to live quite happily in their own somewhat more innocent worlds include *Moone Boy* (about a boy and his imaginary friend growing up in 1980s and 1990s Ireland) and *Detectorists* (about two best friends who are dedicated to their metal detecting hobbies). Fans of Hart can also find her playing a nurse midwife with an upper-class background in the first four seasons of the historical drama *Call the Midwife*.

Moone Boy

Run Time

The series aired from 2012 to 2015, and consisted of eighteen episodes in three seasons. Episodes were twenty-two minutes long, making for a total run time of just a touch under seven hours.

Creator and Writers

Chris O'Dowd created the show (it's based on his childhood in 1980s and early 1990s Boyle, County Roscommon, in Ireland), and co-wrote it with Nick Vincent Murphy.

What It's About

Moone Boy is about, quite simply, the "imaginary friend of an idiot boy in the west of Ireland" in the 1980s. The boy is Martin Paul Kenny Dalglish Moone, and although he is twelve years old, his imaginary friend is a grown man named Sean Murphy (who is, of course, invisible to everyone except Martin).

Martin has need of a kindred spirit; his three older sisters have little patience for him, his parents are busy trying to make a living, and although he has one real best friend (who has an imaginary friend of his own, making them a friendly quartet), his school also boasts at least two bullies—they're twins—who keep Martin on his toes.

Idiot boy or not, you cheer for Martin. And he rewards you; nothing really gets him down. Through the onset of puberty and all the challenges that come with being the youngest in a crowded family, he remains cheerful, and he and Sean never stop making or enacting plans that, let's face it, only boys could dream up, including spilling his cereal on his sister's wedding dress and then trying to remove the stain by rubbing it with even messier things.

Why It's Bingeworthy

It's such a great show. It's gentle and wicked and funny and comforting all at once. If you've ever felt like no one in your family listens to you, you'll enjoy this show. If you had an imaginary friend of your own, you'll enjoy this show. If you're Catholic, you're really going to enjoy this show (right up to and including the wedding of the oldest daughter, which takes place WHILE she gives birth).

And if all of that doesn't convince you, Paul Rudd (whose parents were born in Great Britain) makes an appearance in the series's finale. Paul Rudd, people. GO WATCH THIS SHOW NOW.

Main Cast

Chris O'Dowd…Sean Murphy
David Rawle…Martin Paul Kenny Dalglish Moone
Deirdre O'Kane…Debra Moone
Peter McDonald…Liam Moone

Trivia

O'Dowd and Murphy have also published an illustrated middle-grade book based on the series, titled *Moone Boy: The Blunder Years*.

The show won an International Emmy award for Best Comedy in 2013.

What to Binge on Next

Another series that plays out around largely every-day occurrences and can oddly restore your faith in human nature through its humor and gentleness is the sitcom *Detectorists*.

Fans of Chris O'Dowd will also want to check him out in Graham Linehan's comedy *The I.T. Crowd*, about three employees of the I.T. department in a large corporation.

Irish television is a bit of a genre unto itself. In addition to *Moone Boy*, fans of Radio-Television of Ireland (RTÉ) might also enjoy the comedies *Mrs. Brown's Boys*, about another large Irish family (and in which the titular matriarch Mrs. Brown is played by the very male Irish comic Brendan O'Carroll), or *The Young Offenders*, about a group of "two tracksuit-wearing Cork teen scallywags."

The New Statesman

Run Time

The first two series of the show (1987 and 1989) ran for seven half-hour episodes each; the second two series (1991 and 1992) consisted of six half-hour episodes. Add a Comic Relief special and two specials that aired after the second season and the fourth season, respectively, and you're looking at something like a fifteen- to sixteen-hour bingewatch.

Creator and Writers

Although created as a vehicle for comedian Rik Mayall, the series was created and written by Laurence Marks and Maurice Gran.

What It's About

Contemptible conservative Member of Parliament Alan Beresford B'Stard uses his political career to further his own gain, and he doesn't care who knows about it. At thirty-one, he's the youngest MP in Westminster, he's part of the "new money Thatcherites," and his main goal is to stay in power and to reap its many benefits for as long as he can. Sound familiar? Evidently politics everywhere, and in every era, have always been the same.

Most of the action in the series takes place in B'Stard's Westminster antechambers, where he dreams up sociopathic plans to rise through the ranks, with the help of various political employees and toadies. He's also helped in his ambitions by his ruthless wife Sarah, who married him for his money (don't feel bad for him; he married her for her father's Tory connections).

Why It's Bingeworthy

It sounds awful. And it is. But it is also hilariously saucy, particularly for the 1980s, and there's very little B'Stard won't say about and to his constituents or his fellow politicians. As satire this program is top-notch.

It was also a big hit for the network ITV, and its star and its main character Alan B'Stard still loom large in British popular culture: it was further adapted into a successful stage show, and for many years Mayall penned an opinion column (writing as B'Stard) for the *Sunday Telegraph* through 2007.

Main Cast

Rik Mayall…Sir Alan Beresford B'Stard
Michael Troughton…Piers Fletcher-Dervish
Marsha Fitzalan…Sarah B'Stard

Trivia

When Rik Mayall died in 2014 (at the too-young age of fifty-six), Marks and Gran, the creators of this show and of Mayall's most famous character, wrote an obituary for him in the form of a satirical obituary for Alan B'Stard.

Marks and Gran also created a sequel to the show, titled *Son of B'Stard* (or *The B'Stard Legacy*), but the program has not aired, with rumors being that ITV was "too scared" to air it.

What to Binge on Next

Rik Mayall's comedic influence loomed large on the Brit TV landscape of the 1980s and 1990s. Before appearing in this hit he starred on and wrote, along with Lise Mayer and Ben Elton, the cult hit *The Young Ones*, about four young men rooming together at university (and their many obsessions, bad habits, and a truly impressive amount of anarchy and physical violence). He also appeared in several cameos on the *Blackadder* series and starred in a subsequent BBC comedy titled *Bottom*.

Fans of political satire might also consider the series *Yes, Minister* and *Yes, Prime Minister*, although they are much less savage in tone (although they are still funny) or the more recent *The Thick of It*, starring Peter Capaldi as a foul-mouthed and power-hungry political operative.

The Office

Run Time

Twelve thirty-minute episodes in two series and two fifty-minute specials aired between 2001 and 2003: the run time here is nearly eight hours.

Creator and Writers

Comedians Ricky Gervais and Stephen Merchant created, directed, and wrote the entire series, and went on to be involved with adapting the show for American television. It's worth tracking this series down on DVD just to watch the extras and interviews with Gervais and Merchant: Gervais endlessly giggles (and you really have to hear Gervais's giggle to believe it), Merchant is endlessly deadpan (and eye-catching, at over six-and-a-half feet tall, and also familiar from his cameo in this series as the character named Oggy), and when you hear the two of them together you truly start to understand their comedy dynamic.

What It's About

Although the "mockumentary" format is familiar to most of us, primarily from Christopher Guest's film *Spinal Tap* (and his multiple similar follow-ups), this Britcom elevated the concept to a true art form. Although never shown onscreen, the idea is that a documentary is being made about middle manager David Brent and his employees at the Wernham Hogg paper supply company in Slough. This is not, as you can imagine, a documentary that will be dripping in action and glamour.

Nearly every appearance of David Brent on-camera will make the viewer cringe, as he cracks countless racially and sexually tone-deaf jokes and clearly believes that both the people he supervises and the bosses who try to supervise him absolutely love him for his stellar management skills and his humor. Mostly what the people around Brent do is ignore him; they have enough to keep up with in their own lives: Gareth Keenan, Assistant Regional Manager (or is that actually "Assistant to the Regional Manager"?), tries to instill militaristic order to an office of non-followers; sales rep Tim is hopelessly in love with receptionist Dawn and enacts, with her, countless pranks on Gareth; Dawn has a good-looking but dim boyfriend who arguably sees her as less of a person with artistic talent than she is simply his girlfriend who, after they marry, will most likely "get a few kiddies under her belt."

Over the course of the show's two seasons Wernham Hogg's employees worried about corporate downsizing and redundancies, pub challenges, soul-sucking management retreats and trainings, and interoffice co-dependent friendships and unrequited love affairs. In other words, everything office workers still deal with on a daily basis.

Why It's Bingeworthy

Although the American version of this show went on to become hugely popular and was not without its charms, the British original is just so much better, and accomplishes its goals in a mere eight hours. First you'll watch it for the relationships; the tortured enemyship between Tim and Gareth; as well as the love triangle of paper salesman Tim, receptionist Dawn, and Dawn's insensitive boyfriend Lee; then you'll want to watch it again the following weekend to appreciate the true genius of Ricky Gervais's nervous, painful, high-energy portrayal of David Brent (for whom the viewer does eventually start to feel some sympathy, despite oneself). Finally, you'll need to watch it at least one more time to pick up all the one-liners ("Under weaknesses, you've put…eczema") and leave yourself enough time for a good weep after watching the Christmas special (which also wrapped up the series) in all its British Christmas-pop-music fueled goodness.

It's a classic, pure and simple. But don't watch it if you feel like quitting your own job (which is fun, I know, but not always financially prudent). Its drab white, tan, and gray color palette, the flicker of fluorescent lights throughout, and the spot-on portrayal of dreadful training seminars and corporate team-building exercises will really put you in the mood to hand in your notice.

Main Cast

Ricky Gervais…David Brent
Martin Freeman…Tim Canterbury
Mackenzie Crook…Gareth Keenan
Lucy Davis…Dawn Tinsley

Trivia

The Office was the first British comedy in twenty-five years to be nominated for a Golden Globe, and the first ever to win one.

When the first series of *The Office* was offered for sale on DVD in the U.K., it sold 80,000 units in its first week.

The American version of the show would eventually last for nine seasons and 201 episodes.

What to Binge on Next

Gervais and Merchant have been involved together in several other comedy series worth watching: *Extras* (about film extras working in Hollywood, also starring Gervais); *An Idiot Abroad* (in which the duo send their homebody friend Karl Pilkington traveling in search of different cultures and experiences primarily so that they can enjoy his discomfort from afar); and *Life's Too Short*, another mockumentary sitcom about "the life of a showbiz dwarf."

Mackenzie Crook, who played Gareth Keenan in this series, went on to write and star in another critically acclaimed series for the BBC, titled *Detectorists*. It's another ensemble piece that perfectly mixes the best of human relationships (between friends and romantic partners) with the worst (between rivals and ex-romantic partners).

Jackie on...
Christmas Specials, Comedies, and Reruns

In the holiday season the main TV channels tend to be filled with new content. In recent years we've been treated to Christmas specials from *Call the Midwife, Still Open All Hours, Birds of a Feather, Doctor Who* and *The Great British Bake Off*.

Many classic TV programmes have produced Christmas specials, but these don't tend to be repeated each year. You might catch glimpses of episodes of *Blackadder, Porridge,* and *Steptoe and Son* on a compilation clip show, but they don't tend to show repeat episodes on the main TV channels – unless you're watching at 3am!

The only programmes that do seem to be repeated each year are *Morecambe and Wise* and *The Two Ronnies*.

Some kids' programmes are repeated every season, like. Raymond Briggs's *The Snowman*, and, more recently, *The Snow Dog*, and are timeless classics that can be enjoyed by the whole family.

Only Fools and Horses

Run Time

This series was hugely popular and is one of the longer-running British sitcoms; it is also well-known (and loved) for its many Christmas specials. This all makes it a bit complicated to attempt to give a total run time, but I'm going to try. Through the first four seasons, the episodes and the specials all had a length of thirty minutes. The Christmas special for the fourth season was the first episode to deviate from that format, and ran for ninety minutes. Thereafter, there was another series of thirty-minute episodes, but the subsequent specials had different lengths, and the regular episodes themselves changed to fifty-minute programs starting with series six. Overall, sixty-four episodes and sixteen specials? They make for a total viewing time of nearly forty-six hours.

Creator and Writers

The show was created and written by John Sullivan.

What It's About

Del Boy Trotter and his brother Rodney comprise the Trotters Independent Traders—making a life in Peckham, the somewhat seedy side of London in the 1980s and 1990s by buying low (anything, even combination-lock briefcases that come with the combination written on pieces of paper locked INSIDE the cases) and selling high (hopefully; if the police don't catch them with stolen goods first). Del Boy thrives on the lifestyle, he's a "trier," as their Grandad, who lives with them, says. Rodney, on the other hand, chafes a bit under the thumb of his older brother and always dreams of a lifestyle that's a bit more honorable and upscale.

Changes come to the lives of the Trotter brothers regularly throughout the series: first they live with their Grandad, but in later series the role of their elderly family statesman is filled by their Uncle Albert, who is certainly a match for Del Boy in terms of coming up with (not often successful) schemes. Likewise, the brothers' respective love lives make for many plot twists, although Rodney eventually marries and the issues of that relationship also have an impact on his decisions and the business.

But the heart of the program is always Del Boy's and Rodney's relationship with one another. Business profits may never materialize and arguments may often be the top order of the day, but one thing they always have (even if they don't admit it) is their love for each other.

Why It's Bingeworthy

This is another classic show that looms large in British pop cultural history (I first heard about it when it was referenced by a character in another popular sitcom, *The Vicar of Dibley*). David Jason and Nicholas Lyndhurst, the show's stars, would go on to star in many other programs, but have always probably been best loved for their roles as the scrappy Trotter brothers. Perhaps more than any other this sitcom showcases the British love for the underdog and the less-than-glamorous star characters. And when the Brits portray underdogs they really mean it; most of these episodes end with the latest Trotter get-rich-quick scheme failing miserably. It's funny, and it's totally right, but I'm still enough of an American that after watching multiple episodes I started thinking, "Ah, come on, can't the boys win one for once?"

The supporting cast members are also very funny actors, and the show's many Christmas specials made this program must-see viewing in most homes during the holidays (viewership numbers routinely topped fifteen and twenty million viewers per episode).

Main Cast

David Jason…Derek ("Del Boy") Trotter
Nicholas Lyndhurst…Rodney Trotter
Lennard Pierce…Grandad
Buster Merryfield…Uncle Albert

Trivia

In 2004 *Only Fools and Horses* was voted the best British sitcom by the BBC and public votes.

David Jason was not actually the producers' first choice to play the role of Del Boy (particularly as he and Nicholas Lyndhurst look nothing alike); they originally wanted Jim Broadbent to play the part.

A sequel of sorts to this program, featuring the supporting character Boycie and his family and about their move to the country to escape some of the rougher elements of Peckham, ran for four series in the 2000s, and was titled *The Green Green Grass*.

What to Binge on Next

There were two "sort of" sequels to this show that might be fun to watch, if you can find them: *The Green Green Grass* focused on the further exploits of Boycie, one of the supporting characters in *Only Fools...*, and a three-episode "prequel" titled *Rock & Chips* aired in 2010.

Any number of long-running and classic Britcoms might work when you have finished watching *Only Fools and Horses*. Consider *Are You Being Served?*, which ran in the 1970s and 1980s and focused on the employees of a department store who sniped at one another constantly but nonetheless remained united in their disdain for management; *The Vicar of Dibley*, in which a female vicar is sent to a conservative rural parish where she somehow manages to charm the locals; or the long-running *Last of the Summer Wine*, which ran for thirty-one seasons and 295 episodes, and which featured a group of crotchety old friends who remained both crotchety and friends throughout the entire run of the series.

Fans of David Jason will want to check out another classic program he was in, the police procedural *A Touch of Frost*, and those viewers charmed by Nicholas Lyndhurst as Rodney might check out the 1990s Britcom *Goodnight Sweetheart*.

Outnumbered

Run Time

In five series between 2007 and 2014, this show included thirty-one thirty-minute episodes and four forty-minute specials, resulting in a total run time of roughly eighteen hours.

Creator and Writers

The series was created by Andy Hamilton and Guy Jenkin, and written by them as well, although the show is infamous for allowing its young stars to create their own dialogue after giving them only a story prompt or outline.

What It's About

I have two kids, so technically, we aren't outnumbered by them, but I can still empathize with the parents in this sitcom. Not only are the two Brockman parents outnumbered by their three children, but what children they are. The eldest, Jake, a young teen when the series starts, relies heavily on sarcasm and is more than a little interested in girls; the middle son Ben is an evil genius who excels at exploiting the dynamics of the household to get what he wants; and the youngest, Karen, is a relentless questioner who is oblivious to the discomfort of the adults she is questioning. Throw in a grandfather who believes in telling the unflinching truth (and who is slipping into dementia) and you definitely have a household where the parents end up feeling under siege. It doesn't help that neither parent is particularly in love with their respective careers; in early seasons, Pete works as a teacher in an inner-city school and Sue works as a personal assistant for a particularly mercurial boss (who is often referenced but never seen).

As the series progresses the kids grow up, but they're still a handful. In one story Ben decides to get into the Guinness World Records, preferably for some kind of act involving knives; in another, a psychology-obsessed Jake tells his parents every wrong move they have made while parenting Karen.

Why It's Bingeworthy

The show achieves its tone of surreal realism by making itself semi-real; the adult actors are given scripts but the children are only generally advised by the writers of how they want the scene to run. If the parents often seem befuddled by their offspring (and they do), that, too, is intentional.

This series has a rhythm and tone all its own among television shows, but after a while spent watching it you will realize with a jolt why you can't look away from it: it perfectly matches both the frenetic and totally dull pace of your own household of a spouse or partner, children, aged parents, pets, and everyone else who comes and goes. Luckily it's very, very funny, not only thanks to the children's improvisations but also in large part due to the reactions and skills of the actors Claire Skinner and Hugh Dennis as Sue and Pete (the parents).

Main Cast

Claire Skinner...Sue Brockman
Hugh Dennis...Pete Brockman
Tyger Drew-Honey...Jake Brockman
Daniel Roche...Ben Brockman
Ramona Marquez...Karen Brockman

Trivia

The series included four Christmas specials, which first aired in 2009, 2011, 2012, and 2016.

Life imitated art in 2017, when it was confirmed that Hugh Dennis and Claire Skinner were in a relationship (although both have children with other partners).

What to Binge on Next

Outnumbered was written by the same creative team that was behind the Channel 4 sitcom *Drop the Dead Donkey*, which was set in a news production company and ran for six seasons in the 1990s.

Friday Night Dinner is a sitcom about a North London family who keep the tradition of having Friday night dinners with their two grown sons, who are not sufficiently grown to stop tormenting one another (or their parents) with pranks and generally obnoxious behavior.

If you like sitcoms focusing on family life (or ways in which it does not always meet one's expectations), you might also enjoy *Moone Boy*, *My Family*, and *Spy*, or the family dramas *The Durrells in Corfu* and *Wild at Heart*.

Peep Show

Run Time

Peep Show is a long bingewatch; it ran on Channel 4 from 2003 to 2015 (nine series in all), and the entire series contains fifty-four twenty-four-minute episodes, for a total run time of nearly twenty-two hours.

Creator and Writers

Although the program stars popular comedians David Mitchell and Robert Webb (otherwise best known for their variety/comedy program *That Mitchell and Webb Look*), it was actually created by Andrew O'Connor, Jesse Armstrong, and Sam Bain. Armstrong and Bain were the primary writers, with Simon Blackwell getting writing credits on four episodes, and Mitchell and Webb being credited with providing "additional material."

What It's About

Mark Corrigan and Jeremy ("Jez") Usborne have two things in common: they're flatmates, and their friendship is completely dysfunctional.

That is, of course, because they're completely dysfunctional individuals. Although a perfectly respectably-employed loan officer, Mark hides his feelings of social anxiety with an overwhelmingly cynical attitude; Jez, on the other hand, is an underemployed musician and full-time slacker whose problem is over-confidence. We see their friendship and their relationships with others through a variety of different point of view shots (hence the title) and through their inner monologues delivered as voice-overs.

Over the course of nine series the men endure awkward situations, dating and work conflicts, and a lot of completely juvenile hijinks that never end well. The flatmates' other friends are no help; mostly they manage to land the flatmates in ever bigger problems, from drug addictions, job losses, and Jez's failed career as a life coach (among many others).

Why It's Bingeworthy

If you can stand watching two grown men being total idiots, you're going to love this series.

Now that's harsh. Because Mark and Jez are quite unlikable, it's easy to miss that they're also underdogs in their own way (which is underscored by the series' finale, which I'm not going to tell you about, because I don't give spoilers). It actually is quite funny, particularly when you consider that the boys' various idiocies mostly blow up in their own and each other's faces.

Although the show never garnered huge viewership numbers, it's long been viewed as a cult favorite in the U.K.

Main Cast

David Mitchell…Mark Corrigan
Robert Webb…Jeremy ("Jez") Usborne
Matt King…Super Hans
Paterson Joseph…Alan Johnson
Olivia Colman…Sophie Chapman

Trivia

When the program started in 2003 and was still on the air until 2010 (it would eventually run until 2015), it became Channel 4's longest-running comedy (and Channel 4's longest-running show, full stop) ever.

Russell Brand auditioned for the role of Super Hans.

There have been three attempts to adapt the show for American television, but all three attempts failed. One failed attempt starred Johnny Galecki, while for the third attempt the Starz network assembled a team to start production but scrapped the project before filming anything.

What to Binge on Next

A very similar comedy to this one is HBO's *Flight of the Conchords*, although it features a slightly gentler friendship between the two main characters, who are trying to start a career as a singing duo. (*Peep Show* creators Armstrong and Bain were originally slated to assist with *Flight of the Conchords*, but had to bow out due to scheduling conflicts.) If you're a fan of *Peep Show* you might also enjoy two other series created by Armstrong and Bain: *Fresh Meat*, a comedy about college students; and *Babylon*, a comedy about employees of the Metropolitan Police Service.

Of course these fans are also going to want to catch the stars' other well-regarded program, the sketch comedy *That Mitchell and Webb Look*.

Red Dwarf

Run Time

Red Dwarf is another British comedy exception to the rule that most British shows run for only a few series or a handful of episodes: it is comprised of seventy-three half-hour episodes, over twelve seasons. It first aired on BBC Two from 1988 to 1993 and 1997 to 1999, and then on Dave (a digital British TV channel, owned by U.K.TV) in 2009 and from 2012 to 2017.

Creator and Writers

The creator of the show is credited as "Grant Naylor"; this is actually a combination of the creators' names, Rob Grant and Doug Naylor. It is based on radio comedy sketches written by the creators, and titled *Dave Hollins: Space Cadet*, which aired on a BBC 4 Radio program in 1984. Through the first six series, the duo also wrote all of the episodes, but after 1993 Rob Grant left the program to pursue other projects. Many subsequent episodes were written by Doug Naylor, but he worked with other writers on series VII and VIII (that's the way *Red Dwarf* seasons are labeled), including Paul Alexander, Kim Fuller, Robert Llewellyn, and James Hendrie.

What It's About

The last man on Earth, Dave Lister, isn't actually on Earth—he's on a mining spaceship named the *Red Dwarf*, and he's only there because when a radiation leak on the ship killed everyone else, he was in suspended animation (and somehow his pregnant cat survived too). He was subsequently kept there by the ship's computer, which only brought him around when the radiation had sufficiently dispersed for him to live safely…three million years in the future.

At least Lister isn't alone. There's always the ship's computer (Holly) to keep him company, as well as, less fortunately for Lister, a hologram of his previous supervisor (Arnold Judas Rimmer), who actually perished in the radiation. And don't forget Cat—a humanoid feline who evolved from a race birthed by Lister's pregnant cat.

Confused? Don't be. Even if it never makes any kind of real sense, the interactions between those characters, and several others who manage to join them in the course of the show's many series, will keep you so busy watching that you'll forget all about your troublesome need for a linear storyline. Just relax and enjoy.

Why It's Bingeworthy

There's a lot of reasons to love *Red Dwarf*, even if it doesn't lend itself to being easily summarized (or perhaps that's just another reason to love it). It's a classic, for one thing, its creators and viewers are clearly still not ready to give it up, as a series XIII is being planned for 2019.

It's astounding that most of the actors who started on the program in the late 1980s are still showing up to reprise their roles in the latest episodes, lending the show a truly immortal air. And speaking of characters, Dave Lister is the type of character the Brits love to love, a true underdog; he was, after all, the lowest-ranked of all 169 of the original ship's crew members.

Main Cast

Craig Charles…Dave Lister
Chris Barrie…Arnold Judas Rimmer
Danny John-Jules…The Cat
Robert Llewellyn…Kryten
Clare Grogan/Chloë Annett…Kristine Kochanski
Norman Lovett/Hattie Hayridge…Holly

Trivia

Alan Rickman auditioned for the role of Arnold Rimmer, while Hugh Laurie was considered for the role of Dave Lister.

Red Dwarf is the second longest-running science fiction program on British TV, after *Doctor Who*.

After Series VIII ended in 1999, Doug Naylor hoped a feature film based on the series could be made, but even though a script was written and filming was planned, insufficient funding scuttled the project in 2005.

In April 2018 it was announced that a thirteenth series would be made in 2019.

Red Dwarf is completely unique, but its fans might enjoy any show where the comedy stems from the same characters being stuck with each other in nearly claustrophobic circumstances. These include but are not limited to *Father Ted*, about three misfit priests and their slightly barmy housekeeper, stuck together on an Irish island; *Fawlty Towers*, in which all the workers and guests in a hotel are stuck together with the snobbishly unhinged proprietor Basil Fawlty; and *The Brittas Empire*, about the employees of a community leisure center (which also stars Chris Barrie, who plays Arnold Rimmer in *Red Dwarf*).

If you like the science fiction trappings of *Red Dwarf*, and the sheer number of its episodes and its importance in the pop culture canon, you might also like any (or all) seasons of another venerable science fiction classic: a little show known as *Doctor Who*.

Jackie on...
Programming for Kids

The quality of programmes for children seems to have increased a lot recently. They used to just be on for a couple of hours in the morning and then between 3pm and 5.30pm, but now they are on all day. I haven't watched CBeebies for a while, but many of the programmes are engrained in our culture. Have you ever seen *In the Night Garden*? That is a bizarre programme that no one really understands!

Another mention must be for Justin Fletcher—a giant of children's TV. He does *Mr Tumble*, *Justin's House* and *Gigglebiz*. He is so good with children and I love the fact he includes people with disabilities in his shows. It is really weird seeing him being interviewed as he is so different in real life.

CBeebies is a channel for children under the age of 5. Many of the programmes have been produced for years and were originally on BBC1 and BBC2, but were then all transferred across to their own channel in 2002. (At the same time CBBC, Children's BBC, for kids aged 6 to 12, was also launched.) CBeebies have a bedtime story every night (6.50pm - 7pm) just before it goes off air for the evening. They are normally read by the CBeebies presenters, but they occasionally get big celebrities in. Tim Peake even read one from space!

Reggie Perrin

Run Time

This 2009-2010 series, which is a remake of the earlier comedy classic *The Fall and Rise of Reginald Perrin*, ran for two series of six half-hour episodes each, making for a total run time of six hours.

Creator and Writers

The original program was created and written by David Nobbs; he co-wrote this version as well, along with Simon Nye.

What It's About

Corporate cog Reginald Perrin is having a doozy of a midlife crisis: his commute is always at least eleven minutes longer than planned; he's bored with his job as the head of the disposable razor division of Groomtech, the corporation to which he's sold his soul; his boss is an egomaniacal manipulator; his marriage has lost its zing and he spends many of his work hours fantasizing about a colleague.

He's Everyman, and by that I mean he's every middle-aged corporate shill who's ever annoyed you, and yet you can't help liking him. When, in the second series, he unexpectedly saves the company with a new invention, he also tries to make sure none of the current employees are made redundant (laid off). Turns out he's a mostly decent bloke: it's modern life that's the problem.

Why It's Bingeworthy

The 1970s program on which this remake is based is regarded as a classic, but if you can't find that series, this updated version will fit the bill nicely. Even though it aired less than a decade ago, it does seem a bit more dated than many other programs from its time: Perrin's fantasizing about his colleague, for example, may not play well in this (hopefully) more enlightened time.

But it's still dark and cynical in all the right places, with relatable characters, and if you're at all feeling the ennui of modern corporate jobs you'll feel for these characters' plights). Hang in there after the first series; the second series displays more heart.

Main Cast

Martin Clunes...Reggie Perrin
Fay Ripley...Nicola Perrin
Lucy Liemann...Jasmine Strauss
Neil Stuke...Chris Jackson

Trivia

In the original series Reginald Perrin faked his own death at the end of the first season and came back with his own wildly successful business idea, although it still didn't make him happy. In this new series Reggie contemplates actual suicide.

One of the most popular catchphrases of the original program, which was re-used in the remake was Perrin's boss stating, "I didn't get where I am today by...," a phrase which could be followed by either a sensible thing to do or a surreal impossibility.

What to Binge on Next

Of course purists will want to go back and watch the full twenty-one-episode run of the original *The Fall and Rise of Reginald Perrin*, starring Leonard Rossiter.

If you can't get enough of cheering for the underdog and/or laughing at the inanities of office life, you might also enjoy the sitcom *The Office*, featuring a clueless but largely harmless boss and several complex office friendships.

Martin Clunes did a great job with this role; his fans might also want to consider his earlier comedy *Men Behaving Badly* (it's about exactly what its title says it's about); *Doc Martin*, his dramedy about a surgeon who leaves the big city and decides instead to enter general practice in rural Cornwall; or his drama *William and Mary*, about an undertaker's tempestuous midlife relationship with a single mother who works as a midwife.

Spaced

Run Time

Spaced is a perfect little snack of television, consisting of fourteen twenty-five-minute episodes in two series, making for a total run time of just a touch under six hours.

Creator and Writers

Co-creators Simon Pegg and Jessica Stevenson created, wrote, and starred in all of the episodes.

What It's About

Tim Bisley's just been kicked out of the flat he was sharing with his girlfriend Sarah and Daisy Steiner has been squatting in various locations until she can find a more permanent place to live, so it seems like good luck when the two twenty-somethings meet one another in a north London coffee shop and decide to join forces to find a place to live together. Soon they find the perfect flat; so what if the landlady only wants to rent to a "professional couple"?

So that's what they set out to become, learning one another's (many) pop culture interests, strengths and weaknesses (primarily their truly awesome abilities to procrastinate and avoid finding real jobs), and other personal issues. In fact—do they become so good at acting a couple that maybe, just maybe, they should become a couple?

Why It's Bingeworthy

You'll just have to watch to find out what happens between Tim and Daisy. But don't make the mistake of thinking this sitcom has only a "will they or won't they?" plot…there's plenty of other things going on. The pop culture references fly thick and fast and very cleverly and the supporting and cameo characters are all well-known in Brit acting circles (they include Nick Frost, Bill Bailey, John Simm, even Mark Gatiss and Ricky Gervais). It's gentle and somewhat drug-addled (there is a lot of pot smoking in this show) and funny and a classic.

Main Cast

Simon Pegg…Tim Bisley
Jessica Stevenson (Hynes)…Daisy Steiner
Julia Deakin…Marsha Klein
Nick Frost…Mike Watt
Mark Heap…Brian Topp
Katy Carmichael…Twist Morgan

Trivia

One of the few restrictions placed on the show by the network that produced it was that the writers could only use the word "fuck" twice in each episode.

Pegg and Stevenson have stated that they were influenced by the heavy use of fantasy sequences in the American show *Northern Exposure*.

What to Binge on Next

Fans of Simon Pegg (and Nick Frost) are obviously going to want to see the trilogy of movies for which those two are best known: *Shaun of the Dead*, *Hot Fuzz*, and *World's End*. Jessica Stevenson (now known as Jessica Hynes) also played a supporting role on the comedy *The Royle Family*, as well as on the short-lived comedy series *Asylum*.

Other shows in which flatmates' relationships are front and center might appeal to *Spaced* fans, including the comedy/drama/horror hybrid *Being Human* (in which the roommates are a vampire, a werewolf, and a ghost) and *Peep Show* (although the two male roommates in this show are not nearly as fond of one another as Tim and Daisy are).

Spy

Run Time

Spy's run was short, but sweet. It aired in two series in 2011 and 2012, for a total of sixteen twenty-five-minute episodes and one forty-five-minute Christmas special. Total run time is roughly seven and a half hours; call in sick to work and you can do the whole program in one eight-hour day!

Creator and Writers

The show was created and written by Simeon Goulden.

What It's About

You know how sometimes it happens that you're casting about for a new career, your ex-wife and evil genius son are disdainful of your very existence, and your best friend is a bitter tech services worker with a questionable sense of ethics? Tim Elliot, mild-mannered computer sales associate and disdained former husband and current part-time father, feels your pain.

When Tim decides he has to get a better job and arrives for what he thinks is a typical civil service job interview, he finds himself recruited into MI-5 by a spy trainer known only as The Examiner, whose own grasp on reality is tenuous at best. Tim realizes fairly early on (like when he drops the gun he's issued the minute he steps outside headquarters) that he may be unsuited for the work, but it also occurs to him that working as a super-spy may be the best way to impress his son Marcus, who keeps himself busy running Godfather-like schemes and power plays at his school and largely can't be bothered to notice what his father is doing.

A life of intrigue is not all Tim finds at his new job: he also falls in love with one of his co-workers, only to have that situation complicated when her former boyfriend, a CIA agent, joins their workplace.

Why It's Bingeworthy

Spy is a perfect example of what makes British television, and its comedy in particular, so great. It's equal parts ridiculous, gentle, unexpected, brash, and all with a bit of physical comedy thrown in (much of it being supplied more than ably by the great Robert Lindsay in his role as The Examiner). And it's a really quick watch; anytime you're feeling down and you need the quick endorphin hit that only the best Britcom can provide, you can watch a season of *Spy* after dinner and still make it to bed on time.

Main Cast

Darren Boyd...Tim Elliot
Jude Wright...Marcus Elliot
Mathew Baynton...Chris Pitt-Goddard
Rebekah Staton...Caitlin Banks
Dolly Wells...Judith Elliot
Robert Lindsay...The Examiner

Trivia

Darren Boyd won a BAFTA (British Academy of Film and Television Arts) award for Best Male Comedy Role in 2012, for his portrayal of Tim Elliot.

What to Binge on Next

If you like your British comedy series short and sweet, there's plenty of other very funny choices for you: the complete runs of the classic *The Office*, *Moone Boy*, *Detectorists* can all be watched in under ten hours.

The offbeat nature of *Spy* is very similar to the thriller spoof *The Wrong Mans*, which Mathew Boynton (who plays Tim Elliot's strange and morally ambiguous friend in *Spy*) co-wrote and starred in, along with James Corden.

To The Manor Born

Run Time

The show's entire run from 1979 to 1981 consisted of twenty episodes (at thirty minutes) and two Christmas specials (at an hour) across three series. In 2007 an hour-long anniversary and Christmas special brought the total watch time to thirteen hours.

Creator and Writers

The series was created and written by Peter Spence; script associate Christopher Bond wrote the series' final episode that aired in 1981.

What It's About

Audrey fforbes-Hamilton is trying to look the part of the grieving widow and largely failing: when her mostly ineffectual pedigreed husband Martin dies and is finally out of the way, she looks forward to exercising full control over her family's estate, Grantleigh. She is, therefore, more than just a little put out to find that Martin had gotten Grantleigh deeply into debts and the property must be sold to cover them.

Audrey's mood does not improve when her estate and manor house (she always thinks of the estate as hers, you must understand, even when she doesn't technically own it) is sold at auction to the nouveau-riche supermarket magnate Richard DeVere. She wreaks her own brand of revenge by buying the small cottage on the manor grounds and keeping a close eye (often with binoculars) on the manor and its new occupants (DeVere and his mother). Ever at the ready to instruct the new lord of the manor in his community responsibilities, she largely fails to notice that the neighborhood is enjoying both the largesse of its new benefactor, as well as Audrey's corresponding loss in fortune and influence.

Why It's Bingeworthy

For my money this is one of the most romantic sitcoms out there. Penelope Keith and Peter Bowles as Audrey and Richard have fantastic chemistry (even in the twenty-five-year anniversary special) and the three seasons' worth of "will they or won't they" tension was very believably and satisfyingly resolved in the end. A rich supporting cast (particularly John Rudling as Audrey's loyal butler Brabinger, Angela Thorne as Audrey's rather fluffy but good-hearted friend Marjory Frobisher, and Daphne Heard as Richard's mother Mrs. Polouvicka) and a lot of very funny small moments make this series ideal for comfort watching when you need a break from the world.

Much is made of the importance of the class system in Great Britain, and this show provides a short but comprehensive education in matters of class, aristocracy, and many cultural attitudes that were in place in the 1980s (and are still in play today, although perhaps less obviously).

Main Cast

Penelope Keith…Audrey fforbes-Hamilton
Peter Bowles…Richard DeVere
Angela Thorne…Marjory Frobisher
Daphne Heard…Mrs. Maria Polouvicka
John Rudling…Brabinger

Trivia

Keith and Bowles did all of their own stunts—primarily of the horse-riding variety—for the show.

At its peak the show was watched by twenty million viewers.

Actor Penelope Keith became aristocracy in 2014, when she was made a Dame Commander of the Order of the British Empire (DBE), for "services to the Arts and to Charity." She has also served as the High Sheriff of Surrey (only the third woman to ever hold the post) and Deputy Lieutenant of Surrey.

What to Binge on Next

Keith practiced her comedy chops on an earlier series, *The Good Life*, in which she played the snobby neighbor to Richard Briers's and Felicity Kendal's married couple attempting to live on the land of their suburban tract house. For his part, Peter Bowles was in several other well-regarded comedy series, including Yorkshire Television's *The Bounder* and Thames Television's *Executive Stress*.

If you're in need of more romantic television you'll also want to check out *As Time Goes By*, *May to December*, or *The Vicar of Dibley*, all from the same era or a bit later.

The Vicar of Dibley

Run Time

The Vicar of Dibley had a somewhat irregular number of episodes and series. The first series was a fairly typical run of six half-hour episodes, while the second series consisted of four similar episodes (although episode one of series two ran for forty minutes rather than thirty). Those two series were followed by two seasonal specials, titled "The Easter Bunny" and "The Christmas Lunch Incident," and then four "seasonal specials" (at forty minutes each). Finally, a two-part Christmas special was aired over the 2004-2005 holidays, and the series concluded with another two-part Christmas special the following year (with each of the final two episodes running for fifty-five minutes). The series began in 1994, ended on January 1, 2007, and if you add up all those episodes, you get a run time of nearly thirteen hours.

Creator and Writers

The series was created specifically for Dawn French by Richard Curtis, with the majority of the episodes being written by Curtis and Paul Mayhew-Archer (with "contributions" from Kit Hesketh-Harvey).

What It's About

The small rural village of Dibley is getting a new vicar…and a female one at that! And what a female she is: Geraldine Granger, a "babe with a bob cut and a magnificent bosom."

From the moment she arrives in the village she begins to change it for the better, livening up church services, council meetings, and the town's social life. Whether she's busy holding a church service to bless all the parish animals, trying to help Dibley line up Elton John for their village fête, or just generally trying to help the decidedly odd parish residents keep on with their oddness in the most productive way possible, she truly is a vixen of a vicar.

Why It's Bingeworthy

When you watch *The Vicar of Dibley* you are in the presence of comedy royalty. It was created and written by Richard Curtis, one of the most influential Brit TV writers of recent years, and Dawn French is half of the influential comedy duo of French and Jennifer Saunders, who has appeared in numerous TV comedies and dramas alike.

But even if you didn't know all that (or if you don't care about it now that you do know) you'll want to catch this show because you wouldn't believe a show that works to advance a rather new idea (women priests in the Church of England started being ordained in 1994) and that is so gentle in its portrayal of a community comprised of eccentrics could also be so funny. The show boasts some truly wicked innuendo and Geraldine herself is a very earthy vicar whose search for true love rarely runs smooth but about which she is always very enthusiastic. Visual gags and great physical humor moments are a huge part of the show, and the aforementioned eccentric characters are all great fun in their own way, from the village idiot (son of the village's most wealthy man) to the lonely farmer preoccupied with the state of his bowels, from the elderly lady whose culinary masterpieces are not so much masterpieces as they are random combinations of unexpected ingredients to the elderly gentlemen who often surprise with their tales of village life in the past. Vicar Geraldine meets them all on their own insane ground and the village (and your TV viewing experience) is all the richer for it.

Main Cast

Dawn French...Vicar Geraldine Granger
Gary Waldhorn...David Horton
James Fleet...Hugo Horton
Emma Chambers...Alice Tinker
Roger Lloyd-Pack...Owen Newitt
Trevor Peacock...Jim Trott
John Bluthal...Frank Pickle
Liz Smith...Letitia Cropley

Trivia

Dawn French originally wanted to play the role of the much funnier (she thought) Alice Tinker. She specifically requested that her character have her fair share of faults—including her vanity and her obsession with chocolate—to make her more interesting.

Actor Emma Chambers, who played Alice Tinker to perfection, died of a heart attack in 2018, at the too-young age of fifty-three. Rest in peace, Alice.

The Vicar of Dibley is also well known for its frequent Comic Relief specials. Six of them were made between the years of 1997 and 2015, and they're all worth watching, if you can find them.

What to Binge on Next

As already noted, Richard Curtis (who is actually from New Zealand) is a popular and prolific writer who not only penned the movies *Love Actually*, *Four Weddings and a Funeral*, and *Notting Hill* but also the television shows *Blackadder*, *Mr. Bean*, and *Robbie the Reindeer*. His co-writer, Paul Mayhew-Archer, also wrote the sitcoms *My Hero* and *Office Gossip*.

Dawn French showcases her great comedic and acting talents in everything she's in, and that's quite an impressive list. In addition to her work on the sketch comedy program *French and Saunders* she has appeared in the comedies *Psychoville* and *The Wrong Mans* as well as the historical drama *Lark Rise to Candleford*.

If you like the community aspect of this program you might also like other Britcoms in which geographical or work communities take center stage: the work mockumentary *The Office*; the classic program about elder residents in a retirement community (who aren't necessarily happy to be there), *Waiting for God*, and the romantic sitcom *Gavin & Stacey*, which also boasts a number of eccentric characters.

Jackie on...
Five Comedies You Should Start With

The Vicar of Dibley

The Vicar of Dibley is my favourite comedy series. It perfectly captures English village life - gently poking fun at everything we do. I love the innocence of Alice and the gentle mocking she receives from Geraldine, the Vicar. There is a real love and warmth that runs through the whole programme, and it showed ridiculous ideas about what women can and can't do, (and then gently squashed them with humour).

Father Ted

I'm not sure what it is about vicars that make them such a good match for comedy, but maybe it's their special position in society, enabling them to comment on events like birth and death. *Father Ted* is surreal, but the bizarre satire and unique characters make it impossible not to laugh. It is occasionally crude, but it is also brilliantly bonkers!!

Fawlty Towers

Fawlty Towers is a classic of British comedy. Some scenes are no longer acceptable, due to their racism, but with these removed it really is one of the funniest things ever made. I especially love Basil Fawlty's overreaction to tiny errors. The physical comedy in it can't be beaten. A real classic.

Black Books

Black Books is less known than my other choices, but as a book lover, I love Dylan Moran's portrayal of frustrated bookshop owner Bernard Black. The dialogue is incredibly funny and I love how Bernard hates book shoppers, particularly when they disturb his peace to ask ridiculous questions about books! It is original and the addition of Bill Bailey is comic genius.

Outnumbered

Outnumbered is the most recent of my choices. It perfectly captures the frustration of family life. It isn't as polished as the others, but this is because the child actors were often left to improvise, giving everything an authentic and bizarre feel. I recommend it to anyone, but if you have children it is especially worth watching

Dramas

At Home with the Braithwaites

Run Time

This comedy-drama ran for four seasons, from 2000 to 2003, and consisted of twenty-six forty-five-minute episodes, for a total run time of nearly twenty hours.

Creator and Writers

The show is an early creation of writer Sally Wainwright, and all its episodes were written by her, with the exception of the episodes in the last series, several of which were written by Katie Baxendale and Jonathan Harvey.

What It's About

When housewife and mother Alison Braithwaite wins thirty-eight million pounds in the lottery, the first thing she doesn't do is tell her family.

In all fairness, her whole family has a lot going on and don't really take the time to notice that Alison is distracted: her husband is having an affair that he is beginning to regret; their oldest daughter has been sent down from university and is struggling with her unrequited love for their next-door neighbor (and older woman) Megan; their middle daughter is desperate for all the wrong kind of male attention, and their youngest daughter (and the one who bought the lottery ticket for her mother as a birthday gift) is secretive and mainly keeps her own company.

Subsequent seasons find the family learning about Alison's lottery win and dealing with all the changes it brings in their lifestyle and relationships. Whoever thinks that money can buy happiness would do well to watch this program.

Why It's Bingeworthy

In addition to their love for the underdog, the British also seem to have a cultural aversion to the happy ending or spiritually uplifting family drama. (And this is one of the many reasons I love them.) In America this series would be all about how the family uses their lottery winnings to be guardian angels to those around them and solve problems with the God-given gift of money; in the U.K. this show is a drama with moments of dark comedy that shows money contributing to the downfall of an already shaky marriage, multiple teenaged pregnancies, and the tendency of people to lose track of their better natures when great wealth becomes involved.

Main Cast

Amanda Redman…Alison Braithwaite
Peter Davison…David Braithwaite
Sarah Smart…Virginia Braithwaite
Sarah Churm…Sarah Braithwaite
Keeley Fawcett…Charlotte Braithwaite

Trivia

Peter Davison, who plays the patriarch of the Braithwaite family, has said that this was "his favourite role on television."

The show regularly garnered seven to nine million viewers when it was first shown.

What to Binge on Next

If you like this very British mix of drama and comedy, you might also enjoy *Cold Feet*, which is an ensemble show exploring the relationships and relationship difficulties of six friends in their thirties (and eventually forties).

Wainwright is a prolific writer who first honed her melodramatic craft by writing for such soaps as *Emmerdale* and *Coronation Street*; she is also the writer of the more recent family drama *Last Tango in Halifax* and the crime drama *Happy Valley*. An earlier production of hers that also started Sarah Smart (who appears in this program as Virginia Braithwaite) is the drama *Sparkhouse*, which is a modern take on the story of *Wuthering Heights*.

Ballykissangel

Run Time

The entire series spanned six seasons (1996 through 2001) and fifty-eight fifty-minute episodes, leading to a total run time of a tad over forty-eight hours. However, the show has a bit of a split personality; the first three seasons focused on the growing relationship between Father Peter Clifford and Assumpta Fitzgerald, while the latter three seasons were more of an ensemble piece. If you're inclined only to watch the Peter/Assumpta romance, you can watch those episodes in about twenty-two hours.

Creator and Writers

The series was created by Kieran Prendiville, who has writing credits on all fifty-eight episodes. Other writers who wrote multiple episodes included Ted Gannon, Mark Holloway, and Rio Fanning.

What It's About

The first three seasons of *Ballykissangel* focuses primarily on the growing relationship between Father Peter Clifford, an English Catholic priest sent to serve the congregation in Ballykissangel, Ireland, and Assumpta Fitzgerald, the feisty, organized-religion-and-especially-priest-hating owner and proprietor of the local pub. There's no denying the chemistry between the two, just as there's no denying the characters' mutual confusion and frustration about their attraction: as a priest, Father Clifford is supposed to be celibate, and there's really no place for a romantic relationship to grow while he remains a priest. A further complication is that he's a good priest: his parishioners like him and he's the thoughtful, serious kind of priest you wouldn't mind confessing all your sins to, especially as he's a total sweetie who also has a good sense of humor. You wouldn't mind grabbing a pint with him after mass, all told.

In addition to this relationship, which is soap-opera-y and sexual tension-y enough to fulfill all your viewing needs, *Ballyk* also hosts a cast of robust characters and community storylines. There's Assumpta's friend Niamh, married to the village police officer Ambrose (the prickly scenes between Niamh and her old-school mother-in-law provide a lot of comedy bang for the buck); Niamh's father, the village wheeler and dealer Bryan Quigley; a triumvirate of best friends who work as a school teacher, veterinarian, and garage owner, who spend much of their time in Assumpta's achingly cozy pub; the old-school parish priest who is not interested in Peter Clifford's kinder and gentler ways; and the two village workmen/stooges who are always doing some type of dodgy job for Quigley. Later seasons, after the Assumpta/Peter storyline had run its course, featured new cast members and new storylines, all incorporated well into the broader neighborhood life of Ballykissangel village, which is what the show is really all about.

Why It's Bingeworthy

As long as we're in Catholic mode here I'll confess: I've never actually watched the full run of *Ballykissangel*. I've seen a lot of episodes from the latter three seasons at one time or another, and always enjoy them when I catch them on public television (yes, I'm just that old: I've been watching British TV since the dawn of time, when the only place you could find offerings from the BBC was on PBS), but I never felt the need to watch them in sequence the way I still re-watch the first three seasons. For me the most powerful draw of the program is the heartbreaking relationship between Peter and Assumpta, as well as the community's gentle and forgiving response to its development and end. Fans of programs that focus on offbeat communities (such as *Northern Exposure* or *Gilmore Girls*) will love that aspect of this show.

It also includes a great deal of humor and many lighthearted storylines, and pokes good-natured fun at the community's big business fish (Bryan Quigley). The result is a drama that is thoughtful and sentimental without ever becoming too bleak or saccharine.

Ballykissangel was a hugely popular "dramedy" for its time, regularly scoring ten million viewers at the height of its first-run popularity (which ain't too shabby, considering that the combined population of the U.K. now is sixty-four million).

Main Cast

Stephen Tompkinson...Father Peter Clifford
Dervla Kirwan...Assumpta Fitzgerald
Tina Kellegher...Niamh Egan
Peter Hanly...Ambrose Egan
Tony Doyle...Bryan Quigley
Niall Toibin...Father Macanally
Don Wycherley...Father Aidan O'Connell

Trivia

Stephen Tompkinson and Dervla Kirwan (Father Clifford and Assumpta) actually became an item while filming the show and were engaged for two years.

Who's that who pops up in season four? Why, that's a very young, and already very good-looking, Colin Farrell, that's who!

Travel companies still advertise tours to Wicklow and Avoca…the region and town in Ireland, an hour south of Dublin, where *Ballykissangel* was filmed.

What to Binge on Next

Viewers who like their stories of offbeat communities and their residents, along with a little romance, might also consider the series *Doc Martin*, starring Martin Clunes as a standoffish surgeon who becomes a family doctor in a small town in Cornwall (and falls in love with one of the residents), or *Monarch of the Glen*, in which the son of a Scottish laird (lord of the manor, basically) returns home to try and keep his family and community afloat (and falls in love with one of the residents).

Those viewers who enjoy older British television might also consider the classic *All Creatures Great and Small*, set in rural Yorkshire during the 1930s and about a vet who joins a practice there (and falls in love with one of the residents).

Being Human

Run Time

Being Human ran for five seasons and a total of thirty-seven episodes, between 2008 and 2013. Each episode is very nearly an hour long, making for a total run time of thirty-seven hours.

Creator and Writers

The show was created by Toby Whithouse, and he wrote most of its episodes. Other writers include Jamie Mathieson, Lisa McGee, John Jackson, and Brian Dooley.

What It's About

When roommates George and Mitchell rent a flat together in Bristol, they are a bit disturbed to learn they have another roommate who is not on the lease: Annie, the ghost of the woman who lived there before them, and who died falling down the flat's stairs. Matters are complicated further by the facts that George is a werewolf, Mitchell is a vampire, and they are rooming and working together primarily so they can help each other "pass" as normal among the humans around them. Befriending a ghost does not seem, on the face of things, the best way to fit in (particularly if they ever want to bring dates home).

Over time, however, the trio form deep friendships with one another and seek to help each other with their rather specialized challenges. Annie wants to discover why she's stuck on earth as a ghost, while also trying to figure out what her much-loved fiancé might have had to do with her death. George wants to figure out a way to not hurt anyone during his full-moon transformations, and also how not to end up far from home, naked, and not remembering how he spent his werewolf time. Mitchell's is perhaps the most complex situation of all; he was once part of vampire society, but now seeks to live without draining victims and without ties to his former community. What all three seem to want, more than anything, is simply to be human.

Most of the seasons have longer story arcs, as when Mitchell has to fight the current leader of Bristol's vampire community, or George falls in love with his co-worker at the hospital. Eventually the main characters face a greater challenge in the face of an organization that wants to study them (not always humanely), so they move from Bristol to Barry Island, Wales, but even as the first season's main characters leave and new ones take their place, friendship remains a main theme of the program.

Why It's Bingeworthy

Being Human covers a lot of ground: its scary bits are genuinely scary and there's more than enough villains to go around, but most of the program focuses on the growing friendship between the flatmates and the rather commonplace situations they find themselves in (how best to ask people out; whose turn it is to do the dishes, etc.) The chemistry between Annie, George, and Mitchell is lively and might I just say, Aidan Turner (as Mitchell)? Aidan Turner is much worth watching in anything. Actually, I could say that about Lenora Crichlow (Annie) and Russell Tovey (George) as well.

You just don't see a lot of programs that combine elements of horror, comedy, and drama. It's a wild mix and *Being Human* hits all the high points of all three of those genres.

Main Cast

Lenora Crichlow...Annie Sawyer
Aidan Turner...John Mitchell
Russell Tovey...George Sands
Tom McNair...Michael Socha
Damien Molony...Hal Yorke
Kate Bracken...Alex Millar

Trivia

A pilot that aired before the first series properly began starred Andrea Riseborough as Annie and Guy Flanagan as John Mitchell; these actors were replaced by Lenora Crichlow and Aidan Turner.

In 2011, when the show's third series premiered on BBC Three, it was watched by 1.8 million viewers—the largest viewing audience for a series premiere in BBC Three history.

A U.S. remake of the show aired on Syfy from 2011 to 2014, and ran for four seasons and fifty-two episodes.

What to Binge on Next

Viewers who enjoy the unique blend of drama, comedy, and the supernatural that *Being Human* offers might also find a lot to like in the five-series-long program *The Misfits*, a drama/comedy/science fiction blend about a group of young offenders, sentenced to work community service together, and who all gain supernatural abilities when they're caught in a freak electrical storm.

Another show that blends stories of contemporary friendships and relationships with fantastic elements might also like *Primeval*, a series in which a group of scientists study temporal accidents in which both ancient and futuristic animals enter our present world and wreak all sorts of havoc.

Flatmate humor meets relationship humor in another recent sitcom, *Him & Her*, that also stars Russell Tovey.

Jackie on...
The Differences between the BBCs

BBC1 is the main BBC channel. It was launched in 1936 and strives to produce "impartial, high-quality and distinctive content and services that inform, educate and entertain". It is the most watched channel in the UK and it is paid for through a licence fee (which is currently £145.50/household, per year). This means that there are no ads on the channel at all - a massive bonus! A typical day begins at 6am with 3 hours of breakfast news and discussion. The main day-time slots are filled with programmes like *Homes Under the Hammer* (about buying property at auction) or *The Antiques Roadshow* (about the price of antique items). The evening is filled with popular programmes like new dramas, wildlife documentaries (we love David Attenborough!), *EastEnders* (very popular soap opera) or the latest cookery show.

BBC2 was launched in 1964. It tends to show less mainstream programmes than BBC, focusing more on culture. On a typical day it will have quiz shows, news, politics, documentaries and sporting events.

BBC3 was launched in 2003 and aimed at 16- to 34-year-olds. It moved online in 2016.

BBC4 was launched in 2002 and is very "high-brow". It is filled with arts programmes, historical documentaries, international films, music, and current affairs.

Black Mirror

Run Time

All told, the four series of *Black Mirror* that have aired through 2018 are 1,098 of the strangest (and often most horrifying) minutes you will find anywhere on television. Nineteen episodes aired between 2011 and 2017, and they all vary in length, from forty-one to ninety minutes, but in all it'll take you just a bit over eighteen hours to watch them all.

Creator and Writers

The show was created by Charlie Brooker, and he has written almost all of its episodes, with the exception of one by Jesse Armstrong, and another by Rashida Jones and Mike Schur. William Bridges also assisted Brooker on several episodes.

What It's About

In order to fully tell you what *Black Mirror* is about, I would have to tell you nineteen separate stories; this is an anthology program, meaning that each episode presents a new storyline and characters, acted by entirely different characters (like the classic program *The Twilight Zone*). That said, there is a theme to all of the stories: creator Charlie Brooker has said they are about technology and culture, and "the way we live now; and the way we might be living in ten minutes' time if we're clumsy."

Many of the stories involve technological advances that cause unforeseen distress; such as the implant that allows you to replay all your memories and see every single past moment of your life (which drives one couple to separation when infidelity is replayed); a rating system that allows you to "rate" all of your interpersonal interactions with other people (and which leads to empty relationships, as everyone desires to be seen as pleasant and upbeat to ensure a higher socioeconomic status); a group of blackmailers who download users' Internet-history secrets and then forces them to commit crimes or they'll release those secrets to the individual's friends and family; and many more.

Consider yourself warned: it's not really a series you can bingewatch right before going to bed; either it'll keep you up thinking or it'll give you nightmares.

Why It's Bingeworthy

I find it horrifying to watch, personally, but *Black Mirror* is also really creative and might actually serve a function as a variety of cautionary tales about the dangers of such now-omnipresent features of our lives, like constant surveillance, enhanced senses, and social media (to name just a few).

The show also employs a wide variety of actors, many you'll know from other programs and movies, including Rory Kinnear, Jon Hamm, Tobias Menzies, Jodie Whittaker, Rupert Everett, and Georgina Campbell.

Mainly, though, it's just a fascinating show that you won't be able to look away from, and every episode is a whole new story in a whole new world.

Main Cast

There isn't one, not really, but check out the names given above or go through the series' unbelievably long list of actors at imdb.com.

Trivia

The show was originally produced by British production company Zeppotron and by Channel 4, the network that commissioned the first two series. The latter two series, which began airing in 2016, were produced by Netflix.

Charlie Brooker and William Bridges won the 2018 Emmy Award in the Outstanding Writing for a Limited Series, Movie or Special category for the episode "USS Callister."

What to Binge on Next

There's just not a whole lot on television, British or otherwise, that is similar to *Black Mirror*. Creator Charlie Brooker has also written a short-lived horror/zombie series titled *Dead Set*, that aired on E4 in 2008.

For some reason I always have to stop and think which show is *Black Mirror*, and which is *Orphan Black*. These shows are not really alike in format; *Orphan Black* is a much more straightforward and linear narrative, but it is also dystopian in tone and counts as science fiction due to its plotlines revolving around cloning and other technological advances.

Bodyguard

Run Time

As of 2018 this BBC series has run for one season of six episodes, and has a total run time of just a bit over six hours. Future seasons are planned.

Creator and Writers

This hugely popular drama was created and written by Jed Mercurio.

What It's About

If only all David Budd had to deal with was a terrible case of Post-traumatic stress disorder after a tour of duty in Afghanistan, his life would be a lot easier.

It's not, though. From the very first episode of this political thriller, former soldier Budd is dumped straight into the deep end, also known as the train he's traveling on to return his children to their mother (his estranged wife), which also happens to be the target of a suicide bomber. Budd is able to detect and defuse that situation, and for his diligence is rewarded with a job in a special branch of the London Metropolitan Police, responsible for providing protective services to high-profile targets. If he thought he was in the deep end before, his new job will prove that he's still in the water, and he's been joined by piranhas.

The person he is assigned to guard is the staunchly Conservative Home Secretary Julia Montague, a politician for whom he feels little affinity but whose life he is sworn to protect. What follows as the protected and the protector get to know one another is one of the darkest cat-and-mouse games ever seen on television.

Why It's Bingeworthy

More than fourteen million viewers watched this show when it debuted on BBC One in 2018, giving the network its highest viewing figures since 2008. It was a media sensation, and viewers spent a lot of time on social media discussing the show's twists, turns, and series finale. It was the darling of that year's television season, and deserves a watch for that reason alone.

It is also packed with action and suspenseful sequences, as well as a plot guaranteed to keep viewers guessing about its main characters' motivations at every single moment. Headlined by actors Richard Madden (better known for his role as Robb Stark on another program of which you may have heard, *Game of Thrones*) and the always-exceptional Keeley Hawes, it's a program that is, quite literally, difficult to tear your eyes away from.

Main Cast

Richard Madden…David Budd
Keeley Hawes…Julia Montague
Sophie Rundle…Vicky Budd
Vincent Franklin…Mike Travis

Trivia

Journalists play a key role in this drama, and many real-life journalists made appearances in this series, including Laura Kuenssberg and Andrew Marr.

The series was mostly filmed on location in London, and its events are clearly shown to be taking place in the autumn of 2018, which is also when the show first aired.

What to Binge on Next

Jed Mercurio has a long history of making extremely bingeworthy television; earlier series of his include the medical dramas *Cardiac Arrest* and *Critical*, as well as the unbelievably watchable police procedural/thriller *Line of Duty* (which also featured Keeley Hawes in several seasons).

If you find yourself jonesing for another twisty-and-turny political drama, you're in luck; that is a genre they do extremely well in the UK. Consider watching the classic 1990 series *House of Cards* (American television came up with its own remake of that program, but the original British version is better) starring Ian Richardson. You're also going to want to watch *State of Play*, a thriller about journalists investigating the death of a young woman which turns out to be connected to all sorts of government cover-ups, and which featured a stellar cast, including David Morrissey, Bill Nighy, James McAvoy, Kelly Macdonald, and John Simm.

Cold Feet

Run Time

Cold Feet first aired in 1997; eventually it would go on to span seven series and forty-eight episodes. The first five series ran from 1997 to 2003; then the show overcame a thirteen-year gap and aired two new series in 2016 and 2017. Total run time, including a pilot episode, the slightly truncated fifth season, and the 2016 and 2017 reboots, comes in around thirty-eight hours.

Creator and Writers

The series was created and primarily written by Mike Bullen.

What It's About

Three very different couples experience their relationship ups and downs together, as well as commiseration about the challenges of changing and aging (including friendship, work, and health concerns). It's a drama, but many parts of it are as (unintentionally?) funny as real life can be sometimes. The three primary couples are Adam and Rachel, who fall in love in the beginning of the series, get married, and eventually experience great tragedy; Pete and Jenny, who struggle in the first season to conceive and who struggle in later seasons to stay married; and David and Karen, an upwardly mobile couple with one son (and later twin daughters), who also experience problems and infidelities in their marriage.

The series takes place in Manchester and is noted for its use of fantasy and flashbacks to augment the storylines. The pace of coupling, de-coupling, and re-coupling is such that the viewer almost needs to make a flowchart to follow who is currently in a relationship with who (particularly in later seasons, when new characters are introduced and try to fit in among the historical remains of the primary couples' relationships). From the very first pilot episode the show has offered offbeat moments of comedy: consider Adam winning Rachel back while serenading her in the nude, with a rose tucked jauntily in an uncomfortable place.

Why It's Bingeworthy

Cold Feet premiered to rather lackluster reviews and viewership, but eventually became hugely popular and topped out at nearly ten million viewers per episode in its third and later seasons. The fact that three series have been commissioned to air in 2017, 2018, and 2019, after the show was last seen in 2003, is testament to its staying power.

The program is not as lighthearted as its American counterpart, the sitcom *Friends*, but its mix of dramatic moments, fantasy elements, and dark comedy make it addictive watching.

Main Cast

Helen Baxendale…Rachel Bradley
James Nesbitt…Adam Williams
Fay Ripley…Jenny Gifford
John Thomson…Pete Gifford
Hermione Norris…Karen Marsden
Robert Bathurst…David Marsden

Trivia

Helen Baxendale also starred in several episodes of the American sitcom *Friends*, but her storyline as Ross Geller's wife (and then ex-wife) was cut short due to her first pregnancy.

The show was originally meant to be set in north London, but the setting was changed to Manchester (largely because it was cheaper to film there).

Over the years the show collected many awards, including a BAFTA for Best Drama Series and the British Comedy Award's Best TV Comedy Drama prize.

What to Binge on Next

Although much lighter in tone, the Britcom *Coupling*, which also featured the dating exploits of six friends and aired around the same early 2000s time period, might also appeal to fans of *Cold Feet*. Another comedy/drama that mixes relationship humor with nontraditional family groups and lives is the series *Stella*, written by and starring Ruth Jones (who also played one of the main roles in the relationship sitcom *Gavin & Stacey*).

Each of the primary stars of this program have starred in a wide variety of other British TV classics, including Helen Baxendale in the crime drama *An Unsuitable Job for a Woman*; James Nesbitt in the police drama *Murphy's Law*; Hermione Norris in *MI-5*; and Robert Bathurst in the comedy *Toast of London* and *Downton Abbey*.

Cucumber

Run Time

Cucumber was a short series, running for only one season and eight forty-five-minute episodes in 2015. Total run time is six hours.

Creator and Writers

Russell T. Davies created and wrote all of the episodes.

What It's About

Henry Best is middle-aged, has had a huge row with his boyfriend of nine years, and is besotted with two younger men with whom he works. He is, in short, in unfamiliar and confusing territory.

And that territory only becomes more tenuous as Henry temporarily moves in with the younger men, Dean and Freddie, but is unable to leave his own complicated personal life behind. His former partner Lance and he cannot resolve their differences; his sister visits with her son and reconnects with a former flame (now married); and Henry's forays into a new dating life do not go well.

The end of the series includes a shocking tragedy and story arc, after which Henry and his friends must find a deeper understanding of one another to move toward forgiveness and their futures.

Why It's Bingeworthy

Russell T. Davies, better known as the TV producer who revived the *Doctor Who* franchise in 2005, worked on developing this series for many years, and conceived of it as a sequel of sorts to the popular and groundbreaking earlier British series *Queer as Folk* (which he also created and developed). It has been critically lauded for its LGBT focus, but, more importantly, for its storylines that deal with broader themes such as the breakdown of "respectability" and the complexity of interpersonal relationships.

The writing and the actors share double billing for this show's unique ability to find the humor (and humanity) in even the darkest of situations.

Main Cast

Vincent Franklin...Henry Best
Cyril Nri...Lance Sullivan
Julie Hesmondhalgh...Cleo Whitaker
Fisayo Akinade...Dean Monroe
Freddie Fox...Freddie Baxter

Trivia

Cucumber and its two companion series, *Banana* and *Tofu*, all "exploring what it means to be gay in modern Britain," take their titles from a scientific study that classified the male erection into four categories: tofu, peeled banana, unpeeled banana, and cucumber.

What to Binge on Next

Davies also created a companion series to this show, titled *Banana*, which is considered an "anthology series," and which focuses on multiple storylines of young gay characters in Manchester; its plots occasionally overlap with the stories told in *Cucumber*. A third companion program, *Tofu*, is a documentary program that aired online on the video on demand service 4oD and explores individuals' attitudes toward sexuality, love, and relationships.

Davies is a one-man television creation industry; he was also the creator of the earlier British series *Queer as Folk* (also exploring the love lives of young people in Manchester; please note this is a different series than the longer-running American version which shares the same title) and *Bob & Rose*, about a gay man who, tired of the clubbing scene, pursues a relationship and shared parenthood with a woman (and which was based on a true story). The success of these earlier programs helped give Davies the influence necessary to revive the *Doctor Who* series (with Christopher Eccleston as its new Doctor) after its long hiatus.

Doc Martin

Run Time

This ITV drama is one of your longer-running British programs; it aired between 2004 and 2018 and ran for a total of sixty-two episodes in eight series. Episodes were roughly fifty minutes long (one episode, a TV film/Christmas special that aired after series two, was two hours long), making for a total run time of nearly fifty-three hours.

Creator and Writers

The series was created by Dominic Minghella (based partially on the 2000 movie *Saving Grace*). Minghella is also credited at the show's primary writer, although other writers who have been credited on various episodes include Jack Lothian, Richard Stoneman, and Julian Unthank.

What It's About

Doctor Martin Ellingham has a bright career as a talented and well-known surgeon...when he develops a sudden phobia about blood which, as you can imagine, makes continuing his career as a surgeon difficult.

He applies for and is hired as a community general practitioner in the small seaside town of Portwenn, in Cornwall; a location he sought out because an aunt (Joan) with whom he had a close bond during his childhood lives there. The village turns out to be anything but quaint; its inhabitants insist on calling him Doc Martin, popping into his surgery simply to say hello and be served tea and biscuits, and when they find out he cannot stand the sight or smell of blood, they are merciless in their teasing and practical jokes.

Eventually his proficiency at doctoring (if not at interpersonal relationships) endears the doctor to Portwenn's residents, particularly one of its resident school teachers, Louisa Glasson, with whom he embarks on an on-again, off-again love affair (which is usually off whenever Martin engages in some of his more egregious moments of interpersonal stiffness).

Why It's Bingeworthy

You know, I never used to be a big Martin Clunes fan, although I've enjoyed several programs he's been in, including *Men Behaving Badly* and *Reggie Perrin*. However, the character of Doc Martin finally allows him to play a more nuanced individual: he's completely clueless about most human interactions, he can be ridiculously stiff and brisk, and yet there's a vulnerability about him that makes you want to love him, and Clunes does a great job showing all those attributes from the very first episode.

The scenery of Cornwall is beautiful and the storylines, focusing as they do on a community of both eccentric and commonplace characters, makes for a wonderful ensemble program. And a lot of it is really very, very funny. When I did start watching it, I started with the later seasons that were airing on my PBS station, but once I started watching the series from the very first episode, the great humor of the program, most of it based on its characters' quirks, became much more obvious.

Main Cast

Martin Clunes...Doctor Martin Ellingham
Caroline Catz...Louisa Glasson
Stephanie Cole...Joan Norton
Ian McNeice...Bert Large
Joe Absolom...Al Large
John Marquez...Joe Penhale
Jessica Ransom...Morwenna Newcross
Eileen Atkins...Ruth Ellingham

Trivia

Portwenn is a fictional village, but the program is filmed in the real-life Cornwall village of Port Isaac.

The series is loosely based on the movie *Saving Grace*, written by comedian and talk show host Craig Ferguson. Ferguson is credited as a writer/creator on this series, although the main character's name changed from Martin Bamford in the movie to Martin Ellingham, and a new backstory was created for him.

American actress Sigourney Weaver made a cameo appearance in two episodes of series eight.

What to Binge on Next

Another series set in an insular community (this time in Scotland) is the somewhat cozy mystery series *Hamish Macbeth*, for which Dominic Minghella wrote several episodes, and which stars Robert Carlyle as Hamish Macbeth.

Martin Clunes is an acting institution in Great Britain and has starred in many comedies, dramas, and even documentaries. His role in the comedy/drama series *William and Mary*, about a somewhat staid funeral director who falls in love with a more free-spirited midwife, might appeal to his *Doc Martin* fans. Likewise, Caroline Catz's role as a no-nonsense police detective in the mystery series *Murder in Suburbia* might also appeal to her fans.

Other programs which feature a "fish out of water" character theme include the long-running program *Death in Paradise* (in the first seasons of which a very British police detective struggled to adapt to life in the tropics) and *Ballykissangel*, in which a British priest struggled to adapt to his new life in an Irish community.

Jackie on...
Sports on TV in the UK (Part One)

The most popular sport in the UK is football (or soccer, as it is known in the US). Most people support their local team, or their nearest team in the Premier League, and will watch their matches every Saturday afternoon throughout the football season (August to May). Almost everyone in the country will watch an International game—especially during the World Cup.

Football used to be shown on BBC1, but recently Sky purchased the rights to many football games and only those with a subscription to Sky sports can watch those. BBC1 show highlights from the Premier league every Saturday afternoon, but those wanting to watch the full match often head to the pub, where they can support their local team together. The atmosphere is often as good as at the stadium itself, but you must be careful to wear the right colour shirt when entering pubs during a football match, as football supporters are very loyal and don't like to watch a match with those who support a different team!

The second most popular sport in the UK is rugby. There is less of a following for local teams, but the International sides play more regularly. The six nations championship (England, France, Ireland, Italy, Scotland and Wales) is played annually and there is a friendly rivalry whenever the home countries play each other. Rugby matches are generally shown live on BBC1.

Hustle

Run Time

Hustle consisted of forty-eight hour-long episodes in eight seasons. The first four seasons, aired from 2004 to 2007, comprised a unified series with most of the main characters in place; for series five through eight, *Hustle* returned in a slightly different version and with two new main characters (as well as a new, techno-fied theme song) and aired from 2009 through 2012. To watch all eight seasons would take forty-eight hours.

Creator and Writers

The show was created by Bharat Nalluri and Tony Jordan. Tony Jordan was the primary writer of the series, although other writers included Ashley Pharaoh, Matthew Graham, Howard Overman, and Julie Rutterford.

What It's About

The show follows a cast of con artists who form a team and undertake the "long con"—a con set up over a long period of time for a bigger payoff. The man who brings them all together is just out of prison for his last con gone wrong, but you're way off if you think Michael Stone is just another petty criminal. Sure what he does is illegal. But he only picks marks who deserve it—after all, you can't cheat an honest man—and he'll do anything to protect his team.

So who's on the team? Well, in addition to Michael Stone ("Mickey Bricks"), the team is comprised of Albert Stroller, the distinguished elder gentleman, as played by Robert Vaughn, whose role is to "rope in" the mark; Danny Blue, the new kid, who's all flash and brash and raw talent for Mickey to shape; Stacie Monroe, the beauty with more than her share of brains; and Ashley Morgan, "the Fixer," who can beg, borrow, or steal anything needed to run the con.

Why It's Bingeworthy

Sure, the stories and the details of the cons sometimes stretch believability. But it's all in good fun and there's often "ah-ha" moments at the end where you realize the con artists have set something up that completely fooled the mark—and you.

One of my very favorite things about this series is its setting and filming techniques; if you love London, this show is serious exterior skyscraper and glamorous interior eye candy. One of the most frequent interior locations is a bar whose bartender, Eddie, is simultaneously amused and frustrated by his clientele. Whenever I watch this show it always ends up making me want a whiskey, neat, in a cut-glass highball glass. But I digress. The show's cast also has great chemistry and the theme song can't be beat.

Main Cast

Adrian Lester…Michael Stone
Robert Glenister…Ashley Morgan
Robert Vaughn…Albert Stroller
Jaime Murray…Stacie Monroe
Marc Warren…Danny Blue
Later seasons:
Matt Di Angelo…Sean Kennedy
Kelly Adams…Emma Kennedy
Ashley Walters…Billy Bond

Trivia

Robert Vaughn is a well-known American actor, perhaps most famous for his role as Napoleon Solo in the 1960s classic TV series *The Man from U.N.C.L.E.*

Creator/writer Tony Jordan is a prolific television writer who also turned out scripts for popular soap *EastEnders* and the awesome crime drama/time travel series *Life on Mars*.

What to Binge on Next

Creator Tony Jordan also created the completely unique police procedural/time travel drama *Life on Mars*, about a modern-day police detective who is somehow transported back to the 1970s and must pursue his crime-fighting career using (what seem to him) prehistoric techniques.

Bharat Nalluri helped create *Hustle*; another show he directed, the spy drama *MI-5*, matches the beautiful cinematography and fast pace of *Hustle*.

The dark comedy/drama series *Hotel Babylon* also features a tight-knit group of hospitality workers who strive to extract as much money as possible from the (mostly) degenerate guests of their five-star hotel, while also dealing with their own complex private lives.

Last Tango in Halifax

Run Time

This BBC One drama ran from 2012 to 2016, and consists of twenty sixty-minute episodes in four seasons (with the entire final series composed only of two Christmas specials). The total run time is twenty hours.

Creator and Writers

The show was created and written by Sally Wainwright.

What It's About

Thanks to the wonders of social media, childhood sweethearts Celia and Alan find each other once again, meet in person, and shortly thereafter rekindle their romance and decide to get married. Their rush to marry alarms their respective children: Celia' daughter is a school headmaster and parent who has marriage troubles of her own, while Alan's daughter is raising her teenage son alone in the aftermath of her husband's death (as a suicide, the circumstances of which are questioned throughout the series).

Although they recognize their attraction and love immediately, Alan and Celia do experience rocky patches on their way to (and within) married bliss. When Celia's daughter Caroline leaves her unfaithful husband, and decides to embark on a relationship with another woman, Celia struggles to accept this aspect of her daughter's life. Likewise, a past infidelity of Alan's (to his first wife) is revealed when his illegitimate son enters his life.

But throughout the series both families learn to navigate their relationships and growing friendships with one another, and Alan and Celia remain committed to maximizing their love and new leases on life together.

Why It's Bingeworthy

Last Tango in Halifax, although it certainly has its moments of both drama and dark humor, is something lovely that you don't see on television very much: an uplifting and romantic storyline featuring more mature characters. It's also a complex family drama which portrays human relationships as still very much worth the effort (even after forming bad first impressions of one another, Alan's and Celia's daughters become important sources of support for each other).

It's also delightful to watch this cast work together; both the main and the supporting characters, including Caroline's cheating husband John (played by Tony Gardner) and Gillian's lighthearted son Raff (played by Josh Bolt).

Main Cast

Anne Reid…Celia Dawson
Derek Jacobi…Alan Buttershaw
Sarah Lancashire…Caroline
Nicola Walker…Gillian

Trivia

Wainwright has said she created this show and based it on the story of her mother's later-in-life second romance and marriage.

In the program Sarah Lancashire plays a character who struggles with her sexuality, leaving her marriage and engaging in a relationship with another woman. The actor has said she has received the most fan mail of her life for playing this role.

What to Binge on Next

A completely different depiction of an older couple's love is provided in the sitcom *Vicious*, which stars Derek Jacobi and Ian McKellen as elderly lovers, and which is filled with their (indeed very) vicious snipes at one another, although the series also includes loving moments between the two as well.

Sally Wainwright is said to have been so taken with Sarah Lancashire's portrayal of Caroline that she created another role and show for her: *Happy Valley*, in which Lancashire plays a world-weary police officer in a rural district plagued by drugs and violence.

Another lovely series which shows romance between older characters is the classic *As Time Goes By*, in which Judi Dench and Geoffrey Palmer star as lovers who lost touch with another during the Korean War, and who meet again many years later. Older characters are also the focus of the sitcoms *One Foot In the Grave* (in which the main character is offered early retirement and doesn't really know how to relax into all of his spare time) and *Waiting for God* (in which residents of a retirement home become friends and concentrate on making life difficult for their families and the home's administrator).

MI-5

Run Time

MI-5 ran for ten series between the years of 2002 and 2011. Its eighty-six episodes were nearly an hour in length, making the total binge time for watching this show eighty-six hours.

Creator and Writers

MI-5 was created by David Wolstencroft, who wrote many of the show's episodes through its first three seasons. Writers of multiple episodes in later seasons include Ben Richards, Howard Brenton, Jonathan Brackley, and Sam Vincent.

What It's About

MI-5, titled *Spooks* in the U.K., is espionage drama that features an ever-refreshed cast as old characters give their all—truly—in the defense of Queen and country, and new characters take their place in MI-5, the British domestic spy service. From the very first episode the tension between doing the job and trying to maintain outside relationships is apparent, as Tom Quinn, Spy Extraordinaire, finds himself spinning ever less likely tales to explain to his girlfriend and her daughter why he, a run-of-the-mill tech worker, has to rush to work at a moment's notice, or even, on one memorable occasion, has a bomb planted at the home where he lives with them. That's the sort of thing significant others tend to wonder about.

Throughout the series, the threats to British national security (and the safety of MI-5's intrepid officers) vary from homegrown extremists to religious terrorists, from the Russian government as well as the American one (which often oversteps its bounds in taking over joint operations). In addition to threats from outside, there are many subplots involving betrayals and unclear loyalties within the secret services and the British government. In short, you never really know who is on what side, and you feel a real sympathy for agents trying to remain true to their own codes of honor in the face of swiftly changing loyalties among MI-5 and government leaders.

In such confusing professional surroundings, it's little surprise that many of the main characters in this show have difficult and complex personal lives. Two agents are actually married to one another, while the others engage in relationships with outsiders with whom they can't be honest about their work. The top man on the totem pole, Harry Pearce, has perhaps the most difficult love affair of all: in love with one of his subordinates (and she with him), they continually deny their attraction to one another so that they can focus exclusively on their work. It's all just so heartbreaking.

Why It's Bingeworthy

The very first things I noticed about *MI-5* were its unique and ingenious filming and storytelling techniques. From the very first episode the viewer is treated to split screens, showing simultaneous action; other tricks are used to showcase different characters' points of view and provide fast-moving but very watchable and suspense-filled action sequences. Thematic music is also used to great effect, and the result is a series in which nearly every episode seems as lovingly filmed and edited as most feature films.

Spy stories are typically not my thing, James Bond notwithstanding (Ian Fleming, Bond's creator, was a Brit, after all). What I also love about this series is its emphasis on the domestic role of MI-5 (as opposed to its more internationally concerned secret service cousin, MI-6), and on the defense of the country of Great Britain. Geopolitics come into play, of course, but basically the MI-5 spooks are doing everything they can to keep bad things from happening on their home soil, which is a mission I can understand.

MI-5 is also great and British in its startling willingness to kill off or otherwise jettison established characters and introduce new ones. Although all the characters here are fascinating in their own way (and the casting directors must also pay attention to how the actors they cast work with one another; the chemistry among the co-workers here is astounding as well), they each bring something different to the show and make the whole stronger than its individual characters. It's a true ensemble piece in the very best way.

Lastly, the storytelling is top-notch. It's never simplistic, but by and large there's very few plot holes to distract you, and the action in each episode is easy to follow and understand, even when the director is showing you more than one scene happening at a time.

Main Cast

Peter Firth...Harry Pearce
Nicola Walker...Ruth Evershed
Matthew Macfadyen...Tom Quinn
Hugh Simon...Malcolm Wynn-Jones
Keeley Hawes...Zoe Reynolds
David Oyelowo...Danny Hunter

Rupert Penry-Jones...Adam Carter
Hermione Norris...Ros Myers
Raza Jaffrey...Zafar Younis
Richard Armitage...Lucas North
...and too many others to list.

Trivia

"Spook" is British slang for spies, explaining the show's U.K. title of *Spooks*.

The Wikipedia page for this program lists a whomping total of forty-seven main characters, twenty-four of whom died during the course of the series (the characters, that is, not the actors!).

Although their characters on the show were never romantically linked, stars Matthew Macfadyen and Keeley Hawes married one another in 2004.

A spin-off of the original program, titled *Spooks: Code 9*, aired for one season in 2012, and was meant to offer a "more maverick, younger perspective." A feature film, also titled *MI-5*, and starring Peter Firth as Harry Pearce and Kit Harrington (of *Game of Thrones*/Jon Snow fame), was released in 2015.

What to Binge on Next

Although different in tone, the crime drama *Sherlock* is also visually beautiful and makes use of a lot of different storytelling and filming techniques. Its frenetic pacing and taut plotting may also appeal to fans of *MI-5*.

The creator of *MI-5*, David Wolstencroft, also wrote the 2013 three-part drama thriller *The Escape Artist* (starring David Tennant), and the historical drama *Versailles* (about Louis XIV, which he co-created with Simon Mirren and co-wrote with several others); either or both of those shows might appeal to you as well.

Fans of great drama and the primary actors in this show will have tons of great shows to consider next: *Ripper Street*, a crime drama set in London's East End six months after the last Jack the Ripper killing (Matthew Macfadyen); *Line of Duty*, a police procedural focusing on the fine line between corrupt cops and too-earnest cops (Keeley Hawes); *Whitechapel*, a crime drama/horror hybrid set in modern-day Whitechapel (Rupert Penry-Jones); and *Unforgotten*, a crime drama about police detectives investigating cold cases (Nicola Walker).

Monarch of the Glen

Run Time

Monarch of the Glen eventually ended up running for seven series and sixty-four episodes, between 2000 and 2005. The episodes in series one through three were fifty minutes long, and in the latter four series they were sixty minutes long, making for a total run time of nearly sixty hours.

Creator and Writers

This drama doubles as a literary adaptation, as it is loosely based on Compton Mackenzie's Highland novels. It was created by Michael Chaplin and it was written by him and several other writers, including Niall Leonard, John Martin Johnson, Mark Holloway, and Andrew Taft.

What It's About

Although he lives in London and has his own career, Archie MacDonald nonetheless is drawn back to his family's estate in Glenbogle, Scotland, where his father, the aging laird (large estate owner), is running the entire place into the ground. Archie steps in and tries to make the estate a paying concern, help his father's employees, and the local village, but it's an uphill slog. Particularly when one of the fiery locals keeps distracting him!

Throughout seven seasons Archie, his parents, the estate's employees, Archie's love interests, and several newly arrived family members (in later seasons) try to keep Glenbogle afloat, all while caring for each other and the estate. Love affairs loom large, and so do family intrigues, but in the end, the estate and its surrounding community are always there for one another.

Why It's Bingeworthy

Monarch of the Glen is kind of an early prototype of the historical drama *Downton Abbey*, only set in the modern day and with even more financial pressures facing the estate owners. The estate and Highland scenery used in the filming of this show work as their own characters; anyone who's ever wanted to visit misty, wild, Scotland will find this show a beautiful watch.

But for me the fun of the show is in the characters. The people who are supposed to have chemistry do (even the aging laird and his wife), and even the estate's staff members are fully drawn individuals in their own rights.

It's dramatic and soap opera-y and even when sad events happen (and they do), it's not too sad, or dark. It makes for relaxing weekend watching.

Main Cast

Alastair Mackenzie…Archie MacDonald
Dawn Steele…Lexie McTavish
Susan Hampshire…Molly MacDonald
Richard Briers…Hector MacDonald
Lloyd Owen…Paul Bowman
Alexander Morton…Golly Mackenzie
Hamish Clark…Duncan McKay
Lorraine Pilkington…Katrina Finlay

Trivia

Several of the series' regulars (including Alastair Mackenzie and Lorraine Pilkington) left the show after the first three series, but new family members stepped up to take their place in slightly different storylines.

Julian Fellowes, who plays neighboring estate owner Kilwillie, is not only *Downton Abbey*'s creator, but is also a real-life peer in the House of Lords.

The estate where much of the show was filmed, Ardverikie Estate, is a popular tourist destination and cottages on the estate are available to rent (although the castle is still privately owned and closed to the public).

What to Binge on Next

For most of my formative college years, *Ballykissangel* and *Monarch of the Glen* played on my local PBS channel on Saturday nights. For this reason, the two will be forever linked in my mind and affection. Do watch *Ballykissangel* as well; it's got great location shoots (only in Ireland rather than in Scotland), great romance, and great community storylines.

Another drama about family life and starting something new is the popular series *Wild at Heart*, in which a British family moves to Africa and buys a nature preserve/resort to run as a business. As an added bonus, it stars Dawn Steele (who played Lexie McTavish in *Monarch*).

If you don't mind historical drama, you might enjoy *Poldark*, set in 1700s Cornwall, in which the estate owner Ross Poldark is constantly fighting to keep his mining concerns (and his employees) and his estate afloat.

Orphan Black

Run Time

Orphan Black consisted of fifty episodes in five series, and aired from 2013 to 2017. Each episode had a run time of forty-five minutes, making its run time nearly thirty-eight hours.

Creator and Writers

Screenwriter Graeme Manson and director John Fawcett created the series. Numerous writers helped develop and write the series; authors who wrote more than one episode each include Chris Roberts, Tony Elliott, Renée St. Cyr, Alexandra Mircheff, Hannah Cheesman, Lynn Coady, and Aisha Porter-Christie.

What It's About

Brit Sarah Manning is trying to lay low; she's got a lot of burnt bridges behind her and a lot of people she'd rather not see (and who she'd rather didn't see her). So when she looks across a train station at night and sees a woman who is her physical double, she is stunned…and becomes even more so when the woman steps in front of an oncoming train, killing herself. Never one to miss an opportunity, Sarah takes the purse she left behind, finds the woman's apartment and assumes her identity: that of Beth Childs.

Little does she know that if she expects to take the identity of every one of her "doubles" in town, she's going to be taking a lot of identities. Shortly she and her foster brother Felix realize that Sarah and her multiple "twins" are in fact clones, who, as they start to find each other, become fixated on learning who created them and why (as well as on staying alive; someone is trying to kill them, and some of them are obviously afflicted with a genetic disease). For Sarah, the whole scenario is entirely too personal: she has a biological daughter she is trying to raise and protect.

Eventually Sarah learns that she and her clones are not the only experiments that were performed by unscrupulous scientists; there is another group of male clones in the area, and it's nearly impossible to keep track of who is on whose side. But you'll need to find out; no matter how confusing this series gets, you're going to want to stay with it until the very last episode.

Why It's Bingeworthy

Now, technically, this may not qualify as Brit TV, as it is considered a Canadian science fiction thriller series, co-produced by BBC America and two Canadian media and production companies (Temple Street Productions and Bell Media), but I'm including it here because, well, close enough, and also because it is so awesome.

The plot twists, conspiracy theories, characters who aren't who they say they are, and dystopian technological issues all combine to make this a series that you literally can't stop watching. Every episode ends at a tense point in the action, making it a necessity just to start the next episode after finishing one. There's some plot holes, but for how many characters and changing allegiances and constantly evolving scientific advances and issues the writers had to keep track of, they actually did a really good job keeping the show story-driven and coherent.

And let's not overlook the acting jobs of Tatiana Maslany and Ari Millen, who had to portray multiple characters who all looked exactly alike, but who exhibited very different personalities (it's been noted that Maslany had a continuity assistant to help her keep all the individual behavior and physical tics of each of the clones she played separate and consistent). Also of note in this program is the great chemistry, not only between characters who fall in love with each other, but also between friends and family members.

Main Cast

Tatiana Maslany…Sarah Manning/Multiple clones
Jordan Gavaris…Felix Dawkins
Maria Doyle Kennedy…Siobahn Sadler
Ari Millen…Mark Rollins/Multiple clones
Kevin Hanchard…Art Bell
Evelyne Brochu…Delphine Cormier
Dylan Bruce…Paul Dierden

Trivia

The show was time-consuming to shoot and edit. Tatiana Maslany played multiple characters, many of whom had to interact together, so she had to shoot multiple scenes in which she would act as one character alongside acting doubles, and then the different shots would be "layered" together.

The show's science consultant is named Cosima Herter—and one of Maslany's main clone characters is named Cosima as well.

All of the episodes' titles come from groundbreaking scientific and cultural works: in the first season, the titles come from Charles Darwin's *On the Origin of Species*; in season two, they are from Francis Bacon's *Novum Organum*, in season three they are from Dwight D. Eisenhower's farewell speech referencing the military-industrial complex; and in season four they were inspired by the works of Donna J. Haraway, a professor who has written extensively on the ethical considerations around cloning; in season five they were quoted from the poem "Protest" by Ella Wheeler Wilcox.

Although the program is filmed in Toronto, the characters never overtly refer to the city or the location.

What to Binge on Next

Another program which considers how near-future technology will affect human lives and relationships is the anthology program *Black Mirror*.

The short supernatural series *In the Flesh* might also appeal to *Orphan Black* fans. It is about a zombie apocalypse that has already occurred, and has been somewhat controlled by the military and scientists' advances that have found medication and other ways to control individuals who died and were re-animated as zombies (they are called sufferers from PDS, or Partially Deceased Syndrome). It's an interesting mix of horror and science, and very story-driven as well.

Our Friends in the North

Run Time

The show only had one season, for a total of nine seventy-minutes episodes. It aired in 1996, and its total run time is ten-and-a-half hours.

Creator and Writers

The show was created and written by Peter Flannery.

What It's About

Four friends, three men and one woman, grow from teenagers in the 1960s, to idealistic twenty-somethings, to disillusioned (but still resilient) forty-somethings in 1990s Newcastle, the heart of industrial northern England.

The revolutionary of the group is Nicky, who wants to make a difference in the world. His friends Geordie and Tosker, however, have different dreams: Tosker is trying to leverage his mediocre talent into a big-time singing career, while Geordie first plans to go with him into music, but then leaves Newcastle to seek his fortune elsewhere. Nicky also leaves to start making his way in politics, leaving Mary and Tosker to go on a disastrous date that ends, eventually, in an unplanned pregnancy and their eventual marriage.

Although most of the friends lose contact with one another, their paths gradually start merge back together, with Geordie falling in with a criminal element in London but then returning home after serving prison time, Tosker and Mary divorcing after Mary's feminist awakening, and Nicky and Mary eventually marrying (although their relationship is also fraught with difficulties). At the end of the series not all of them find their "happy ending" (even the happy endings here are a bit ambiguous), but the program still manages to end on a hopeful note (and on the inspirational notes of the band Oasis's song "Don't Look Back in Anger").

Why It's Bingeworthy

This program first aired in 1996, but it remains relevant today for its storylines of commerce and corruption, as well as its exposure of class matters. It was groundbreaking (and very popular) for its time; few programs were set in northern locales and fewer still dealt so frankly with political issues, illness and abuse, sexuality, and criminal activity.

The casting, too, makes this one a must-see. Nicky and Geordie were played by a young Christopher Eccleston and Daniel Craig, respectively (that's right: Dr. Who and James Bond), and Mark Strong and Gina McKee (as Tosker and Mary), would also go on to strong stage and movie careers.

It's dark and heartbreaking and yet you won't be able to stop watching it.

Main Cast

Christopher Eccleston...Nicky Hutchinson
Gina McKee...Mary Soulsby
Mark Strong...Terry ("Tosker") Cox
Daniel Craig...George ("Geordie") Peacock

Trivia

BBC Two spent about four million pounds producing the series, which was its entire drama budget for the year.

The corrupt Newcastle politician and builder characters were based on real people (T. Dan Smith and John Poulson) who built poor-quality high-rise housing projects in that city.

Each episode's title reflected simply the year in which its action took place: 1964, 1966, 1967, 1970, 1974, 1979, 1984, 1987, and 1995.

What to Binge on Next

Peter Flannery is also the writer who adapted Alan Hunter's Inspector Gently novels for the crime drama series *Inspector George Gently*. Although those novels were originally set in the Essex region, not in the north of England, Flannery changed the setting to northeast England. Viewers who enjoy *Our Friends in the North* will find a lot to like in the Gently series as well; it's very dark and gritty but the relationships between the characters are strong and the compassion they show one another (and the dedication they show to solving crimes) is inspirational.

Although much longer running, and much lighter in tone (at times; at other times it's every bit as dramatic), the drama *Cold Feet*, which follows the lives and fortunes of three couples and their children across many years, might be a good program to watch after finishing *Our Friends in the North*.

Of course the four main cast members of this program have appeared in numerous other television programs and movies: Christopher Eccleston would go on to be the new Doctor Who in the 2005 reboot of the series; Gina McKee played the heartbreaking role of a woman who marries a man she doesn't love for financial security, which turns out to be a huge mistake, in the 2002 adaptation of *The Forsyte Saga*; Mark Strong has starred in a ton of programs and movies, including *The Long Firm* (about a 1960s mobster) and *RocknRolla* (about even more gangster types); and Daniel Craig became James Bond, as well as Mikael Blomkvist in *The Girl with the Dragon Tattoo*.

Jackie on...
Sports on TV in the UK (Part Two)

Other sports besides football are watched throughout the year - including Formula One, cricket, tennis at Wimbledon in June (when everyone likes to watch with a bowl of strawberries and cream!), and the Grand National (a big horse race in April for which many offices will do a sweepstake).

Since London held the Olympics in 2012 there has also been a growing interest in other sports, such as cycling, swimming and athletics. These are shown on a variety of channels, either live or on highlight shows.

University sport doesn't have the same following in the UK as it does in the US. In fact it is almost nonexistent. The only exception I can think of is the University Boat Race. This takes place every March between teams from Oxford and Cambridge. The race involves the teams rowing 4.2 miles along the River Thames. We British love it when the boats capsize or collide with something (as long as no one is injured) - it makes everything much more interesting!

Shameless

Run Time

Shameless is another series that will keep you busy bingewatching for some time. It aired from 2004 to 2013, and eventually grew to eleven series and a whopping (by British television standards) 139 hour-long episodes. You'll need nearly 140 hours, or nearly six days, to watch the whole thing.

Creator and Writers

Paul Abbott created the series and has writing credits on 130 episodes; other writers include Ed McCardie, Tom Higgins, and Jimmy Dowdall.

What It's About

In the decidedly urban gritty setting of a Manchester council estate, this drama features Frank Gallagher, the patriarch of a large family, who mostly can't be bothered to provide for, look after, or even remember the names or ages of most of his children, as he spends most of his time being extremely drunk. The kids are the story: headstrong eldest daughter Fiona, who is the de facto head of the household; her various younger siblings, and her friends and love interest Steve (who seems like the most law-abiding character on the program—emphasis on *seems*).

Fiona's and Steve's love affair plays out over the first two series, and thereafter other characters in the show, mostly Fiona's younger brothers and sister, have main storylines of their own. Another family, the Maguires, despite their oftentimes antagonistic dealings with the Gallagher clan, also start to feature more prominently in the show's later series. Life on the council estate is complicated, with everyone's love affairs and relationships and criminal activities becoming more complex by the minute.

Why It's Bingeworthy

I've got to be honest with you; when I say *Shameless* is gritty, what I really mean is, it's a little too gritty for me, what with all the parental neglect and the kids having kids, etc. And yet still the program is addicting to watch; there's no denying both the Gallaghers and the Maguires have their own peculiar codes of honor, and ways of being loyal to one another, and they largely are able to co-exist with one another even in difficult circumstances and less-than-perfect surroundings. To call this show "uplifting" is not really right, but you have to respect the sheer energy with which the residents of Paul Abbott's fictional world live their lives.

Main Cast

David Threlfall...Frank Gallagher
Anne-Marie Duff...Fiona Gallagher
Jody Latham...Lip Gallagher
Gerard Kearns...Ian Gallagher
Elliott Tittensor...Carl Gallagher
Rebecca Ryan...Debbie Gallagher
Rebecca Atkinson...Karen Maguire
...and too many more to list.

Trivia

Creator Paul Abbott drew largely on his own personal experiences when making the show. He has been forthright in the media about how he grew up as the second-youngest in a family of nine children, his mother left their home when he was only nine, and his eldest sister ended up raising her siblings when their father left two years after their mother had. Eventually he was placed with a foster family and began work toward a psychology degree, and became a successful television writer in his late 20s.

Shameless was hugely popular in the U.K., and is also one of the few shows to be successfully remade for an American audience; its Showtime adaptation starring Emmy Rossum and William H. Macy, also titled *Shameless*, ran for nine seasons from 2011 to 2019.

What to Binge on Next

Fans of Abbott's forthright storytelling might also enjoy a later drama series he created, *No Offence*, about a female detective inspector whose methods are unorthodox, and the 2003 miniseries *State of Play*, about corruption in government and journalism, which also stars James McAvoy.

If you're looking for slightly more lighthearted laughs in a story about a large family, the Irish sitcom *Mrs. Brown's Boys*, starring comedian Brendan O'Carroll as the Brown matriarch, might be just right.

The same type of brash humor and no-holds-barred lifestyles highlighted in *Shameless* also appear in the series *Skins*, which focuses on the intense lives of teenagers living in Bristol.

Silk

Run Time

This drama aired for three seasons and eighteen episodes between 2011 and 2014. Each episode had a run time of sixty minutes, so this is an eighteen-hour watch from start to finish.

Creator and Writers

The show was created by Peter Moffat, and he is credited as the writer on all eighteen episodes, but other writers credited with single episodes include Mick Collins, Debbie O'Malley, and Christian Spurrier.

What It's About

Silk is referred to as a legal drama, but it derives as many of its storylines from its barristers' (often very complex) personal lives as it does from the court cases that they argue.

The series focuses on two competing barristers, both hoping to be promoted to QCs (Queen's Counsel): the driven, ambitious, and smart Martha Costello, and the also very smart but even more smooth (and extremely interested in pursuing physical relationships with the opposite sex) Clive Reader. They both work for the same criminal defense firm, and they both find themselves defending individuals for a wide variety of crimes, from drug offenses to rape and manslaughter.

Why It's Bingeworthy

There are a lot of crime dramas on British TV, and the Brits do them extremely well, but there are fewer dramas that focus on the legal side of crime and the court system. This program can be a nice change of pace from the multitude of other series featuring the lives and work of police detectives and investigators.

This show has the ring of accuracy; creator Peter Moffatt based the show on his experiences working as a barrister and at the Bar. Both main characters (Maxine Peake as Martha and Rupert Penry-Jones as Clive) also offer nuanced character portraits of individuals who are driven in their professional lives, but who also have a lot to keep track of in their personal lives, and in their rivalry with one another.

Main Cast

Maxine Peake...Martha Costello
Rupert Penry-Jones...Clive Reader
Neil Stuke...Billy Lamb
Theo Barklem-Biggs...Jake Milner
John Macmillan...John Bright

Trivia

The title, *Silk*, refers to the certain type of gowns that Queen's Counsel (QCs) are entitled to wear in court, and which are usually made of silk.

What to Binge on Next

A more classic program about barristers is the long-running and popular drama *Kavanagh QC*, which aired on ITV from 1995 to 2001 and starred John Thaw.

Peter Moffat also created two other legal dramas that you might like (but which might be difficult to find): *North Square*, which also featured actor Rupert Penry-Jones, and *Criminal Justice*, which featured actor Maxine Peake in its second series. Please note, however, that *Criminal Justice* also features a lot of very graphic prison violence scenes and is really, really hard to watch.

Another program that is about the justice system but which is not a police drama is the spy drama *MI-5* (in which Penry-Jones also stars, in later seasons).

Jackie on...
Four Dramas You Should Start With

At Home with the Braithwaites

This programme isn't that well known in the UK, but it is one of my personal favourites. It revolves around a woman who wins the lottery but doesn't tell her family. It's fascinating to see how money changes the dynamics of her relationships, and the way comic moments are interspersed with real drama make this show both entertaining and thought-provoking.

Bodyguard

Bodyguard was first broadcast on British television in August 2018 and news of its brilliance quickly spread via word-of-mouth; enabling it to become the new BBC drama with the highest viewing figures for a decade. The series revolves around a former war-veteran with PTSD who becomes a bodyguard for the Home Secretary (one of the highest ranking politicians in the UK). The tension builds over the course of the series, and its series finale is one of the most thrilling I've ever watched.

Cold Feet

Cold Feet is one of the only British comedy dramas with real staying power. It first aired in 1997 and is still running today (albeit with a ten-year gap in production)! The characters have all become household names in the UK and many of the scenes from this programme are still referenced—the one in which Adam serenaded Rachel naked, with a rose clutched between his buttocks, being one of them! The three main couples in this show go through a rollercoaster of storylines and emotions and I think you'll be hard-pressed not to fall in love with them all.

MI-5

Known as *Spooks* in the UK, *MI-5* is an intelligent, gripping drama about a group of secret agents trying to prevent terrorist acts on British soil. Its clever storytelling means that each episode is a tense, thrilling ride in which you'll never predict what the outcome will be. It's hard hitting and they don't shy away from killing off the main characters, or torturing others in graphic ways, but if you've got a strong stomach you'll be rewarded with one of the most intelligent shows on television.

Historical Dramas

All Creatures Great and Small

Run Time

This series ran for seven series and a grand total of ninety forty-eight-minute episodes, making for a total view time of seventy-two hours. The first three series aired from 1978 to 1980, and the second batch of four series aired from 1988 to 1990.

Creator and Writers

The program is based on the classic vet books of James Herriot (a.k.a. Alf Wight), including the novels *If Only They Could Talk* and *It Shouldn't Happen to a Vet*. The first three series were based exclusively on Herriot's books, while the remaining four series featured original story ideas and plotlines.

What It's About

It's Yorkshire in the 1930s, and new veterinarian James Herriot joins the practice of the highly eccentric (and extremely likable) Siegfried Farnon. It's a life of late-night phone summons out to isolated farms, as well as hard physical work performed in all seasons and locations. Later they are joined in the practice by Siegfried's cheerful brother Tristan, who pursues pints at the local pub and relationships with local women much more fervently than he pursues his veterinary studies.

Much like the gruff but sincere Yorkshire residents the vets visit, this is a show with some earthy scenes involving animals (you may actually start to wonder if you need to see this many physical details of animal husbandry, particularly those including their back ends), but it also includes many charming moments of friendship, community spirit, and joy.

Why It's Bingeworthy

Both James Herriot's books (such as *All Creatures Great and Small*) and this show are well-known and loved throughout Great Britain. Likewise, the cast of this program are all well-regarded actors, two of whom in particular (Robert Hardy and Peter Davison) would go on to become two of the U.K.'s most frequently working actors.

The chemistry between all of the cast members here is noteworthy; you really believe they are all one another's closest friends and colleagues. The scenery of the program, which was filmed in North Yorkshire and the village of Askrigg, is spectacular (if you like that wild and ruggedly beautiful Yorkshire countryside kind of thing). And the animals! Although this program was about a point in history when animals were really one's workmates, more so than friends, the vets' and farmers' dedication to giving the best care to all of the animals portrayed in these stories is inspiring.

Main Cast

Christopher Timothy…James Herriot
Robert Hardy…Siegfried Farnon
Peter Davison…Tristan Farnon
Carol Drinkwater/Lynda Bellingham…Helen Alderson Herriot
Mary Hignett…Mrs. Hall

Trivia

The show employed two veterinary consultants: Jack Watkinson and Eddie Straiton. The scenes in which the various vet characters had to examine a cow by, ahem, inserting an arm into their bottom, were real: the actors were instructed by Watkinson on this technique.

Christopher Timothy and Carol Drinkwater (who played Herriot and his wife Helen) had an affair during the filming of the first season.

During the filming of the show's fourth season, in 1977, Timothy was in a serious car accident, but returned to filming in nine weeks: members of the crew had to physically help him move around the set.

What to Binge on Next

Other dramas with a focus on community life and work might appeal to you if you love *All Creatures Great and Small*, such as *Monarch of the Glen*, set on a failing Scottish estate that the new laird (estate owner) must save in order to preserve his family's living and community jobs; *Call the Midwife*, a historical drama about midwives and nurses working in 1950s East End London; and *Upstairs, Downstairs* (the classic version from 1971, which feels surprisingly contemporary), about an upper-class family and their servants.

If you love animals, you might also like the drama *Wild at Heart*, about a British family that buys and maintains a wildlife sanctuary in Africa, and the classic comedy *The Good Life*, which featured main characters raising animals in their backyard to become self-sufficient back-to-the-landers.

Call the Midwife

Run Time

From 2012 through 2019, there have been eight seasons and a total of sixty-nine episodes (sixty-two regular episodes and seven Christmas specials). The regular episodes are sixty minutes long and the Christmas specials vary between seventy-five and ninety minutes, making for a total run time of roughly seventy-three hours. At least two more series are planned.

Creator and Writers

The show was created by Heidi Thomas and is based partially upon the nursing memoirs of Jennifer Worth (*Call the Midwife*, *Shadows of the Workhouse*, and *Farewell to the East End*). Many episodes were also written by Heidi Thomas, but many other writers have also worked on the series, including Harriet Warner, Damian Wayling, Carolyn Bonnyman, and Louise Ironside.

What It's About

Anybody who is at all squeamish about childbirth should definitely not watch the BBC historical drama *Call the Midwife*.

Set in the 1950s and 1960s, in a particularly poor area of London's East End, the program follows the adventures of numerous nurse midwives who serve the community, as well as the institution that supports them: Nonnatus House, where a community of nuns in the Anglican religious order also work to support the community's residents with maternity, child, and adult medical (as well as spiritual) care.

The stories and experiences of these two very different groups of women are the core of the program. In early seasons the action is narrated by midwife Jenny Lee, who is at first shocked by the poverty (and the astounding birth rate—eighty to one hundred babies born per month) of the neighborhood, but who comes to know the people and their problems, as well as their dreams, as she provides their health care. Several other characters who appear in the first series are main or recurring characters throughout the entire series: Sister Julienne, the "sister in charge" of Nonnatus, who displays both wisdom and kindness, but who must also sometimes make the unpopular decisions that come with being in charge; midwife Trixie, one of the saucier nurses, but also one with a big heart and a willingness to accept people as they are; and Dr. Patrick Turner, the community's (and the nuns' and midwives') doctor who eventually marries former nun and midwife Shelagh. Numerous other characters and storylines, many based on historical events like the founding of the National Health Service and the incidences of birth defects caused by the drug Thalidomide, are also featured throughout the program's run.

Why It's Bingeworthy

Make no mistake: this show may be set in the 1950s (although latter series have entered the 1960s and it is thought the final season will take place in 1965), but it tackles a number of topics that were taboo in that time: illegitimate children, infidelity, homosexuality, illegal abortion, and birth control and women's rights.

The show's incorporation of real historical events, and its writers' skill at writing believable and interesting characters, make this a show well worth watching (if you don't mind some fairly graphic childbirth and medical procedure depictions). Although the poverty portrayed on the program is disheartening, the episodes do strive to end on an upbeat note (particularly in the early series, when the program is narrated by nurse Jenny), and the Christmas specials are guaranteed to make you feel all warm and fuzzy.

Main Cast

Jessica Raine…Jenny Lee
Jenny Agutter…Sister Julienne
Judy Parfitt…Sister Monica Joan
Miranda Hart…Chummy Noakes
Bryony Hannah…Cynthia Miller
Helen George…Beatrix ("Trixie") Franklin
Stephen McGann…Dr. Patrick Turner
Cliff Parisi…Fred Buckle

Trivia

Stephen McGann, who portrays Dr. Turner on the show, is married to show creator Heidi Thomas. The couple's struggles to conceive and Thomas's near-death surgical experience when their baby was only a few weeks old, helped inspire Thomas to create the show.

Memoirist Jennifer Worth, on whose books the series is largely based, worked closely with the creators and writers of the program, although she died in 2011, shortly before the first episode aired. When helping develop the show, Worth claimed that Miranda Hart was perfect to play the role of the somewhat awkward nurse Chummy Noakes; Hart eventually committed to the role before it was even written.

The program uses real infants in its filming; they can only film for fifteen minutes at a time.

Actors Helen George and Jack Ashton, who play Trixie Franklin and Tom Hereward (and have a relationship on the show), are partners in real life and had a daughter together in 2017.

What to Binge on Next

Heidi Thomas was also a writer on the literary adaptation serialization of Elizabeth Gaskell's *Cranford* novel: *Cranford* (2007) and the Christmas special *Return to Cranford* (2009). Set in the 1840s, the shows focuses on the strong community of women living in the rural village of Cranford. Another historical drama which might appeal to these viewers is the more gentle *Lark Rise to Candleford*, which is narrated by the young female character at the center of the plot, who leaves her rural village of Lark Rise to work as an assistant to a postmistress in the town of Candleford.

Fans of medical dramas have plenty to choose from on British television, including the popular nighttime soap opera *Casualty* and the short-lived but still very intense *Trust Me* (starring Jodie Whittaker, before she left to become the BBC's first female Doctor Who).

The Crown

Run Time

As of 2018, there have been two series of this program, with each series containing ten hour-long episodes, making for a run time of twenty hours. However, promotional materials for the program note that a six-series run, comprised of sixty total episodes, is hoped for; a third and fourth series have already been confirmed. The show began airing on Netflix in 2016.

Creator and Writers

The program is based on the creator Peter Morgan's 2006 film *The Queen* and his 2013 stage play *The Audience*. Thus far all the episodes have been written by Morgan, although other credited writers include Amy Jenkins and Tom Edge.

What It's About

The Crown is a historical drama, that, in its entirety, is meant to portray Queen Elizabeth II's life, from the beginning of her reign to its later years. The series that have aired thus far have dramatized her marriage to Philip, the early years of her reign, her sister Margaret's relationship with Peter Townsend (a divorced man of whom the Queen Mother disapproves), her relationship with Winston Churchill and other government members, and several foreign relations crises from the 1950s era.

The accuracy of some of the historical details and storylines have been challenged, and the *Daily Express* newspaper reported that Queen Elizabeth herself was "displeased" about the portrayal of Prince Philip's decision to send their son Charles to Gordonstoun, and his less-than-sympathetic response to reports that Charles was being bullied there.

Why It's Bingeworthy

Although interest in and sympathy for the monarchy and the royal family seems to wax and wane, tabloid sales and the number of headlines about the royals in my Yahoo news feed would indicate that plenty of people are still very interested in the royal family, their lives, their relationships, and whatever "inside dirt" we can possibly read (I count myself among the number of those so obsessed). That interest in royalty is what has made *The Crown* a very popular and generally well-regarded by critics program for Netflix.

No expense has been spared to make this a gorgeous series to look at; it has been noted that the first series alone cost Netflix more than £100 million to produce. Between the lush settings and even more lush costumes and details, this series is extremely easy on the eyes.

It doesn't hurt that the program is sometimes a bit risqué. Titillating details about the early days of Elizabeth's and Philip's marriage in particular have kept fans busy discussing the program on social media. Future series plan to introduce storylines about Camilla Parker-Bowles and Princess Diana, so the gossipy appeal of the program will probably continue to grow.

Main Cast

Claire Foy...Queen Elizabeth II
Matt Smith...Philip, Duke of Edinburgh
Victoria Hamilton...Queen Elizabeth, the Queen Mother
Vanessa Kirby...Princess Margaret
John Lithgow...Winston Churchill
Future cast members will include Olivia Colman as Queen Elizabeth II and Helena Bonham Carter as Princess Margaret.

Trivia

This program was commissioned by and premiered on Netflix, but a British production company, Left Bank Pictures, was involved in its production.

As the series movies through the years and historical events, cast members will change to reflect the aging of the main characters. Although Claire Foy began the series as Queen Elizabeth II, it has been announced that Olivia Colman will next play the Queen, and Helena Bonham Carter will take over the role of Princess Margaret from Vanessa Kirby.

In 2018 the producers admitted that Claire Foy had received a lower salary than Matt Smith for her work on the show. They apologized for the discrepancy and promised that, going forward, the actors playing the roles of the Queen and Prince Philip would receive equal pay.

What to Binge on Next

Another sumptuously produced historical drama about the British monarchy is *Victoria*, which depicts the life of Queen Victoria. Although much more racy, the historical drama *The Tudors*, starring Jonathan Rhys-Meyers as King Henry VIII, is also beautifully produced, but has been criticized even more fervently than has *The Crown* for its historical inaccuracies. A recent television movie imagining a near future when Charles becomes the king, *King Charles III* (starring Tim Pigott-Smith) might also appeal to you.

Those viewers more interested in British history of the twentieth century, and the many political machinations between the British government and members of the monarchy, might also consider the political drama *House of Cards*.

Morgan's film *The Queen*, which starred Helen Mirren as Queen Elizabeth II, is also a must-see.

Jackie on...
Soaps in the UK (Part One)

Coronation Street is the longest running soap in the world. It was first broadcast in 1960 and many people continue to watch the three new episodes that are broadcast every week. It is set on a terraced street in Weatherfield, a fictional town in Northern England, and follows the lives of ordinary working class people. The storylines mainly concentrate on the relationships between the families; but occasionally the action becomes more dramatic—they have been known to hold each other up at gun point and commit murder! In 1998 it was ground-breaking for including the first transgender character in a British soap and it celebrated its 50th birthday with a live episode dealing with a gas explosion and tram crash! Millions of British people love *Coronation Street*.

EastEnders was first broadcast in 1985 and has been shocking audiences ever since. The soap is set in inner-city London and often covers taboo subjects—child grooming, schizophrenia and euthanasia have all been covered. There are currently four half-hour episodes every week, with occasional live episodes to draw in more viewers. *EastEnders* is famed for including many elderly people, although more younger characters have recently been cast (which has been controversial, as the loyal viewers prefer the mature cast). *EastEnders* isn't for those looking for light-hearted entertainment, but if you're after a gritty insight into London-life it may well be for you.

Downton Abbey

Run Time

The series ran for six seasons and is comprised of forty-seven (roughly) hour-long episodes, and five Christmas specials at ninety minutes each, for a total run time of about fifty-four hours. The series started in 2010 and ended in 2015.

Creator and Writers

Julian Fellowes created and wrote the series (along with co-writers Shelagh Stephenson and Tina Pepler); he just also happens to be a Conservative peer in the House of Lords.

What It's About

Do I really have to do the recap of *Downton Abbey*? Has anyone who has any interest in British TV not heard all about *Downton Abbey*?

But I suppose, despite the show's massive popularity, including (or particularly) in the United States, a summary would still not go amiss. The year is 1912, and the setting is the Yorkshire-area estate known as Downton Abbey. Populated by the Earl of Grantham, his heiress wife Cora (the American heiress, that is, who brought her fortune to her marriage to help bolster the estate's finances), and their three daughters, the house is filled with family (upstairs) and servants (downstairs). All of the family lives well, but the daughters know that the estate is entailed and will not pass to them on their father's death...which is why the eldest daughter is set to marry their second cousin, who *will* inherit the estate. When the news arrives that the heir has died, everyone is upset, but everyone also knows that what they are mourning is not so much a man, but rather their best chance at continuing their residence and lifestyle.

Downton is now set to pass to an even more distant male cousin, a doctor-in-training named Matthew Crawley. From then on the stage is set for matrimonial hijinks: will any of the estate's daughters be able to convince Matthew to marry them? Or will their parents, the current Earl and his wife, have an even greater surprise for all of them, in the form of a new baby who might be a male heir?

Whew...all of that happens within a few episodes, and believe me when I say the below-stairs action is every bit as juicy as that upstairs. The staff is headed by the conscientious butler and housekeeper (Mr. Carson and Mrs. Hughes), but that's where the crisp subservient professionalism ends: Cora's lady's maid Miss O'Brien is a known troublemaker, and she is often joined in her schemes by Thomas Barrow, the footman; another storyline throughout the series concerns that of Earl Grantham's valet Bates and his wife Anna (lady's maid to Lady Mary Crawley), and Bates's past. Let's just put it this way: there's a lot going on.

And it continues at that pace through its entire six seasons, eventually encompassing the events of World War I, class and race relations in early twentieth-century Britain, and the economic challenges of the age.

Why It's Bingeworthy

Everything you ever wanted in a soap opera is here. Forbidden love affairs, strategic marriages, children who feel stifled by their parents, those with great wealth living close by (or being served by) those in great poverty, abusive husbands, crimes and trials and wrongly accused innocent men, deaths by childbirth, deaths by car, deaths by sexual excitement, it is ALL here. I promise you, like the other millions of Americans who first watched this program on PBS's Masterpiece Theatre, you will not be able to look away.

Main Cast

Hugh Bonneville…Robert Crawley
Elizabeth McGovern…Cora Crawley
Maggie Smith…Violet, Dowager Countess of Grantham
Michelle Dockery…Mary Crawley
Laura Carmichael…Edith Crawley
Jessica Brown Findlay…Sybil Crawley
Dan Stevens…Matthew Crawley
Lily James…Rose MacClare
Allen Leech…Tom Branson
Jim Carter…Mr. Carson (butler)
Phyllis Logan…Mrs. Hughes (housekeeper)
Rob James-Collier…Thomas Barrow
Siobhan Finneran…Miss O'Brien
Brendan Coyle…Mr. Bates
Joanne Froggatt…Anna Bates

Trivia

As of 2018, a feature film based on the series was being filmed.

The castle where the series was filmed is called Highclere Castle, and is still inhabited by the Carnavon family (and has been since 1679).

Each episode of the show reportedly cost £1 million to film and produce.

What To Binge on Next

If you've run out of episodes of *Downton Abbey* on which to binge, you might also enjoy other shows in which both family and staff dramas are portrayed: the classic series *Upstairs, Downstairs* is one such program, and although it ran from 1971 to 1975, you'll be surprised at how current it seems, and the risqué nature of some of its storylines (I think British TV has always taken a few more chances than has American). In 2010 a remake of that series, also titled *Upstairs, Downstairs*, that consists of two series and nine episodes, aired; you might like that one too.

Otherwise any number of recent historical dramas (melodramas?) might hit the spot: *The Crown*, a dramatization of the life of Queen Elizabeth II; *Call the Midwife*, about a group of nuns and nurse midwives working in the poor East End of London in the 1950s and 1960s; *Poldark*, a drama about a mining family in late 1700s Cornwall; and *Outlander*, which is based on the novels by Diana Gabaldon and largely set in the mid-1700s in Scotland (and later America).

The Durrells in Corfu

Run Time

From 2016 to 2018, twenty episodes in three series have aired. Each episode is nearly forty-five minutes long, making the total run time fifteen hours and change.

Creator and Writers

The series is based on the memoirs of author Gerald Durrell, but the episodes were written by Simon Nye.

What It's About

It's the 1930s in Bournemouth, and young widow Louisa Durrell finds herself and her four children in bleak circumstances. She is drinking like a fish ("if fish liked gin," as her oldest son Larry points out) and all of her children are struggling in various ways. Larry hates his job; her middle son is too fascinated with guns; her daughter lives in a dream world of her own, and her youngest son is interested only in animals and nature and as a result is getting caned by his strict school headmaster for failing in his studies.

Larry notes that all his friends are living cheaply and well on the Greek island of Corfu, so Louisa decides it is time to start afresh in what they think will be an island paradise. When the family arrives, however, it soon becomes clear that even a cheap location is going to strain their finances.

Finally the family has some good luck when they meet a local cabdriver, Spiros, who soon becomes their housing agent and friend. Soon the family starts to gel: all four children have the space to pursue their own interests, and even Louisa feels sufficiently strengthened by the sunlight to find her own romance, although, for all the family members, their strongest love affair remains the one they share as a family bond.

Why It's Bingeworthy

The series is based on British author Gerald Durrell's memoirs about his family's life in Corfu: *My Family and Other Animals*; *Birds, Beasts, and Relatives*; and *The Garden of the Gods*. It stars the superb Keeley Hawes, whose performance as the indefatigable Louisa Durrell is a sly, heart-filled, generous inhabitation of one of the most unique women in British literature. The actors who play her children are also uniformly excellent, which is all the more disgusting because they are all actually very young.

The sense of a uniquely quirky community in this show rivals that shown in one of my favorite American programs, *Northern Exposure*. But this show has at least one thing *Northern Exposure* lacked: beautiful and sunny Greek landscapes and shots of the gorgeous ocean, making this a warming program to watch if you are stuck in a Northern hemisphere winter.

One's family and one's love of it, in spite of said family's quirks, is on full display here, without any softening through sentimentality.

Main Cast

Keeley Hawes…Louisa Durrell
Josh O'Connor…Larry Durrell
Milo Parker…Gerry Durrell
Callum Woodhouse…Leslie Durrell
Daisy Waterstone…Margo Durrell
Alexis Georgoulis…Spiros Halikiopoulous

Trivia

In the U.K. the program is known simply as *The Durrells*.

Milo Parker, who plays the role of the animal-loving Gerry, now also acts as an official ambassador for the Durrell Wildlife Conservation Trust.

What to Binge on Next

Consider the comedy series *Jeeves and Wooster*, based on P.G. Wodehouse's novels, set in the same era, and starring Stephen Fry and Hugh Laurie.

Likewise, if you can't get enough of the tropical sunshine in this program, you might enjoy the cozy detective program *Death in Paradise*—it includes more murders but is set in the French Caribbean and will warm you when you're stuck in the depths of a British or northern North American winter.

Those viewers who love the "my family against the world" aspect of this program might also enjoy the (rather more broad but still enjoyable) comedy *Mrs. Brown's Boys*, or, if you have a darker sense of humor and don't mind a much more urban setting, Paul Abbott's series *Shameless*, following the adventures of a large family that lives in a Manchester council flat.

Lark Rise to Candleford

Run Time

The series consisted of forty episodes over the course of four series, and each episode was sixty minutes long, making for a total run time of forty hours. It aired on BBC One between 2008 and 2011.

Creator and Writers

The show is based upon the *Lark Rise to Candleford* trilogy of semi-autobiographical novels published by Flora Thompson in the 1930s and 1940s. Bill Gallagher is credited as the show's creator, and wrote most of the show's episodes, with other episodes being written by Gaby Chiappe, Carolyn Bonnyman, and others.

What It's About

It's the turn of the nineteenth century, and teenager Laura Timmins is ready to broaden her horizons from those of her small home village, Lark Rise. Her logical first step is to accept a job as an assistant in the post office in the neighboring town of Candleford, and it is her good luck that her boss is Dorcas Lane, an independent woman with strong ideas of her own.

The drama of the show largely comes in the interplay of the residents of the two communities; the more rural and poor Lark Rise, and the larger and more cosmopolitan Candleford. There is also plenty of drama in the lives of both Laura and Dorcas; both work hard to succeed in their careers, and both also have their share of love affairs. Perhaps most importantly, their friendship grows throughout the series, and they are able to provide help and support for one another.

Why It's Bingeworthy

Although this is a gentle program (watchers looking for a lot of romance but not very explicit love scenes need look no further), it also is surprisingly forthright about dealing with issues such as prejudice, the role of women in a society, family problems, and love relationships gone wrong. The appeal of the strong women main characters (played beautifully by Julia Sawalha, one of the most versatile actors around, and Olivia Hallinan) and their stronger friendship is one of the main draws of this historical adaptation.

Viewers might also enjoy the period detail and the diverse settings, particularly the many pastoral rural scenes. The series also boasted many cameo and guest appearances by such well-known Brit actors as Dawn French, Brendan Coyle, Ben Miles, Claire Skinner, and Richard Harrington.

Main Cast

Julia Sawalha…Dorcas Lane
Olivia Hallinan…Laura Timmins
Claudie Blakley…Emma Timmins
Brendan Coyle…Robert Timmins
Linda Bassett… Victoria May ("Queenie") Warrener Turrill
Karl Johnson… Thomas ("Twister") Turrill
Mark Heap…Thomas Brown
John Dagliesh…Alf Arless
Sarah Lancashire…Narrator

Trivia

The popularity of the show was proven when, after it was announced that it would end after its fourth season, many fans created online campaigns to ask that the program be renewed.

One of the many locations used for the shooting of the program, Chavenage House (which stands in for Candleford House), is rumored to be haunted.

What to Binge on Next

Fans of gentler costume dramas similar to *Lark Rise* might also consider the very gentle *Cranford* and *Return to Cranford* (based on Elizabeth Gaskell's nineteenth-century novel *Cranford*); the relatively gentle *The Paradise*, about a department store in late nineteenth-century London and a young woman from Scotland who gets a job there; and *Victoria*, a series about Queen Victoria's young life and new marriage, which is not as gentle but which is definitely of the right time period.

Other dramas in which the community (or communities) shines as one of the stars of the show might also appeal to *Lark Rise* fans, such as *All Creatures Great and Small*, about veterinarians in World War II-era Yorkshire; or even *The Bletchley Circle*, which features its own small but strong community of female former World War II codebreakers who continue to be friends and actually begin to investigate crimes on their own.

Mr. Selfridge

Run Time

Mr. Selfridge ran for four series and forty episodes between 2013 and 2016. Most of the episodes clocked in at forty-five minutes, making this a bingewatch of just a little over thirty hours.

Creator and Writers

The show is based on *Shopping, Seduction, and Mr. Selfridge*, a biography by Lindy Woodhead about the real Selfridge and his glamorous store. Andrew Davies first adapted it and wrote many episodes; other writers include Kate Brooke, Kate O'Riordan, Lindy Woodhead, and Helen Raynor.

What It's About

American Harry Selfridge is in London to open a luxurious retail palace, and he plans to get rich while doing so.

But the road to business success is not always so smooth; before he is able to open Selfridge & Co. on Oxford Street, he loses his financing, has to install his family in their new British home, and he also has to supervise construction and hire a staff that he will find suitable for his business.

The store is a one-of-a-kind experience in London, and for the employees (and eventually his family members) working there, it begins to function as a second home. And of course, that home comes with all the drama that you find in families: people with different working styles clash; love affairs are begun and ended; and through it all the store becomes an institution where everyone goes, not only to shop, but also to rub shoulders with some of the famous people who put in promotional appearances at the store.

Why It's Bingeworthy

Imagine *Downton Abbey* set in a glittering luxury-goods store and you'll pretty much have the appeal of *Mr. Selfridge*. Although a few characters are mainstays throughout all four seasons, the cast is large and varied and there are always multiple plot lines going on involving the Selfridge family, the store's employees, and the wealthy shoppers who flock to the store. And many of those storylines are every bit as juicy and scandalous as anything ever seen in *Downton*!

The story is set during the first two decades of the twentieth century, so the set decoration and the costumes are gorgeous. An added bonus is a number of "cameos" by famous individuals of the day: in the first season alone dancer Anna Pavlova, Arthur Conan Doyle, Ernest Shackleton, and even King Edward VII (all played by modern actors, of course) drop in to shop.

Main Cast

Jeremy Piven…Harry Selfridge
Ron Cook…Mr. Crabb
Tom Goodman-Hill…Mr. Grove
Amy Beth Hayes…Kitty Hawkins
Amanda Abbington…Miss Mardle
Greg Austin…Gordon Selfridge
Frances O'Connor…Rose Selfridge

Trivia

There's a reason this show is so magnificent to look at: from chocolates to jewelry, perfumes to crystal, so many actual products (for product placement purposes; over 1.7 million dollars' worth, in season two) were used that extra security on the set was necessary.

Selfridges the store is still open, and is located on Oxford Street in London.

What to Binge on Next

A very similar show in subject to this one (although it is not as salacious or as long-running) is the period drama *The Paradise*, which is about a British department store and its workers, set in the 1870s.

History buffs who love to see recent(ish) historical dramas that include big names might also like *The Crown*, which shows the life of Queen Elizabeth II from her marriage through recent years, and includes storylines about Winston Churchill, Princess Margaret, and many other notable figures.

Andrew Davies, who first adapted this series, is well known, of course, as the king of period drama adaptations. He is famous for other such series as 1995's *Pride and Prejudice*, 1994's *Middlemarch*, 2001's *The Way We Live Now*, and 2016's *War and Peace*.

Outlander

Run Time

As of 2019, a total of fifty-five episodes in four series have aired. Most episodes are just under an hour long, making the run time fifty-five hours.

Creator and Writers

Outlander is based on the Outlander novels by Diana Gabaldon. It was developed by Ronald D. Moore, and although Gabaldon is credited as the writer, many others have worked on the series, including Moore, Toni Graphia, Matthew B. Roberts, Anne Kenney, and Ira Steven Behr.

What It's About

The year is 1946, and nurse Claire Randall is enjoying a second honeymoon with her husband Frank, as the two have long been separated by their World War II service. While traveling in Inverness, the pair visits a standing stone site, and when Claire goes back on her own and touches a stone, she blacks out (so she thinks) and wakes up to find herself in the same location, but not in the same time. She has traveled back to the year 1743.

As she has traveled to a dangerous time, with tensions high between the Scots and the occupying Brits, she must act fast to gain protection from an influential local family and one of their members, Jamie Fraser, whose wounds she initially tends and with whom she finds herself falling in love.

In later seasons the links between Claire, Jamie, Frank, and Frank's unpleasant 1740s relative "Black Jack" Randall, become clear, as Claire travels back and forth through time and makes choices for herself and the two men she loves. The show also incorporates many historical events of the time, including the Jacobite uprising and Scottish emigration to the American colonies, and those aren't the only educational bits: this series (book and television) is noted for its quite spicy romantic and sex scenes.

Why It's Bingeworthy

Technically, this show is produced by Starz (an American network),but it's included here because its stars are primarily Brit actors (well, Caitriona Balfe is Irish and Sam Heughan is from Scotland), the first three seasons are set in England, and it's produced by the British company Left Bank Pictures.

Also? It's a fascinating period drama about a time period that isn't shown as often as are the Victorian and Georgian eras. The story is compelling, the chemistry between the characters is real and the acting is fabulous (even Tobias Menzies, pulling double duty as two characters the audience doesn't really want to like, hits it out of the park), and the setting and costuming is taken very seriously (I wouldn't really know how accurate it is, but even though all of the actors are fantastically good-looking, they do often look realistically uncomfortable in heavy woolens and primitive shoes).

Oh, and did I mention those love scenes? If the Scottish setting is cold, the sexy bits are anything but.

Main Cast

Caitriona Balfe...Claire Randall
Sam Heughan...Jamie Fraser
Tobias Menzies...Frank Randall/Jonathan Randall
Duncan Lacroix...Murtagh Fraser
Sophie Skelton...Brianna Fraser

Trivia

The castle that stood in for Castle Leoch during filming is Doune Castle. It was used in *Monty Python and the Holy Grail*, as well as *Game of Thrones*.

The author of the novels on which the series is based, Diana Gabaldon, has stated that watching an episode of *Doctor Who*, in which actor Frazer Hines played a Scotsman (in a fetching kilt), inspired her to write the novel.

When a motion picture adaptation was planned in 2010, its producers wanted Katherine Heigl to play Claire. That adaptation was never made.

What to Binge on Next

Another popular historical drama set in the 1780s and 1790s, is *Poldark*, which also features strong male and female leads in Ross Poldark and his wife Demelza (played by Aidan Turner and Eleanor Tomlinson).

Although even more graphic in its depictions of both violence and sexuality, the historical drama series *Versailles* about the reign of France's Louis XIV and the building of his palace at Versailles might also appeal to these viewers. (The third season of *Outlander* also happens to be set in France during the reign of Louis XV.)

Peaky Blinders

Run Time

As of 2018, *Peaky Blinders* has aired for four seasons and twenty-four hour-long episodes. The series began in 2013, and a fifth season is planned (for another six episodes) that will air in 2019. Right now the run time is twenty-four hours, but when the fifth season concludes it will be thirty hours.

Creator and Writers

Peaky Blinders was created by Steven Knight, and Knight is also credited as the writer of all its episodes (with periodic assistance from other writers).

What It's About

Turn of the twentieth century: Birmingham, England. It's a time and place when violent street gangs became more organized and often fought with rival gangs in the region and beyond; one of those gangs was known as the "Peaky Blinders," young men who were known for the practice of sewing razor blades into the peaks and brims of their flat caps to use as weapons.

In the show the Blinders are re-imagined slightly as a family-run enterprise. Just after the Great War, Arthur Shelby and his family are one of the most influential gangs in town, although their influence grows after Arthur's younger brother, Thomas Shelby, returns and assumes power of the family. Their schemes become riskier, including trying to sell a cache of war weapons that falls into their hands, and which is traced to them by Chester Campbell, a detective sent from Ireland to break their hold on the city.

In the first seasons the battles of will are mostly between the Shelby family and Campbell; in later seasons the Blinders decide to try and expand their empire into London and other points south, where they face gangs even more disdainful of human life and decency than they are.

Why It's Bingeworthy

Critics have questioned the historical facts of the show (the real Blinders are thought to have operated primarily from the 1890s to the 1920s, and not in as geographically broad a region), but they have also lauded it for its stylish cinematography and its daring soundtrack choices, many of which are modern or classic rock songs intertwined with the show's action.

The show is tightly plotted and the characters are compelling; viewers will find themselves addicted to watching each episode primarily to see how Tommy Shelby (played with mesmerizing ferocity by Cillian Murphy) will outmaneuver his family's many enemies. The supporting cast also turns in strong performances, and Helen McGrory and other women in the cast provide much more of the action than just "standing by their men."

It's all beautifully filmed, and the period detail is impressive, but there's no denying the program includes a lot of very graphic violence.

Main Cast

Cillian Murphy…Tommy Shelby
Helen McCrory…Polly Gray
Paul Anderson…Arthur Shelby, Jr.
Annabelle Wallis…Grace Burgess
Joe Cole…John Shelby
Sophie Rundle…Ada Thorne
Sam Neill…Chester Campbell
Tom Hardy…Alfie Solomons

Trivia

Actors Joe Cole and Finn Cole (who play cousins John Shelby and Michael Gray) are brothers in real life.

Creator Steven Knight claims that the series is based on Blinders lore from his own family (although his family name was Sheldon, not Shelby).

What to Binge on Next

Peaky Blinders treads a fine line between three genres: Drama, Costume Drama, and Crime Thriller. Other dramas that tread the same line include the crime drama *Whitechapel*, which features elements of cop show, history, and horror; *Life on Mars*, which blends historical (1970s) drama with cop procedural; and *Black Mirror*, which features all sorts of weirdness in all of its stand-alone story episodes.

Cillian Murphy can be seen in the films *28 Days Later* (set in Great Britain), *Perrier's Bounty*, a thriller/comedy also starring Jodie Whittaker (the latest Doctor Who), and *Red Eye*, another thriller in which he is unequivocally the bad guy. Fans of Tom Hardy might also like the dark historical drama *Taboo*, set in the early 1800s, and also created by Steven Knight.

134

Penny Dreadful

Run Time

The show aired from 2014 to 2016, and consisted of twenty-seven episodes that vary from forty-seven to sixty minutes. Assuming an average of fifty-five minutes per episode, the total run time is nearly twenty-five hours.

Creator and Writers

Penny Dreadful was created by John Logan, who also wrote many of the episodes, along with credited writers Andrew Hinderaker and Krysty Wilson-Cairns.

What It's About

In Victorian times some of the most popular periodicals were known as "penny dreadfuls." These publications promised horrific monsters, suspenseful storylines, and larger-than-life battles of good versus evil. This program is based upon those serials, and does a good job of translating their suspense and gothic creepiness from Victorian literature to the television screen.

The series incorporates many classic horror characters of the time into its storylines: Count Dracula and Abraham Van Helsing; Victor Frankenstein and the monster he created; Dorian Gray (and his portrait); Dr. Jekyll. In the first season an enigmatic man named Sir Malcolm Murray and a woman named Vanessa Ives enlist the help of American sharpshooter Ethan to help them investigate the supernatural, most specifically the circumstances of a young woman they both knew. In ensuing seasons the truth behind Vanessa's skills as a medium and her history becomes more clear while Ethan's feelings for her become clearer (although he has a big secret of his own); a broad cast of characters provides a variety of storylines, each creepier than the last.

The show lives up to its name; some of it is truly frightening and downright dreadful, with demonic possessions, Lucifer's seeking of a wife, revelations regarding Sir Malcom's activities among the native residents of Africa, and numerous deceptions and betrayals. The show can be quite graphic, both in violence and sexuality.

Why It's Bingeworthy

The show's creators seem to have perfectly understood the appeal of the historical penny dreadfuls; each of this show's three series offer numerous cliffhangers, plot twists, and ever more sensational revelations and depictions of evil (both human and not so human) in order to keep you watching. It also does a spectacular job of developing and showing its characters' histories so you have a great appreciation for the relationships they form with one another.

Eva Green deserves special kudos for this role, and Josh Hartnett did a nice job in it as well. It's dark and beautiful to look at with gorgeous period detail; you may want to watch it with your hands over your eyes most of the time, but make yourself look: the directors and cinematographers made a gorgeous program on a shoestring budget.

Main Cast

Eva Green...Vanessa Ives
Josh Hartnett...Ethan Chandler
Timothy Dalton...Sir Malcolm Murray
Reeve Carney...Dorian Gray
Rory Kinnear...John Clare (Frankenstein's monster)
Billie Piper...Brona Croft/Lily Frankenstein
Harry Treadaway...Victor Frankenstein

Trivia

Penny Dreadful was a joint production of the American Showtime channel and the U.K.'s Sky Network.

Series creator John Logan was also the screenwriter for the movies *Gladiator* and the Bond movies *Skyfall* and *Spectre*.

Eva Green, who plays the British character Vanessa Ives with all the right Victorian touches, is French.

What to Binge on Next

It's a bit tricky to find this mix of period drama and supernatural horror, but the 2007 adaptation of *Jekyll*, starring James Nesbitt as a modern-day descendent of Dr. Jekyll (and, of course, Mr. Hyde) is thoroughly unnerving as well.

A crime drama set in the same era is *Ripper Street*, starring Matthew Macfadyen as a police detective striving to keep order in the Whitechapel district in 1890s London, where the populace is still reeling from Jack the Ripper's crimes.

Another series that combines atmospheric horror and suspense, and which is set at the end of the nineteenth century, is the six-episode series *The Living and the Dead* (extra bonus: it, too, is as creepy as hell, just like *Penny Dreadful*).

Jackie on...
Soaps in the UK (Part Two)

Emmerdale has a different feel from other soaps as it is set in a rural community. It began as *Emmerdale Farm* in 1972, when it showed the life of a single family; but in 1989 the focus of the soap moved from the farm to the local village. Life in the northern English county of Yorkshire isn't easy though - there is just as much drama as in the city. Over the years *Emmerdale* has included many tragedies, most famously a plane crash in 1993 and a storm in 2004. There are fewer murders than in other soaps, but cast members are killed off just as frequently in accidents or fires. *Emmerdale* is less popular than *Coronation Street* or *EastEnders*, but its audience is just as loyal. They have to be, as six episodes are broadcast every week!

Hollyoaks is the soap for young adults. It was launched in 1995 and follows a group of students who live in Chester, northwest England. The soap mainly deals with issues affecting teenagers, including relationships, substance abuse and mental health. It has been praised for raising awareness of problems which young people face. The young age of the cast means that it has higher character turnover than most soaps, but its teenage audience doesn't seem to mind.

British people don't just enjoy watching soaps on television, many also love listening to them on the radio. Over 5 million people tune into *The Archers* every week, making it the most listened to non-news programme on BBC Radio 4. It was first broadcast in 1950 and is the longest running radio soap in the world. It is set in a small rural community and was originally set up in conjunction with the Ministry of Agriculture, Fisheries and Food, to share information about disease and good farming practices but it has developed into much more. There are currently six thirteen-minute episodes every week, with a 75 minutes omnibus episode broadcast every Sunday.

Poldark

Run Time

Through 2018 there have been four seasons of *Poldark*; a fifth and final series is planned. From 2015 through 2018 the four seasons have been comprised of thirty-five hour-long episodes, making for a total run time of thirty-five hours.

Creator and Writers

Poldark is based upon the twelve-novel historical fiction Poldark series by Winston Graham. In this, its latest adaptation, it was created and written entirely by Debbie Horsfield.

What It's About

Based on the Poldark historical fiction novels by Winston Graham, this drama follows the exploits of late-eighteenth-century Cornish man's man, woman's man, and man about town Ross Poldark. Part of the landed gentry class, Ross left his father's estate to serve in the Revolutionary War in America, and when he returns from being on the losing side of that conflict, he clearly hopes to pick up where he left off with his (he thought) fiancée Elizabeth. When he gets to Cornwall, however, he finds that his father has died, his estate is in ruins and is home to only a pair of middle-aged drunken servants, and his former fiancé is set to marry his cousin Francis. This rightly sends him into something of an existential tailspin; when he emerges from that he finds he has not only committed himself to reviving his family's land and mining interests, he has also taken in a girl orphan, Demelza, who soon emphatically grows up and becomes his wife. All of this, mind you, while he strives to keep out of bankruptcy court (and revives an old feud with banker George Warleggan, a former classmate who has become the wealthiest man in the district) and court in general, as he seems to get into more and more trouble for following his principles and defending his employees and tenants from a corrupt upper class.

Lucky for him he did marry Demelza; she serves as a steadying influence throughout and, although she shows anger at her husband, her love for him is one thing that starts to redeem him.

Why It's Bingeworthy

Winston Graham's series of novels are some of the most engrossing historical fiction books ever written, meaning the source material for this drama is strong. The stories are powerful: Ross wants to do right by his land and by his people; there are angry rivalries all over the place; and the multiple love stories are on the continuum from the convenient and arranged to the difficult and passionate.

The scenery is beautiful and this is not a time period or location that is portrayed in many other programs. All of the actors turn in strong performances, and the stories are quickly paced. Last but not least: the soundtrack is gorgeous.

Main Cast

Aidan Turner...Ross Poldark
Eleanor Tomlinson...Demelza
Heida Reed...Elizabeth Poldark
Kyle Soller...Francis Poldark
Jack Farthing...George Warleggan
Caroline Blakiston...Agatha Poldark
Luke Norris...Dwight Enys
Gabriella Wilde...Caroline Enys
...and too many more to list.

Trivia

Series producer Damien Timmer questioned early on in filming of the first series whether or not women would find Aidan Turner sufficiently attractive as Ross Poldark. Mr. Timmer? No worries: Aidan Turner is way more than "sufficiently attractive."

Actor Kyle Soller, who played Ross's more suitably aristocratic cousin Francis, is an American actor who trained at the RADA in London to perfect his accent for the show.

Robin Ellis, who played Ross Poldark in the 1975 *Poldark* adaptation, plays the role of a merciless judge in the first season of this adaptation.

Caroline Blakiston, the actress who plays Aunt Agatha Poldark, also played the iconic role of Mon Mothma in *Return of the Jedi*.

What to Binge on Next

The first thing you need to do when you're done watching this adaptation of *Poldark* is to go read all of Winston Graham's original twelve novels about the Poldark family and Cornwall; they're AWESOME. And then you're also going to want to go watch the 1970s adaptation, also titled *Poldark*, and starring the strangely magnetic Robin Ellis. It is not as true an adaptation, and it looks as dated and as clunky as all old BBC period pieces do, but it's very different, it's a lot of fun, and Robin Ellis is nothing short of fabulous in it.

Other literary adaptations in which tortured love affairs take center stage might also appeal to these viewers, including Charlotte Brontë's *Jane Eyre* (starring Ruth Wilson and Toby Stephens), Anne Brontë's *The Tenant of Wildfell Hall* (starring Toby Stephens and Tara Fitzgerald), and the 2016 adaptation of *War and Peace* (starring Lily James and James Norton).

Viewers who love the setting of Cornwall might also like the more lighthearted romantic drama *Doc Martin*, set in a seaside village in Cornwall and featuring Martin Clunes as Dr. Martin Ellingham, a surgeon-turned-family-doctor (who also happens to have a phobia about blood).

Robin Hood

Run Time

This lively historical dramedy aired for three seasons between 2006 and 2009, and consisted of thirty-nine forty-five-minute episodes in three series, making for a total watch time of just a touch over twenty-nine hours.

Creator and Writers

The show was created by Dominic Minghella and Foz Allan. Minghella and Allan also have writing credits for all thirty-nine episodes, but other writers credited for multiple episodes include Simon J. Ashford, Bev Doyle, Richard Kurti, and many others.

What It's About

Robin of Locksley is home from the Crusades, and he is not best pleased to find that the Sheriff of Nottingham is a right corrupt and evil bastard, with a staff of henchmen who are all as nasty as he is. They've taken over Locksley's estate, they're taxing the hell out of the locals, and they date (is the nice word for it) all the available women, whether the women are interested or not.

As Robin himself asks, will you tolerate this?

He will not, so he and his faithful manservant, "Much," head out to make a temporary home in the forests of Sherwood. There they stumble across any number of other outlaws, with whom they decide to band together and start stealing from the rich to give back to the poor. While keeping busy with that, they also manage to become fairly large thorns in the side of the thoroughly evil Sheriff and his deputy, Guy of Gisborne, who is intent on marrying the same woman with whom Robin is in love.

There's a lot to do to bring justice back to Locksley and Nottingham. But Robin, Much, Little John, Allan Dale, Will Scarlett, and Marian are all up to the challenge.

Why It's Bingeworthy

This 2006 version of *Robin Hood* is total camp, but in the best possible way. Robin's a lovable scamp; Marian's a brave and feisty maiden; the Sheriff and Guy Gisborne (played by Keith Allen and Richard Armitage) are deliciously evil. There's a lot of action, quite a bit of comedy (mostly delivered by the aforementioned deliciously evil Sheriff), and a lively love story to enjoy. Two lively love stories, actually: of course you know that Marian and Robin are meant to be together, but it's hard to deny the oily yet still sometimes vulnerable charms of Guy of Gisborne.

The natural settings (the program was filmed in Hungary) make it a nice show to watch when you're in a mood for something that isn't set in the city, and the soundtrack makes use of a lot of brassy horns and crashing drums and helps add to the atmosphere.

Everyone in it may be overacting (a frequent charge against this show), but when the result is a show that you just can't stop watching, where's the harm in it?

Main Cast

Jonas Armstrong…Robin of Locksley/Robin Hood
Lucy Griffiths…Marian
Keith Allen…Sheriff of Nottingham
Richard Armitage…Guy of Gisborne
Sam Troughton…Much
Gordon Kennedy…Little John

Trivia

It seems that the actors threw their all into the physical and fight scenes; while filming the second season, Jonas Armstrong broke a bone in his foot, and Keith Allen actually lost a tooth while filming a fight sequence in the first season.

Before the show's premiere, several master tapes of footage were stolen from the program's production base in Hungary. Although it was thought that the premiere of the show would be delayed, the BBC went ahead with plans to publicize the show anyway, and the tapes were recovered by the Hungarian police in September 2006.

The show was meant to provide family-friendly entertainment on Saturday nights, when it aired between seasons of the newly revived *Doctor Who* (which played in the same Saturday night time slot).

What to Binge on Next

In most of the film and television adaptations of the Robin Hood story, Hood takes his mission to steal from the rich and give to the poor very seriously, and he's not often shown with a real sense of humor. The most fun thing about this program is its sense of fun and its stars' willingness to engage in over-acting hijinks. Other programs that are delightfully over the top like this one are the classic comedy *Blackadder* (which is also about pivotal times in British history) and *Hotel Babylon*, about a group of hotel employees who regularly get into troublesome situations involving their hotel's guests. The creator of this show, Dominic Minghella, is also the creator of the comedy drama program *Doc Martin*, starring Martin Clunes as a former surgeon who has developed a phobia of blood and has to restart his career as a general practitioner in a small Cornish village.

Another fantasy adventure series you might like is *Legend of the Seeker*, a drama based on the Sword of Truth fantasy novels by Terry Goodkind, and was filmed in New Zealand.

Another popular adaptation of the Robin Hood legend is the more serious *Robin of Sherwood*, a classic show that aired on ITV in the 1980s. If you're up for a good mystery and a little Derek Jacobi, you might also consider the mystery series *Cadfael*, set in a similar Medieval time period and featuring Jacobi as a crime-solving monk.

Versailles

Run Time

Versailles ran for three series and thirty episodes between 2015 and 2018. Each episode was an hour long; it will take you thirty hours to watch the entire run of episodes.

Creator and Writers

The show is referred to as a joint Franco-Canadian production, and first aired on Canal+ in France, Super Channel in Canada, and BBC Two in Great Britain. It was created by Brits Simon Mirren and David Wolstencroft, who share writing credits with Andrew Bampfield, Tim Loane, and several others.

What It's About

It's France, in the 1660s, and King Louis XIV (the Sun King) is twenty-eight years old and desperate to assert his royal prerogative and power (and to bring his unruly nobles into line). To do so he decides to make his father's former hunting lodge at Versailles into a magnificent palace and the new seat of his power, where he believes he will largely be able to hold his royal court hostage and consolidate power more easily than he would be able to do in Paris.

He faces many challenges in his single-minded drive for power. He needs to hold power, avoid being killed by any of the multiple political operatives and assassins plotting his downfall, conceive another son by his queen, and dominate his relationship with his brother.

Why It's Bingeworthy

If you like your period dramas down and dirty you are going to love *Versailles*. There is a lot of graphic sex and violence in this program. On the other hand, if you're a real stickler for absolute historical accuracy, this is probably not going to be the historical drama for you.

Although movies and histories about the reign of Louis XIV are abundant, there are fewer television shows that dramatize the period and its main characters, making this a different show about a different subject. As noted in the Trivia section, it was an expensive show to produce and a large chunk of its budget went toward its costume and art departments, so it's an absolutely lush program to look at.

Main Cast

George Blagden…Louis XIV
Alexander Vlahos… Monsieur Philippe d'Orléans
Stuart Bowman…Bontemps
Evan Williams…Chevalier

Trivia

As of 2015, this period drama was the most expensive television show ever produced in France.

The costume team on this production consisted of roughly thirty people.

What to Binge on Next

Other period dramas that edge toward the racy are *The Tudors*, starring Jonathan Rhys-Meyers as King Henry VIII (and focusing primarily on his love affairs and wives); *Outlander*, based on the historical time travel novels of Diana Gabaldon, and which is set in eighteenth-century Scotland (mostly); the Victorian-era *Desperate Romantics*, about the Pre-Raphaelite Brotherhood and their saucy hijinks; and *The Borgias*, set in fifteenth-century Rome and featuring Jeremy Irons as Spanish cardinal Rodrigo Borgia.

Victoria

Run Time

As of 2019 there have been twenty-five episodes in three series; it began airing in 2016. Twenty-four fifty-minute episodes and a seventy-minute Christmas special that aired after the second series mean that this program has a total run time of just over twenty-one hours.

Creator and Writers

The series was created by Daisy Goodwin, who also has writing credits on all of the episodes. Also credited is newspaper columnist and historian A.N. Wilson, as well as screenwriters Ottile Wilford and Guy Andrews.

What It's About

Although many stories about Queen Victoria either present an overview of her entire reign or show her as an elderly monarch still in deep mourning for her husband Albert, this series shows Victoria as she has just aged out of childhood and ascends to the throne after the death of her uncle King William IV. There is a lot of political intrigue surrounding her household staff and various family members, and there is also a lot of tension about who she will choose as her eventual husband and consort. Attention is also paid in this story to the personal and household staff of Victoria and at the palace.

Although Victoria commands the screen here as she grasps whatever power she can, there are also strong male presences in this period drama, including the kindly Lord Melbourne, the first prime minister with whom she works, and her eventual husband Albert, whose first meetings with her are both awkward and filled with chemistry. After they marry, the pair must negotiate with one another and Victoria's political ministers about what role Albert will play in the palace. When the children begin to arrive, Victoria must also find a way to be both a mother and a queen.

Why It's Bingeworthy

Victorian-era England has never looked this good. Rufus Sewell as Lord Melbourne is downright dreamy (and that is not, ahem, strictly historically accurate) and the chemistry between Jenna Coleman as Victoria and her love interests (as well as with her family members, in both love and hate relationships) is sparkling.

As is often the case in the newer period dramas, the costumes and interiors are absolutely stunning. The focus on the early years of Victoria's reign, particularly her struggles to balance her constant pregnancies with her political duties, makes for intriguing storylines.

Main Cast

Jenna Coleman…Queen Victoria
Tom Hughes…Prince Albert
Daniela Holtz…Baroness Lehzen
Nigel Lindsay…Sir Robert Peel
Rufus Sewell…Lord Melbourne
Alex Jennings…King Leopold
Nell Hudson…Skerrett
Eve Myles…Mrs. Jenkins
Adrian Schiller…Penge

Trivia

Star Jenna Coleman has brown eyes and wears contacts to change her eye color to blue. When she portrayed the Queen as an eighteen- to twenty-one-year-old in series one, she was thirty years old.

Jenna Coleman and Tom Hughes, the actor who plays Prince Albert, have been in a relationship since 2016.

What to Binge on Next

One of the programs that *Victoria* has been most frequently compared to is *Downton Abbey*, which is a period drama focusing on an aristocratic family in the early years of the twentieth century; it is also sumptuous to look at and features storylines about both the aristocratic family and their servants.

Another new series focusing on the early years of a monarch's reign is *The Crown*, about Queen Elizabeth II's ascension to the throne in the 1950s, as well as the early years of her marriage.

Jenna Coleman has also recently starred in the BBC One suspense drama *The Cry*, about a woman whose child disappears while the family is traveling in Australia, and was a companion (Clara) to Peter Capaldi's twelfth incarnation of the Doctor in *Doctor Who*.

Jackie on...
Two Historical Dramas
You Should Start With

All Creatures Great and Small

All Creatures Great and Small last aired in 1990 but is an important part of British television history. The series is based on books written by the vet James Herriot and show the every-day life of a vet living in rural Yorkshire. The British are known for their love of animals and I think this is why this show takes a special place in our hearts. Much of the programme appears dated now, but this can be overlooked because of the heart-warming scenes showing how much people care for their pets. The beautiful scenery of the Yorkshire Dales is another reason to add this to your watch list.

Call the Midwife

Call the Midwife is a fascinating insight into what life was like in East London in the 1950s and 1960s. Each episode shows the day-to-day life of a group of midwives living in a nursing convent. Through the challenges of pregnancy and birth, the difficulties faced by the poorer members of society are exposed. It's a beautiful blend of trauma and heart-warming stories; showing how a bit of kindness can transform difficult lives. This is a charming series that will probably make you laugh and cry, but is probably best avoided if you're pregnant as some of the scenes are a bit gruesome!

Crime Dramas

Broadchurch

Run Time

Broadchurch ran for three series and a total of twenty-four forty-five-minute episodes between 2013 and 2017. The total run time is eighteen hours.

Creator and Writers

This hugely popular crime drama was created by Chris Chibnall, and written by Chibnall and Louise Fox.

What It's About

When a young boy is found murdered on the beach in the small seaside community of Broadchurch, the town's residents begin to view one another with suspicion and distrust.

That's only natural; nobody knows who killed Danny Latimer or why, and it transpires that everyone in the town has their secrets. Adding to the stress of the situation is the fact that one of the police investigators is a local woman who is biased by her residency in the town, and the other has recently been transferred to Broadchurch after failing to solve his former murder case. The media attention (both local and national) given to the sensational crime also helps to keep community tensions high.

The show is taut and suspenseful and by the end you're not quite sure yourself which lead will be the one that breaks the case. In the end of the first series the detectives make an arrest, but in the following two series it is shown just how little closure an actual arrest can give, and the community continues to struggle with the contentious court battle and other events.

Why It's Bingeworthy

Broadchurch (especially series three, which benefitted from the popularity of the first two series) was ITV's most-watched crime drama ever, and the show's producers and writers kept plot developments a secret even from the actors involved, to increase the feel of the show's suspense and the uncertainty about who the guilty party was. Once you start watching, the cliffhanger at the end of each episode will definitely make you say, "I have to watch just one more," no matter what time of day or night it is.

The scenery in the program, shot in and around West Bay, Dorset, is absolutely gorgeous and the music is haunting as well. Olivia Colman got critical raves for her performance as the local detective; David Tennant is always fun to watch (even when his character is on a downward spiral); and the members of the Latimer family (including Jodie Whittaker and Andrew Buchan) also do a fantastic job at portraying the heartbreak of losing a son.

Main Cast

Olivia Colman…Ellie Miller
David Tennant…Alec Hardy
Jodie Whittaker…Beth Latimer
Andrew Buchan…Mark Latimer
Arthur Darville…Paul Coates

Trivia

The popularity of this show led to it being adapted for America. The title was changed to *Gracepoint* and David Tennant starred in the same role as the lead investigator, but the show flopped and only aired for one season.

More than eleven million viewers watched series three, making it ITV's most-watched crime drama ever.

Creator Chris Chibnall went on to replace Steven Moffat as the executive producer of *Doctor Who*, and also was named head writer of the eleventh series of the program that would air in 2018. His star and the new Doctor Who? None other than Jodie Whittaker.

What to Binge on Next

Another series in which the lead detective finds it difficult to forget his past cases (and their victims) is *River*, starring Stellan Skarsgård as Police Inspector John River. Although it focuses on cold cases and long-ago crimes, in the crime drama *Unforgotten*, Nicola Walker and Sanjeev Bhaskar star as the detectives who seek to bring justice to long-gone victims. Another suspenseful program featuring a driven detective is *Marcella*, considered an example of "Scandinavian noir," a mystery in which the tone is dark and morally complex (a lot like the tone of *Broadchurch*).

Although it is quite different in tone, the drama/mystery/musical series *Blackpool* is also about a community, its members' secrets, and a murder, and also stars David Tennant as a police detective.

Case Histories

Run Time

Case Histories ran for two seasons and a total of nine episodes between 2011 and 2013. In the first series there were six episodes that were sixty minutes each (or three two-part episodes), while the format in the second series changed slightly, into three self-contained episodes at ninety minutes each. The total run time is ten and a half hours.

Creator and Writers

The program is based upon the mystery novels by Kate Atkinson, with some episodes based directly on her books and some featuring new stories written by Atkinson, Peter Harness, Ashley Pharoah, and others.

What It's About

Jackson Brodie, while being a very tough private investigator, has an unexpected weakness: he can't say no to any case that the police won't touch, even cases involving people's lost cats. Of course, because it's Jackson Brodie and he seems to draw all sorts of trouble to him, the elderly lady with the lost cat lives next door to two sisters who, after the death of their authoritarian father, hire him solve the decades-old mystery of what happened to their baby sister.

All of Brodie's cases are like this; seemingly unrelated cases and people all turn out to have connections to one another, and while he solves them and strives to find time to spend with his young daughter (from whose mother he is divorced) he's also still dealing with his own trauma: the unsolved death of his sister Niamh, which happened when he was a boy.

He is also a former police detective, and although he can sometimes access information through a friend of his still on the force (another woman who loves him even though she knows he can be the most frustrating man alive), mostly he and the Edinburgh police treat each other as enemies.

Why It's Bingeworthy

The best thing about this crime drama is how different it seems from many other suspense dramas, which move their stories along at a breakneck pace; what this program offers is a slow burn of revelations, connected storylines, and character insights that will keep you watching and re-watching.

Jason Isaacs hasn't made a whole lot of high-profile British television appearances (you may know him better as Lucius Malfoy in the Harry Potter films), which is a shame, because he is absolutely mesmerizing here. Amanda Abbington does a fantastic job acting his frustrated friend and maybe love interest, police investigator Louise Munroe. Let's also not forget the scenes between Jackson and his eight-year-old daughter Marlee: they're bright little gems in an otherwise somber narrative; you get the feeling Jackson also enjoys his few moments of levity with his daughter as a nice break from all the unrelenting sadness of the cases he pursues.

Main Cast

Jason Isaacs…Jackson Brodie
Amanda Abbington…Louise Munroe
Zawe Ashton…Deborah Arnold
Millie Innes…Marlee Brodie

Trivia

Atkinson's novels are set in Cambridge; for this series the setting was changed to Edinburgh, Scotland, where she currently lives.

The series soundtrack includes plenty of American country singers, including Emmylou Harris, Nanci Griffith, and Mary Gauthier.

What to Binge on Next

The Irish mystery series *Jack Taylor* is about as similar to *Case Histories* as you can find, although it is set in Galway, Ireland. Jack Taylor is also a former police detective who has turned to private detective work to pay the bills. It matches *Case Histories* in tone (both can be quite dark) but also includes somewhat offbeat moments of humor, particularly in the inner dialogue of the main character, Jack Taylor, a sardonic alcoholic type who cannot often seem to help himself, even though it is clear he wants to help others.

The detective series *Rebus*, also set in Edinburgh and featuring John Rebus as a lone wolf police investigator, might also appeal to you if you liked *Case Histories*. Two different actors played the title role: first John Hannah, and then Ken Stott (who is the actor Atkinson originally thought would be perfect for the role of Jackson Brodie, before Jason Isaacs was cast).

Death in Paradise

Run Time

Through 2018, seven seasons have been shown (the show premiered in 2011, and an eighth season is currently being filmed), and there have been fifty-six hour-long episodes, for a total run time of fifty-six hours.

Creator and Writers

The series was created by Robert Thorogood, who also wrote many of the episodes, along with a rotating cast of TV writers including Dana Fainaru, Jack Lothian, Tom Higgins, and Will Fisher.

What It's About

Death in Paradise is a police procedural mixed with a cozy detective story mixed with tropical island eye candy. On the fictional French Caribbean island of Saint Marie, the first episode of the show opens with the murder of its resident British DCI, Charlie Hulme. Soon another British DCI, Richard Poole, is sent to the island to help lead the investigation into his colleague's death.

Poole turns out to be a brilliant investigator, but one whose various neuroses and personality quirks mean that he is little missed by his work colleagues back in Great Britain, so when he is asked by Saint Marie Police Commissioner Selwyn Patterson to stay on and lead their department's homicide investigations, he agrees, even though he is a walking stereotype of all things British, constantly laments the Caribbean heat and sunshine, misses his local pub, and despairs of ever finding a good cup of tea on the island. Eventually he learns that his new colleagues are both dedicated investigators and determined police officers in their own rights, and they are also forgiving and even somewhat affectionate about his curmudgeonly nature.

The series changes its cast frequently, with (to date) three different Brit actors playing three very different British DCIs, as well as many other personnel changes among the police department's resident staff members. Several things remain consistent throughout the show: the endings, which always portray the suspects gathered together so that the investigators can reveal the guilty parties (there's your cozy "everyone gathered at the end" element); the setting, which is gorgeous and drenched in warm sunshine (with the exception of a few episodes set during hurricanes); and the strong interplay between the different British detectives and their long-suffering island colleagues.

Why It's Bingeworthy

Each episode of *Death in Paradise* is so many things: a standard fish-out-of-water story; tropical island vacation porn (in the sense that when you bingewatch it during the winter, you will start to fantasize about planning your own vacation to a tropical island); a cozy police procedural which usually centers on a "locked door" mystery and finds the main detectives gathering all the suspects together at the end to reveal the guilty party or parties; and just a surprisingly fun and lighthearted watch. It's formulaic in the best possible way, with each hour-long episode starting with the finding of a dead body, the incongruently cheerful theme music, the crime investigation, the revelation and flashbacks when the detective suddenly realizes how each crime was done, and the aforementioned reveal with all the suspects gathered together.

The writers and casting directors are also obviously very skilled at shaking up their cast members. The first two seasons featured Ben Miller as DI Richard Poole, the most British of British detectives ever to grace the small screen, who spent equal time solving crimes and wearing uncomfortably warm suits and looking for a good cup of tea; the subsequent three seasons featured Kris Marshall as the decidedly more relaxed DI Humphrey Goodman (who promptly fell in love with the island's detective sergeant, Camille Bordey), and the most recent seasons have featured Ardal O'Hanlon as DI Jack Mooney. The island's police staff also come and go (with the notable exception of Danny John-Jules as the rakish officer Dwayne Myers), but all are strong actors who make their characters unique and memorable even after they've moved on.

Overall the mysteries are not complex (how could they be, when they are committed and neatly solved within sixty minutes?), but they are also not typically gory, making this great comfort watching when you need something to relax with at the end of the day and you can't afford to take your own vacation to a tropical island.

Main Cast

Ben Miller...Richard Poole
Sara Martins...Camille Bordey
Danny John-Jules...Dwayne Myers
Joséphine Jobert...Florence Cassell
Kris Marshall...Humphrey Goodman

Ardal O'Hanlon…Jack Mooney
Elizabeth Bourgine…Catherine Bordey

Trivia

Death in Paradise is filmed on location in the French-owned islands of Guadeloupe (in the town of Deshaies, on the island of Basse-Terre).

Creator and writer Robert Thorogood should provide inspiration for all writers struggling to make it in their chosen field; although he wrote and submitted many scripts to the BBC, ITV, and independent film companies for many years, his writing credit for *Death in Paradise* became his first credit (at age 39).

Thorogood now also writes novels based on his *Death in Paradise* characters and locations. The first was published in 2015 and is titled *A Meditation on Murder*. The novels feature his original detective, DCI Richard Poole.

What to Binge on Next

Death in Paradise is great comfort watching, particularly in the middle of a cold Northern American winter. Other cozy mystery series that will keep you enthralled but which are not too dark in tone include *Campion*, a mystery series set in 1920s and 1930s Great Britain and starring the always charming Peter Davison; *The Mrs. Bradley Mysteries*, featuring Diana Rigg as the lively amateur detective Mrs. Bradley; and pretty much anything by Agatha Christie, including most of the adaptations of her works starring her Belgian expert detective Hercule Poirot or her elderly amateur sleuth Miss Jane Marple.

Viewers who love the tropical setting and sun-drenched locales in this series might also consider the family drama *Wild at Heart*, set on a wildlife sanctuary in Africa, or *The Durrells in Corfu*, featuring the lively escapades of the free-spirited Durrell family members in sunny Corfu.

The Fall

Run Time

The Fall ran for three series and a total of seventeen hour-long episodes, making for a total run time of seventeen hours. The series aired on BBC Two between 2013 and 2016.

Creator and Writers

Television writer and playwright Allan Cubitt is the creator and sole writer of the series.

What It's About

A serial killer is targeting and killing young brunette professional women in Belfast, Northern Ireland. For the viewer, there's no mystery as to who is the Belfast Strangler: very early on he is shown to be Paul Spector, a married man, father of two, and professional bereavement counselor.

For the Police Service of Northern Ireland (PSNI), however, the identity of the killer is elusive and their investigation has been plagued by blunders, missteps, and bad publicity. Eventually they invite Stella Gibson, a Metropolitan Police Service Superintendent from London, to travel to Belfast and investigate the investigation (as well as to provide support in trying to apprehend the killer). Gibson brings to the investigation not only her superlative investigative skills but also her habit of engaging in sexual trysts with men she believes will be disposable and keep their mouths shut, as well as a history of sharing an affair with the man currently in charge of the Strangler investigation, Assistant Chief Constable Jim Burns (who is also a married man).

In series one the crimes take center stage, as Spector falls ever further into his elaborate fantasies and plans and murders several victims, while also struggling to maintain his normal façade at home and keep his job. In series two he is eventually apprehended, but questions about horrific abuse in his child- and adolescent-hood open the door to sympathy, although after he is captured it becomes clear that he has abducted the woman he knows revealed his identity to the police and has hidden her, alive, in a secret location. The third series follows the explosive conclusion of the second, when Spector is hurt while in police custody and spends much of the final series pleading amnesia, insisting he does not remember committing any crimes.

Why It's Bingeworthy

Two words: Gillian Anderson.

Okay, there's a bit more to it than that. (Two more words: Jamie Dornan, who silences all the critics who said he couldn't act in the *Fifty Shades of Grey* trilogy with a stellar performance here.) *The Fall* is also a well-executed, tautly plotted, and thoroughly unnerving and suspenseful police procedural.

Although it may be too dark and violent for some, in addition to being a first-rate crime drama, this show also has a lot of interesting things to say about gender dynamics. What issues are raised by Superintendent Stella Gibson's affairs with her (sometimes inferior in rank, sometimes superior) colleagues? How are female victims treated during criminal investigations? How much do we really know about those we live with and love? Although I was somewhat disappointed by a few loose ends left in the show's conclusion (I was not satisfied, for instance, by the lack of closure given to the story of Spector's wife and family), overall I found this to be a fascinating psychological, as well as crime, drama. I will never forget, for instance, Gibson's suggestion that sometimes victims can be compliant (for a variety of reasons), but that does not mean they have given consent. Think on that one for a while.

Main Cast

Gillian Anderson...Stella Gibson
Jamie Dornan...Paul Spector
John Lynch...Jim Burns
Bronagh Waugh...Sally Ann Spector
Sarah Beattie...Olivia Spector
Aisling Franciosi...Katie Benedetto

Trivia

All of the episode titles in this program are lines in John Milton's epic poem "Paradise Lost."

Actor Jamie Dornan was born in Belfast, Northern Ireland.

Creator and writer Allan Cubitt also wrote the 2004 television adaptation *Sherlock Holmes and the Case of the Silk Stocking*, which starred Rupert Everett as Holmes.

What to Binge on Next

The Queen Mother of all police crime dramas starring a woman as the lead investigator is, of course, the *Prime Suspect* series, created by Lynda La Plante and starring Helen Mirren. Fans of Stella Gibson's are going to find a lot to like in *Prime Suspect*'s Jane Tennison.

Other suspenseful crime dramas in which the mystery of who actually did the crime is not the prime plot point might appeal to these viewers, such as *Broadchurch*, a mystery set in a small community where the perpetrator is actually known through the latter seasons; *Happy Valley*, in which veteran cop Catherine Cawood knows exactly who the bad guy is from the start; or even *Luther*, featuring Idris Elba as detective John Luther, whose problem is not so much knowing who did it as it is in appropriately apprehending and charging such perpetrators.

Jackie on...
Housing Vocabulary in the UK

A **detached house** has nothing attached to it—it is on its own plot of land, surrounded by a garden.

A **semi-detached house** is attached to one other house. There are often whole streets of these, often with neighbouring houses sharing a drive.

A **terraced house** is attached to other houses on both sides. These are normally the cheapest type of house.

A **council house** is owned by the local government and rented out to those on low incomes.

A **council estate** is an area of housing where all the properties are owned by the local authority. Most council estates are made up of semi-detached housing, often built between 1920 and 1950, although some have been built more recently. This definition is blurring as many people now have the opportunity to buy their council house and so some council estates are almost entirely privately owned.

Happy Valley

Run Time

So far the series has had two seasons with six hour-long episodes each; the total run time is twelve hours.

Creator and Writers

Sally Wainwright created and wrote the show. Although critics and fans have indicated a desire to see more seasons, Wainwright has also been busy as the head writer for the shows *Last Tango in Halifax* and *Scott & Bailey*— she just doesn't have the time!

What It's About

In the trailer for series one of this program, veteran cop Catherine Cawood introduces herself to a drunken perp on her urban Yorkshire beat, saying she's divorced; lives with her sister, a recovering heroin addict; one of her kids doesn't talk to her and the other is dead (of suicide); she looks after her young grandson Ryan (conceived through rape, Catherine maintains her daughter told her). And even after that monologue she's still got secrets: she's sleeping with her ex; she's never dealt with her grief over her daughter's death and is having panic attacks and hallucinations; and she's tracking her daughter's rapist, who has just been released from jail after serving time for drug offenses.

There is nothing particularly happy about *Happy Valley*. And yet Catherine persists.

The story arc of the first series follows the events of a kidnapping-gone-wrong, and it features ordinary (not particularly evil, which is what makes the entire thing so unnerving) people often making really terrible decisions. Although the show does include real and horrifying scenes of physical brutality, its psychological creepiness is even more unsettling.

Why It's Bingeworthy

Rural drug rings, kidnapping, rape, horrific violence (both physical and psychological), actually, I'm having to pause a moment here to remember why *Happy Valley* is bingeworthy.

Okay, I've got it. This show is populated by complex characters: you can't count on the "good guys" to be completely good, and sometimes you find yourself having pity for the "bad guys" (most often when they're being intimidated by the "worse guys"). Creator Wainwright has a real knack for displaying human weaknesses and strengths, as well as for telling a quickly paced and suspenseful story. You have to keep watching, because you just keep hoping that someone in Happy Valley will have a happy ending.

Main Cast

Sarah Lancashire…Catherine Cawood
Siobhan Finneran…Clare Cartwright
James Norton…Tommy Lee Royce
Charlie Murphy…Ann Gallagher
Shirley Henderson…Frances Drummond

Trivia

Creator Sally Wainwright was born in the town of Huddersfield, in the Calder Valley area where *Happy Valley* is set.

Wainwright has had a long career in television writing, and wrote the political drama *The Amazing Mrs. Pritchard*. I mention it here because it's one of my favorite shows and stars the talented Jane Horrocks and Steven Mackintosh. (It is more upbeat than *Happy Valley*, although its characters still don't fall neatly into "good" and "bad" stereotypes.)

Wainwright has confirmed that she is open to penning a third series, but as of November 2018, no date has yet been set for such a return.

What to Binge on Next

Creator Sally Wainwright is a cottage industry of television creating and writing all by herself; her other shows that might appeal to fans of *Happy Valley* are *At Home with the Braithwaites*, *Sparkhouse*, and *Scott & Bailey*.

A groundbreaking classic miniseries that was set in the north of England (Newcastle upon Tyne), *Our Friends in the North*, also dealt with economic inequity, crime, relationships, and several similar issues.

You might also enjoy shows featuring strong women detectives, such as *Prime Suspect* (starring Helen Mirren), *An Unsuitable Job for a Woman* (starring Helen Baxendale); or the more recent *No Offence* (starring Joanna Scanlan).

Jackie on...
Guns and the Police in the UK

Question: In a lot of your crime dramas, I never see cops draw guns. When I watched *Happy Valley* and the police officer only had a baton and pepper spray with which to protect herself, I thought, doesn't she have a gun?

Answer: The police over here don't generally carry guns. Up until a few years ago it was very rare to see one as they were only carried by elite gun forces, called out in special circumstances. In the past few years the increased risk of terrorism has meant that armed officers might attend major public events—especially those involving royalty. But the sight of a gun is more likely to scare me, rather than reassure me. I tend to avoid anywhere that has armed police, as it tends to indicate there has been a specific threat.

The crime drama *Happy Valley* is set in a rural area so it would be very unusual to see a gun there. The police officers would probably use Tasers or pepper spray to defend themselves.

Inspector Lewis

Run Time

Inspector Lewis ran for nine seasons between 2006 and 2015. Each episode was a ninety-minute program, and there were a total of thirty-three episodes across the series, making for a total run time of nearly fifty hours.

Creator and Writers

This program is a spinoff of the long-running and hugely popular *Inspector Morse* series, which aired between 1987 and 2000, and which were based on the novels by Colin Dexter. The credit for creating this series is given to Chris Burt and Stephen Churchett, while Dexter himself is given a writer credit on all of the episodes. Other credited writers include Helen Jenkins, Russell Lewis, and Alan Plater (among many others).

What It's About

Inspector Lewis is the sequel to the extremely popular mystery program *Inspector Morse*, which was based on the Morse novels by Colin Dexter and which aired in the 1980s. In this program, Morse's detective sergeant, Robbie Lewis, returns to England after a holiday abroad to try and mourn the sudden death of his wife (in a hit-and-run accident). He steps into a Detective Inspector role in his own right, and takes on his own subordinate, the enigmatic Detective Sergeant Hathaway.

The series is set, as was *Morse*, in Oxford, and many of the crimes and murders feature academic storylines and characters. Lewis and Hathaway are aided in their investigations by the pathologist Laura Hobson, and, in later seasons, by another officer, Detective Sergeant Lizzie Maddox, who disrupts their cozy twosome, but who does so in a way that makes the investigative team as a whole better.

The crimes and their backstories can be quite dark, but each episode concludes with the detectives solving their case and spending companionable non-work time with one another in one or another of Oxford's seemingly endless riverside pubs.

Why It's Bingeworthy

163

This mystery series/police procedural hits a lot of the right notes: the tentative and professional but still rich and satisfying mentor/mentee relationship between Lewis and Hathaway; mysteries that are complex, but which are never so complex that they can't be resolved in ninety minutes; crimes and a tone that can be dark but which is almost never too graphically violent or gory; its satisfying police procedural feel, complete with their no-nonsense supervisor and the subplot of a growing romantic relationship between Lewis and Laura Hobson the pathologist.

Add to all of those attributes beautiful location shooting and sets that just make you ache to visit Oxford and its pubs, as well as a gorgeous soundtrack, and you have a crime drama that is a worthy successor to *Inspector Morse*.

Main Cast

Kevin Whately...Robbie Lewis
Laurence Fox...James Hathaway
Claire Holman...Laura Hobson
Angela Griffin...Elizabeth ("Lizzie") Maddox

Trivia

Colin Dexter, the author on whose books this series and its prequels are based, also made several brief cameo appearances on this show.

The composer who did the music for the *Inspector Morse* series, Barrington Pheloung, also created the music for this series.

Actor Kevin Whately (who plays Inspector Lewis) first played the role in the *Inspector Morse* series, starting with the very first episode in 1987, and the last *Lewis* aired in 2015, meaning he played the same role over the course of nearly thirty years.

The episode and series numbering followed a slightly different pattern in the U.S. (where the show aired on PBS) than it did in the U.K. (where it aired on ITV). In the U.S., two of the early series were combined as one season, so the final season in the U.S. is often referred to as the eighth season (rather than the ninth). Just make sure if you want to watch the entire series to check off the individual episode titles as you go to make sure you get all of them!

What to Binge on Next

Well, obviously, if you haven't seen all of the *Inspector Morse* mysteries yet, you're going to have to go watch those. And when you're done with that you can watch the series that served as a prequel to *Morse* but which started airing in 2012, *Endeavour* (about Morse's early days as a detective).

British crime dramas and police procedurals are a particularly rich source of stories in which partners at work can work effectively together, even when they are not what you would truly call "friends." Two other programs which feature detective teams that work together well despite their differences are *Vera*, featuring a woman detective and her male subordinate, and *The Inspector Lynley Mysteries*, in which the superior officer is also a member of the aristocracy (which can sometimes make things a bit awkward for his more working-class subordinate).

Although usually much darker in tone and in actual look, the historical crime drama *Inspector George Gently*, set during the 1960s, also features a strong relationship between its detective inspector and detective sergeant.

The Inspector Lynley Mysteries

Run Time

This show ran on BBC One between 2001 and 2008 for six series and twenty-four episodes (or, one pilot episode and twenty-three separate episodes), which were ninety minutes in length. The run time is thirty-six hours.

Creator and Writers

The series is based upon Elizabeth George's mystery novels. Through the first two series and part of the third the plots were based on George's novels, but after that the stories were original to the program. The pilot (and a few other episodes) were written by Lizzie Mickery, and other writers included Simon Block, Ed Whitmore, and Valerie Windsor.

What It's About

Detective Inspectors and their Detective Sergeants in British television often have at least a few conflicts; here, DI Thomas ("Tommy") Lynley and his DS Barbara Havers approach their work from completely different ends of the socioeconomic and personality spectrums, as Lynley is also the Earl of Asherton (a titled peer of the realm, and a properly prim and well-attired one at that), while Havers comes from a working-class background and is less than fastidious in terms of her living style and appearance.

But their partnership works and together they are surprisingly effective at solving the murder cases to which they are assigned. This is no small feat: the murder cases and even the locations to which the duo are sent vary widely, from a Scottish mansion to Lancashire, and seaside villages to Lynley's own family's estates.

Why It's Bingeworthy

In most police procedurals, the cases tend to follow a somewhat predictable type of crime or murders, and most often occur within the same geographic area; in this program the crimes and locations are widely varied, making for a program that always keeps the viewer just a little bit on edge.

The relationship between Lynley and Havers, although often difficult and rife with misunderstandings, is also pleasurable to watch when it clicks and their differences are actually what make it possible for them to solve such a wide variety of cases. It's also a pleasure to watch the two develop a grudging respect for one another, and the roles are played to perfection by Nathaniel Parker and Sharon Small.

Main Cast

Nathaniel Parker…Thomas ("Tommy") Lynley, 8th Earl of Asherton
Sharon Small…Barbara Havers
Emma Fielding/Lesley Vickerage/Catherine Russell…Helen Clyde

Trivia

The character of Helen Clyde, who eventually married Tommy Lynley and became Helen Lynley, was played by three different actresses in the series: Emma Fielding in the pilot, Lesley Vickerage in series one through three, and Catherine Russell thereafter.

When the BBC announced in 2007 that the series would conclude, fans protested and launched a petition to try and save the show, but were not successful.

Although Elizabeth George's Lynley novels are set in Great Britain, she is an American who was born in Ohio.

What to Binge on Next

A newer mystery series that turns the dynamics of this program around (that is: the higher-ranking detective is a bit sloppy in her appearance while her subordinates are always a bit more class- and organization-conscious) is *Vera*, starring Brenda Blethyn as the outwardly somewhat messy but inwardly very sharp Detective Chief Inspector Vera Stanhope.

Another mystery series which features a complicated dynamic between its two stars is *Above Suspicion*, a police procedural created by the same author who created *Prime Suspect*, in which Detective Constable Anna Travis is determined to prove herself to her boss, James Langton (with whom she also has a troubling amount of physical chemistry).

Endeavour, which is a prequel to the popular mystery series *Inspector Morse*, also features a detective who, if he is not a member of the aristocracy, nonetheless still considers himself much more educated and a cut above his fellow police officers.

Inspector Morse

Run Time

This hugely popular police procedural ran for seven regular seasons (from 1987 to 1993), and then continued on with annual standalone episodes in 1995, 1996, 1997, 1998, 2000. By my count and most sources, episodes averaged 100 minutes each and there were 33 episodes in all, meaning it would take about 55 hours to watch them.

Creator and Writers

The stories are based upon Colin Dexter's Morse novels, but the series was developed by Anthony Minghella and Kenny McBain. Many writers worked on the series, including Julian Mitchell, Daniel Boyle, and Alma Cullen.

What It's About

Chief Inspector Morse is not your typical detective. His interests run to the opera, crossword puzzles, and classic literature, making him a bit of an enigma to his more working-class sergeant, Robbie Lewis. The two of them are employed with the Thames Valley Police force in Oxford, England, and investigate a variety of murders, many of university-affiliated individuals.

Although brilliant in his own way and able to use his broad interests and knowledge to help him solve their cases, Morse often takes the long way around while doing so. It is his hallmark to get several key things wrong during their investigations (including arresting the wrong people), but working with the level-headed Lewis often helps curb his more excitable errors. He is also unlucky in love; in nearly every episode he flirts with or dates women who end up as either the story's victim or its perpetrator.

Why It's Bingeworthy

This is a completely character-driven mystery series, and the character of Endeavour Morse is one that just keeps on giving. A loner who is always looking for love; an intellectual still drawn to the more prurient and practical aspects of crime, he is a totally unique detective character in the annals of Brit TV detectives.

It's a pleasure to watch John Thaw act (become?) the character of Morse, and the show also provides an interesting working relationship to enjoy between Morse the sometimes snob and his sergeant Lewis, always defensive. The mysteries are suitably dark and believable but the show is not as graphic or as disturbing as even its sequel, *Inspector Lewis*, can be.

Although of its time, with somewhat staid production values and Morse's habit of seeking female companionship everywhere he goes (sometimes inappropriately), this is still a classic mystery program that is a must-watch.

Main Cast

John Thaw…Endeavour Morse
Kevin Whately…Robbie Lewis
James Grout…Chief Superintendent Strange

Trivia

Novelist Colin Dexter made frequent cameo appearances in the program, most often as a drinker in pubs.

Barrington Pheloung wrote the music for the series, and the theme song uses a motif based on Morse code (with various notes standing in for the code and recurring throughout). Pheloung also went on to write the music for this show's sequel, *Inspector Lewis*.

In 2005, one of the cars used during the filming of the show, Morse's Jaguar Mark 2.2.4L car was sold to a U.K.-based businessperson for £100,000.

What to Binge on Next

Two other mystery series that will be must-watches for you if you love *Inspector Morse* are its sequel, *Inspector Lewis* (featuring Morse's former subordinate Robbie Lewis, now an Inspector in his own right and with his own somewhat difficult sergeant James Hathaway); and the prequel *Endeavour*, which stars Shaun Evans as a young Morse.

Another police procedural which features detective partners with very different techniques and personalities is *Dalziel and Pascoe* (which is based on the crime novels of Reginald Hill).

John Thaw, who became almost synonymous with the character of Morse, was also well known for his role in the 1970s classic police drama *The Sweeney*.

Life on Mars

Run Time

Life on Mars was a succinct police drama that ran for two series and sixteen hour-long episodes, making for a run time of sixteen hours. The program aired on BBC One; series one aired in 2006 and series two ran in 2007.

Creator and Writers

The show was created by Matthew Graham, Tony Jordan, and Ashley Pharaoh. Graham and Pharaoh developed the original idea, which was a campier take on 1970s police drama, but the concept was reworked into a more serious drama. The three creators wrote many of the episodes, with help from other writers such as Chris Chibnall, Julie Rutterford, Guy Jenkin, and Mark Greig.

What It's About

Manchester Detective Chief Inspector Sam Tyler is busy enough in 2006, trying to solve a rape and abduction case (in which a colleague might be the next victim), when he's in a car accident and wakes up...in the 1970s.

The rest of the series finds Tyler using his investigative skills primarily to try and understand if he has died, if he's in a coma and dreaming, or if he really has just time-traveled. Luckily for him, he wakes up in the 1970s with papers marking him as a detective who is transferring to a new police station (which is the same police station in which he was working in 2006). Things are very different, though: the detectives are much more casual about their work and forensic methodology, women cops endure endless amounts of sexual harassment, and Tyler's new boss is a sadist named Gene Hunt, who does not take kindly to Tyler's enlightened ways.

So why is Tyler in 1973? Are the cases he solves there related to the ones he was working in 2006? What can he do to get back to his present life? Does he even want to? Don't try to understand it from this summary—just watch it. Even if you never do really get it you'll enjoy the ride.

Why It's Bingeworthy

A mix between time travel drama and a police procedural, *Life on Mars* offers the ultimate "fish out of water" narrative. Sam Tyler finds himself enjoying the old-school nature of police work run more by hunches than by computer work, although he still does try to bring some aspects of modern policing to the 1973 office he has joined. If you're at all prone to nostalgia I think you're going to enjoy this one, even if you weren't alive in the seventies. The appeal is not the decade; the appeal is that sometimes the (by necessity) simpler ways really were nicer, even if they had their limits.

The period detail in this program can't be beat and the soundtrack? The soundtrack is unbelievable. Starting with David Bowie's *Life on Mars*, the music just goes from one great recognizable hit to the next.

Main Cast

John Simm…Sam Tyler
Philip Glenister…Gene Hunt
Liz White…Annie Cartwright
Dean Andrews…Ray Carling
Marshall Lancaster…Chris Skelton

Trivia

There was a popular U.S. remake of this show as well, which shared the same title.

The original title of the show was "Ford Granada," and it was originally conceived as more of a comedy that would make fun of the fashion and attitudes of the 1970s, and which would star comic actor Neil Morrissey.

What to Binge on Next

Life on Mars is a completely unique concept, especially for a police drama, so it's hard to find similar programs. Luckily there was a sequel (of sorts) to the series: *Ashes to Ashes*, which has the same concept, but features a different detective (played by Keeley Hawes) and is set in the 1980s. If you like *Life on Mars*, you should definitely watch *Ashes to Ashes*; it also provides some resolution to story lines that were started in the first program.

Other police dramas that combine crime storylines with historical drama are *Inspector George Gently* (set in the north of England in the 1960s); *Endeavour* (a prequel to the Inspector Morse series, also set in the 1960s, but in Oxford); and *Whitechapel*, which is set in the present day but in which London's East End detectives draw on crime patterns from the 19th century to help solve modern crimes.

Line of Duty

Run Time

As of 2018 there have been four series of this show, and a total of twenty-three hour-long episodes, making for a total run time of twenty-three hours. A fifth series will air in 2019, and a sixth series has been commissioned.

Creator and Writers

Jed Mercurio created the show and has written all of the episodes.

What It's About

There's cops, and then there's the cops who investigate the cops. Stateside you may know them as Internal Affairs, but in the U.K. they're called Anti-Corruption police.

Detective Sergeant Steve Arnott is part of an anti-terrorism task force when an operation he's on goes wrong; when his compatriots cover up what happened, he alone tells the truth. This brings him to the attention of the head of Anti-Corruption Unit 12 (AC-12), Superintendent Ted Hastings, who recruits him to join a case already in progress, investigating a DCI named Tony Gates, who seems always to be in the right place at the right time to make spectacular arrests. Is he truly a superlative officer, or is he "bent" (corrupt) and simply awaiting his chance to help his criminal bosses?

Well, a little of both, actually. In this program you see the cops doing completely straightforward and heroic things while you also are privy to the details of their (often very messy) personal lives and poor personal and professional choices. Very few members of law enforcement in this program, throughout all of its series, are either all good or all bad.

In the first few series, the storyline surrounding Gates and the gangster orchestrating many of his moves dominate the action.

Why It's Bingeworthy

I absolutely love the complexity of this show. The description above barely scratches the surface of the interrelated storylines, plot twists, and character subplots that animate *Line of Duty*. This is also a deeply human show: we can all sympathize with making poor decisions when we are under stress or to keep family members or friends happy, and rarely are characters in this show, much like in real life, "all good" or "all bad."

You'll love the plot twists and suspense, and I think you'll enjoy how every single actor embodies their character so fully that I actually find it hard to watch them when they play different roles in other shows (Martin Compston, for instance, will always be a cop to me now).

Main Cast

Martin Compston…Steve Arnott
Vicky McClure…Kate Fleming
Adrian Dunbar…Ted Hastings
Craig Parkinson… Matthew ("Dot") Cottan
Keeley Hawes…Lindsay Denton
Neil Morrissey…Nigel Morton

Trivia

The city in which the show is set is never really identified; in the first season it was filmed in Birmingham, and in several subsequent seasons it was primarily filmed in Belfast, Northern Ireland.

When it premiered on BBC Two in June 2012, this program became the network's best-performing drama series in ten years (and drew more than four million viewers).

What to Binge on Next

In 2018 Jed Mercurio went on to create and write the hottest event of the U.K.'s fall television season: *Bodyguard*, starring Keeley Hawes and Richard Madden, and about one of the police sergeants charged with protecting Hawes's politically ambitious Home Secretary character. He also created and wrote many of the episodes for the 2015 medical drama *Critical*.

Another police procedural in which it's just heartbreaking to watch people make poor decisions is Sally Wainwright's *Happy Valley*, set in a northern England rural area where drugs and violence have made strong inroads. If you like the complexity and plot twists of *Line of Duty*, you might also want to watch *Luther*, although it is in some ways a much more straightforward police drama. John Luther, however, as played by Idris Elba, is definitely a detective who often has to answer questions of the police who are sent to investigate other police (for his somewhat unorthodox methods).

Luther

Run Time

From 2010 to 2019, five series and a total of twenty episodes of this program have been made. Each episode is an hour long, making for a total run time of twenty hours.

Creator and Writers

Neil Cross created the series and has written all of its episodes.

What It's About

John Luther is emphatically not your typical police detective. He's angrier than most, he's more driven, but most importantly, he's smarter than most of his co-workers and the criminals he tracks. Which is a good thing, because the crimes he investigates are some of the most unpleasant you've ever seen portrayed on television.

He has strong advocates in his supervisor Rose Teller, and in his new partner, detective Justin Ripley, and most of his colleagues are not the type to question the sometimes-rogue brand of justice that Luther sometimes can't help but pursue, but his playing fast and loose with the more by-the-book requirements of modern police work also gain him a number of enemies within the police force.

Another way in which he differs from his colleagues is in his frequent collusion with a woman he knows to be a serial killer. Their relationship is a complex one of co-dependency; he often relies on her for help and insight into the criminal mind, but he is also at her mercy (because he has not arrested her for the crimes he knows, but can't prove, that she has committed).

Why It's Bingeworthy

Critics have charged that there's nothing particularly tight or groundbreaking about the writing in this series, but I think I'm going to disagree with that. Yes, John Luther might engage in a lot of melodramatics, but the storylines in general are suspenseful and the cat-and-mouse game between Luther and Alice Morgan makes for compelling viewing.

It's dark, though. Wow, it's really dark. Some of the crimes depicted are a bit much to watch, and Luther's explosive temper isn't always easy to forgive, either. Just something to keep in mind.

Main Cast

Idris Elba…John Luther
Ruth Wilson…Alice Morgan
Saskia Reeves…Rose Teller
Dermot Crowley…Martin Schenk
Warren Brown…Justin Ripley

Trivia

The first series of *Luther* in 2010 garnered nearly six million viewers per episode.

A seven-minute Comic Relief titled "Meet the Luthers," about all of Luther's similarly melodramatic family members, aired in 2016.

What to Binge on Next

Another "Lone Wolf" police character is former Guard Jack Taylor, in the series also titled *Jack Taylor*. Set in Galway, Ireland, it is also quite dark, and in addition to showing Taylor solving some horrendous crimes that the police weren't able to, it also shows his inability to help himself and address the alcoholism and disobedience to authority that got him fired from the police.

Another police drama that does not shy away from violence, dark themes, and a tortured lead investigator, is *Marcella*, starring Anna Friel as detective Marcella Backland. If you're not opposed to historical crime dramas, a more recent Agatha Christie adaptation of *The ABC Murders*, starring John Malkovich as a much darker Hercule Poirot than you're used to seeing, might also be a program to consider.

Creator Neil Cross was also a head screenwriter for some of the latter series of spy thriller *MI-5*, which was another drama that highlighted the confluence of individuals' personal working styles and problems and their work as intelligence professionals.

Midsomer Murders

Run Time

Midsomer Murders is the rare British program that is going to take you a serious—serious—amount of time to get through. As of 2018 it has run for twenty series (it began airing on ITV in 1997) and a total of 122 ninety-minute(ish) episodes, which means it will take you 183 hours (yes, that's nearly eight whole days) to get through them all. Take some staycation time.

Creator and Writers

The series is based on Caroline Graham's "Chief Inspector Barnaby" mystery books, and was originally adapted for television by Anthony Horowitz. Both Graham and Horowitz have written entire episodes, but so have many other writers, including (but not limited to) Andrew Payne, David Hoskins, Peter Hammond, Michael Aitkens, Douglas Watkinson, and Rachel Cuperman.

What It's About

DCI Tom Barnaby is a straightforward, no-nonsense investigator, and he's the man you want on the case when your small hamlet in the rural (and fictional) county of Midsomer experiences one of its shockingly frequent multiple-murder sprees.

In the course of his investigations, Barnaby works with a variety of detective sergeants, some more dedicated than others. One thing that remains a constant throughout the show is his strong relationship with his wife (her adventurous cooking notwithstanding) and his daughter.

Although the show is always set in one rural village or town or another in the region, the types of crimes and the motivations for them vary widely. Reviewers often note both the tongue-in-cheek humor of the series, and its many gothic touches (I'm calling it a cozy mystery because it's not often very graphic and the themes are not as dark as they are in most British crime dramas, but all the same, sometimes the actual murders are shown multiple times or in flashback, particularly if they are done with nontraditional weapons or in a gruesome manner).

Actor John Nettles stars in the first thirteen series as Tom Barnaby; in subsequent episodes he was replaced in the region by his nephew, DCI

John Barnbay (played by Neil Dudgeon). The tone and the dark humor of the show remained largely the same.

Why It's Bingeworthy

One of the most interesting aspects of this police procedural is Tom Barnaby's highly normal family life, which makes for a pleasant change from the vast majority of detective programs in which the investigators have highly dysfunctional or completely absent private lives. John Nettles plays Barnaby as serious but without the world-weariness portrayed by most detectives, and the various actors who play his detective sergeants all bring a little something different to the investigative team and the program.

As noted, the show sometimes seems to glory in its more gothic and gory touches, but overall these are still "cozy" mysteries in that the possible suspects always come from within a small or local community, and they are apprehended at the end of each ninety-minute installment. These mysteries aren't too complex, but nor are they too simple; they are, in fact, "just right" and make this show a nice bit of comfort watching when you're in the mood for a nice basic whodunit that won't be too scary or depressing.

Main Cast

John Nettles…Tom Barnaby
Jane Wymark…Joyce Barnaby
Laura Howard…Cully Barnaby
Jason Hughes…Ben Jones
Daniel Casey…Gavin Troy
Neil Dudgeon…John Barnaby

Trivia

Well-known guest stars on this show have included Olivia Colman, Sam Heughan, Hugh Bonneville, Robert Hardy, Helen Baxendale, Peter Capaldi, Trudie Styler (Mrs. Sting), and Emily Mortimer. You never know who is going to pop up in the next episode you watch!

Murder instruments used on the show have included: a cricket bat, liquid nicotine, hemlock, a slide projector, toxic fungus, and King Neptune's trident.

The show is one of Great Britain's biggest hits ever: it's been sold to 230 countries.

In 2011, the show's producer, Brian True-May, was suspended after he made comments about racial diversity (or the lack thereof) in the show, including "We just don't have ethnic minorities involved. Because it wouldn't be the English village with them. It just wouldn't work." He apologized and was reinstated but later stepped down from his production role on the show.

What to Binge on Next

Another mystery series about a number of crimes taking place in the peaceful suburbs (where maybe you wouldn't expect such goings-on?) is the aptly named *Murder in Suburbia.*

Cozy mystery staples like *Agatha Christie's Poirot* or *Marple* (particularly the latter) will also appeal to you if you like murders in villages and small circles of possible suspects. Also consider *Father Brown*, based on mystery stories by G.K. Chesterton, about a Catholic priest who solves the crimes that happen in his small village.

Neil Dudgeon, who plays the detective John Barnaby in the latter series of this program, also appears as George the chauffeur and partner-in-crime-solving to Mrs. Bradley in *The Mrs. Bradley Mysteries.*

New Tricks

Run Time

New Tricks ran on BBC One from 2003 to 2015; it consisted of twelve series and 107 hour-long episodes. The total run time is 107 hours (not bad for a show that was originally only ordered for six episodes).

Creator and Writers

The series was created by Nigel McCrery and Roy Mitchell, who share writing credits for all 107 episodes. Other writers who wrote more than five episodes each are Julian Simpson, Lisa Holdsworth, and J.C. Wilsher.

What It's About

When Detective Superintendent Sandra Pullman makes a large and publicly visible mistake on a big case, she is pulled from her more prestigious former position to head up a new initiative: the Unsolved Crime and Open Case Squad (UCOS) of London's Metropolitan Police Service. In addition to her and another uniformed officer, she recruits a number of retired detectives to aid her as "civilian investigators." The three men she initially recruits, Gerry Standing, Jack Halford, and Brian Lane, all had to retire from the force perhaps earlier than they would have liked, and are eager to help Pullman solve any and all unsolved and cold cases that come their way.

These detectives may in fact be considered the "old dogs" (as in "you can't teach an old dog new tricks"), but they certainly aren't past their prime, and they keep both criminals and their new boss on their toes by catching the former and mercilessly teasing the latter. Although they can be somewhat difficult to control, Pullman nevertheless finds that her new colleagues bring unique skills (and the personalities to match) to the job.

Why It's Bingeworthy

It is beyond fun to watch a woman detective who has a low tolerance for bullshit supervise and work with an all-male squad, and to do so with great competence and an even greater sense of humor.

Although many of the major cast members who began with the series eventually left and were replaced by new actors and characters, the show kept its feeling of solidarity and the chemistry was good between all of the characters, regardless of when they joined the team.

The mysteries here are nothing special; the interplay between the characters (both among their investigative colleagues and with their boss, petty bureaucrat Donald Bevan) is what really makes this show sparkle.

Main Cast

Amanda Redman...Sandra Pullman
Dennis Waterman...Gerry Standing
Alun Armstrong...Brian Lane
James Bolam...Jack Halford
Denis Lawson...Steve McAndrew
Tamzin Outhwaite...Sasha Miller
Nicholas Lyndhurst...Dan Griffin
Anthony Calf...D.A.C. Strickland
Susan Jameson...Esther Lane

Trivia

The theme song for the show was sung by cast member Dennis Waterman.

Two of the cast members, James Bolam and Susan Jameson, are married to each other in real life.

Cast members came and went over the course of the series, but the basic team always consisted of three men and one woman, who was their commanding officer.

What to Binge on Next

Another mystery program in which an indomitable and older woman sleuth makes it her mission to solve crimes as a private investigator is *Hetty Wainthropp Investigates*, featuring Patricia Routledge as Wainthropp and Dominic Monaghan as her steadfast assistant.

Other programs in which older characters are definitely not ready to give up living are the drama *Last Tango in Halifax*, in which two elderly former sweethearts reconnect and decide to get married, whether their families think they should or not; and the classic comedy *Dad's Army*, which is a program about older men and men unfit to serve in the armed forces who instead work for the home guard that sought to protect Britain and its small coastal villages from Nazi infiltration and attack during World War II.

Prime Suspect

Run Time

Each *Prime Suspect* episode was the length and quality of a feature film, so it is comprised of seven series that consist of only two or three 100-minute episodes each. In all, fifteen episodes aired on ITV between 1992 and 2006, making the total time to bingewatch twenty-five hours.

Creator and Writers

The series was created and written by Lynda La Plante; each series had a different director.

What It's About

Detective Chief Inspector Jane Tennison doesn't care if you think she's not good enough to be an inspector because she's a woman. She doesn't care if you think less of her because she sleeps with whom she wants when she wants, even if they're junior colleagues. She doesn't care about you or your shit in general, because she is as sharp and as skilled an investigator as ever worked for Greater London's Metropolitan Police Service.

She often works with a detective sergeant or other subordinate, but although she works well with some of them, they never last long enough for Tennison to settle into a mentoring relationship; she always seems to function best as a lone wolf, even when partnered with someone else.

Over the course of several series, Tennison investigates a broad range of crimes, from straight-up murder to serial killings, hate crimes to international crimes of retribution. Along the way she struggles with the sexism and "old boys' club" nature of the Met, as well as with her own conflicting desires (she knew she most likely did not want to have a child on her own, but her choice to have an abortion in the beginning of series four is still not an easy one) and personal life. But she always, always, gets her man, even when it's a woman, and even when it's a perpetrator with whom she feels some small degree of sympathy.

Why It's Bingeworthy

This is another one of those programs that you simply have to have watched if you want to call yourself an Anglophile. It's a classic in every sense of the word: Jane Tennison remains one of Helen Mirren's most well-known portrayals (in her stellar career that contains a lot of well-known portrayals); it's dark and pessimistic and British and it can tell a gut-wrenching story without showing you a lot of blood and gore; it's complex and suspenseful and even though the crimes are terrible the perpetrators are not usually shown as one-note monsters—they too have complex motivations and circumstances.

It's a great, great show.

Main Cast

Helen Mirren…Jane Tennison
John Benfield…Michael Kernan
Richard Hawley…Richard Haskons
Tom Bell…Bill Otley

Trivia

LaPlante created her female detective chief inspector after becoming interested in reality television crime shows and learning that, at that time (the late 1980s), there were only four female DCIs working at Scotland Yard. Her interviews with one of those women, Jackie Malton, would provide character and story inspiration for the series.

The last series, series seven, was dedicated to actor Tom Bell, who played Bill Otley in the program. He died in 2006, two weeks before this series first aired in the U.K.

What to Binge on Next

A prequel to this series and story, titled *Prime Suspect: Tennison*, ran for six episodes in 2017.

Prime Suspect is one of the most well-known mystery series to come out of the U.K. (and Jane Tennison one of the best-known police detectives). Another long-running series which featured a lead police detective who largely operated according to his own internal code was *Inspector Morse* (and John Thaw as DCI Endeavour Morse).

Another crime drama which features an extremely strong female character is *Happy Valley*, starring Sarah Lancashire as police officer Catherine Cawood in a rural region increasingly affected by drug abuse and violence.

Scott & Bailey

Run Time

This program ran from 2011 to 2016, and is comprised of thirty-three forty-five-minute episodes, making its total run time nearly twenty-five hours.

Creator and Writers

The program is based on a concept by actors Suranne Jones and Sally Lindsay, but the "created by" credits belong to writer Sally Wainwright and Diane Taylor, a retired police detective. Several people share writing credits for most of the episodes: Sally Wainwright, Diane Taylor, Suranne Jones, and Sally Lindsay.

What It's About

It's a good thing Janet Scott and Rachel Bailey get along—they spend a lot of time working together as police detectives in Manchester. They also spend time commiserating on various challenges in their personal lives; Rachel's boyfriend is a defense lawyer (who also turns out to be an unscrupulous jerk who maximizes Rachel's mistake in letting certain investigative details about a case slip to him) and Janet's marriage is heading toward the rocks as her children grow up and start to test boundaries.

The crimes being solved by this team of detectives and their colleagues are also quite disturbing. Although the detectives' personal lives are part of the story, most of the narrative here is spent on solving the labyrinthine crimes. Mercifully Scott, Bailey, and their brisk boss Gill Murray are very good at solving crimes.

Why It's Bingeworthy

When this series was developed, writer Sally Wainwright worked with a former Detective Inspector from Greater Manchester Police to ensure that her program had the greatest degree of accuracy possible. This collaboration resulted in a program that focuses less on the drama of the characters' personal lives than it does on the nuances of the crimes and cases they are investigating.

Both leads here are strong characters and are played well by veteran actors Suranne Jones (who plays Rachel Bailey) and Lesley Sharp (Janet Scott), and Amelia Bullmore as Gill Murray is no slouch either. The show is taut and quickly paced and suspenseful, all things you want to see in a good gritty police procedural.

Main Cast

Lesley Sharp...Janet Scott
Suranne Jones...Rachel Bailey
Amelia Bullmore...Gill Murray
Nicholas Gleaves...Andy Roper
Pippa Haywood...Julie Dodson

Trivia

The actors who play Janet Scott (Lesley Sharp) and Nicholas Gleaves (Andy Roper), who have an on-screen affair, are also married in real life.

Creator Suranne Jones has said that she and Sally Lindsay decided there was a need for more women characters on television; she has described this show as the "*Cagney & Lacey* of Manchester."

What to Binge on Next

Another mystery series that features a team of women detectives is *Murder in Suburbia*, starring Caroline Catz and Lisa Faulkner. Although the lead detective in the crime drama *DCI Banks* is a man, that program also features a number of strong women detective characters.

Another crime drama in which a large part of the crime-solving dynamic comes from the personal relationships among the team is Paul Abbott's police procedural *No Offence*.

Suranne Jones and Lesley Sharp both turn in stellar performances here. Their fans might also want to watch the thriller *Doctor Foster* or the horror/family drama *The Secret of Crickley Hall* (starring Jones), or Russell T. Davies's drama *Bob & Rose* (about a gay man who falls in love with a woman) and the crime/thriller drama *Paranoid* (starring Sharp).

Sherlock

Run Time

As of 2018 there are four series of this program, and a total of twelve regular episodes and one Christmas special. The show aired on BBC One between the years of 2010 and 2017, and the total run time (as the episodes are ninety minutes long) is nearly twenty hours.

Creator and Writers

Sherlock is based on the Sherlock Holmes stories by Sir Arthur Conan Doyle, of course, but this series was created by Mark Gatiss and Steven Moffat, who also wrote the episodes, along with Stephen Thompson.

What It's About

Set in modern London, this Sherlock series features a more clearly and self-identified sociopathic Sherlock Holmes. Sherlock's sidekick here is, of course, John Watson, but this Doctor Watson, at the beginning of the series, is suffering from flashbacks to his military service in Afghanistan. After the two are introduced and begin to share quarters at 221B Baker Street, it quickly becomes clear that they each fulfill very important roles for one another: Sherlock gives Watson something to do, in the form of helping solve crimes and then blogging about them afterwards; Watson gives Sherlock someone to bounce ideas off of and someone to insult when he's feeling peevish, which is very nearly all the time. It's a bromance for the ages.

In the early seasons Sherlock faces off primarily against his arch-nemesis Moriarty, and uses his trademark deduction to solve more prosaic mysteries and puzzles. Later series get progressively darker and more psychological as both Sherlock and Watson struggle with inner demons and secrets from their personal histories (and present relationships), and at times their symbiotic relationship with one another falters, but in the end they are still there for one another (even if not in quite the ways the viewer expects).

Why It's Bingeworthy

As good as the stories and main characters were in this program, its strong supporting cast is also a large part of its appeal. Rupert Graves is an absolute treat as the long-suffering police DI Greg Lestrade, as is the incomparable Una Stubbs as a feisty Mrs. Hudson, who often complains that Watson only portrays her as serving the tea (woman power, thy name is Mrs. Hudson). I also have a soft spot for Louise Brealey as Molly Hooper, a "specialist registrar" in the morgue who pops up periodically to help with pathology, corpses, and Sherlock's and John's various schemes (you know, like the small matter of Sherlock leaping off a tall building...).

And let's not forget Andrew Scott as the chilling Moriarty and Amanda Abbington as Mary Morstan, Watson's girlfriend and eventual wife, who has some whopping secrets of her own.

The pace of the show is fast and it has a unique visual feel and pulsing energy, particularly in the early seasons. Latter seasons were more about character development, as we learn more about the relationship between Sherlock and his brother Mycroft (played by co-creator and writer Mark Gatiss), and another character I'm not going to tell you about because I don't believe in giving spoilers.

This show provides a lot of bang for your British viewing buck. Nearly everyone who enjoys British TV or is an Anglophile has seen it (and a shared viewing experience in these days of multiple and disparate streaming services is becoming a rarer experience), so it can be a good conversation starter.

Main Cast

Benedict Cumberbatch...Sherlock Holmes
Martin Freeman...John Watson
Mark Gatiss...Mycroft Holmes
Andrew Scott...James Moriarty
Rupert Graves...DI Lestrade
Una Stubbs...Mrs. Hudson
Amanda Abbington...Mary (Morstan) Watson

Trivia

In episode two of series three ("The Empty Hearse"), the Holmes parents are played in cameo roles by Benedict Cumberbatch's actual parents, Wanda Ventham and Timothy Carlton.

Matt Smith auditioned for (but did not get, of course) the role of Dr. Watson.

John Watson and Mary Morstan married on the show…and Martin Freeman and Amanda Abbington were partners in real life (with two children) for most of the show's run. They separated in 2016.

What to Binge on Next

Another crime drama with a good relationship between the two lead male characters is *Whitechapel*, a police procedural set in London. It stars Rupert Penry-Jones as DI Joseph Chandler and Phil Davis as DS Ray Miles; they are modern-day detectives in Whitechapel investigating crimes that have disturbing similarities to historical crimes (including those of Jack the Ripper) in the area.

A much gentler "bromance" can be seen in the *Poirot* series of cozy mysteries, based on the novels by Agatha Christie, which star David Suchet as the Belgian detective Hercule Poirot, and Hugh Fraser as his friend Captain Hastings.

Fans of the slick and fast-paced cinematography of *Sherlock* might also want to watch the spy drama *MI-5*, which also makes use of different filming techniques and a powerful soundtrack to enhance the dramatic action.

A Touch of Frost

Run Time

A Touch of Frost ran for fifteen series and a total of forty-two episodes from 1992 all the way through to 2010. It's a bit tricky to calculate run time as various sources list these episodes as ranging from seventy-five to one hundred minutes in length; at an average of about ninety minutes per episode, that makes for a run time of sixty-three hours. It'll totally be worth it, though, don't worry.

Creator and Writers

The series is based on the novels featuring Detective Inspector Frost, written by R.D. Wingfield. He also is credited with creating the series and has a writing credit on all forty-two episodes, although other writers listed as writing multiple episodes include Michael Russell, David Gilman, and Christopher Russell.

What It's About

DCI Frost looks like a shambling mess, a walking collection of notes on torn slips of paper and various other effluvia falling out of his pockets, and in his office it appears that file cabinets have exploded. And yet he is capable of keeping the various pieces of multiple crime investigations in his head, and seems to be able to find what he needs in his office (or, more often, paperwork that his bosses need him to find) when he really has to.

He has always put his professional life before his marriage, which the viewer learns in the first series as his wife is dying from a terminal illness and he still spends more time on his case than with her. It's not out of cruelty, but simply the recognition that they had grown apart from each other, and that the job is his first true love.

Unlike in many other police procedurals, which often feature long-term partnerships between inspectors and sergeants, or colleagues, Frost found himself with a new partner nearly every series. He also experienced a bit of turnover in his personal life after his wife died; matters are always complicated by his inability to prioritize his personal life over his crime-solving one.

Why It's Bingeworthy

One of my favorite things about this show is the fact that Frost was assigned a different detective in nearly every series; this means that there is always a new working dynamic to watch, and it's fun to watch each partner learn anew that Frost is not as sloppy in mind as he is in his office. One person with whom Frost had more contact over the course of the series was his supervising officer, Norman Mullett, and that relationship is fun too, as it is often contentious (and that contentiousness is clearly enjoyed by Frost).

Mostly it's just great to watch David Jason here. Much as David Suchet seemed like the actual Hercule Poirot, aging in real life as he aged onscreen, David Jason seems to disappear and become DI Frost, aging and solving ever grittier crimes, over the course of this show's impressive eighteen-year run.

Because Frost's partners and other police officers were replaced so often, this show cast many actors who became notable actors, including Damian Lewis, Robert Glenister, and Neil Dudgeon.

Main Cast

David Jason…William Edward ("Jack") Frost
Bruce Alexander…Norman Mullett
John Lyons…George Toolan
Arthur White…Ernie Trigg
Caroline Harker…Hazel Wallace

Trivia

In the Frost novels, the Frost character was a chain-smoker. David Jason wrote in his 2013 autobiography (*My Life*) that, as he had recently quit smoking in his real life, the decision was made to make Frost a former smoker as well.

A running gag through the show was Frost often drinking other people's coffees or teas, as well as requesting tea or snacks from witnesses or suspects.

Arthur White, who plays officer Ernie Trigg, is David Jason's real-life older brother.

The exact location of the show and its "Denton" police headquarters is never really stated. Because of references in the show to Reading and

Swindon, it is thought that Denton is a South Midlands town. The show itself was shot primarily in West Yorkshire, and was produced in Leeds.

What to Binge on Next

Although the classic police procedural *Dalziel and Pascoe* features a detecting team, rather than a detective who functions perhaps best as a single unit, it is from the same time period and offers a similar "gruff but caring" attitude toward the apprehension of criminals. Although famous detective character Endeavour Morse also had a longtime partner in his sergeant Robbie Lewis, he still seemed to function as somewhat of a lone wolf detective in *Inspector Morse*.

Frost's female counterpart in the "looks ditzy, but is really razor sharp" game is Detective Chief Inspector Vera Stanhope, in the crime drama *Vera*. Set in Northumberland, this darker mystery series presents DCI Stanhope as frumpy and somewhat difficult to get along with, but her partners find that she is relentless in trying to understand the crimes and criminals she investigates in order to apprehend them.

If you really just enjoy David Jason (and I do) you might also consider two other classic programs in which he starred: the comedy *Only Fools and Horses*, in which Jason plays Del Boy (and Nicholas Lyndhurst his brother Rodney), a classic about two brothers trying to make their way through "independent trading"—i.e., selling low and buying high, which never works out for them; and the drama series *The Darling Buds of May*, about a large farm family in the 1950s who are determined to enjoy themselves while also trying to make a living.

Vera

Run Time

There are eight series in this program, and a total of thirty-two ninety-minute episodes, for a total run time of forty-eight hours. It aired on ITV from 2011 to 2018, and as of 2018 a ninth series is planned as well.

Creator and Writers

Vera is based on the Vera Stanhope mysteries by Ann Cleeves, who is credited as a writer on thirty-two episodes. Other writers include Martha Hillier, Paul Rutman, and Paul Matthew Thompson.

What It's About

Detective Chief Inspector Vera Stanhope, employed by the Northumberland & City Police, likes to wear old anoraks and battered wellies. She does not present a particularly sharp image to the world.

Criminals underestimate her at their own risk.

Working first with Detective Sergeant Joe Ashworth and later DS Aiden Healy, Vera solves some of the saddest and ugliest of crimes that her region has to offer—from homicides to cold cases to kidnappings and beatings. She is able to do this even though she is struggling with her own issues, including a difficult relationship with her recently deceased father and her longterm loneliness. Even her weakness is a strength; she often uses her understanding of loneliness to get witnesses and suspects to open up to her.

She is also good at forming relationships that work with her subordinates; through her dedication to her job and her obvious care for the victims, she wins their respect and camaraderie, even though she can also be a very demanding boss (who doesn't really notice when her colleagues have prior or other family commitments that she is interrupting).

Why It's Bingeworthy

It all comes down to Brenda Blethyn. Blethyn is a wonderful actor who obviously has great affection for the woman she is portraying. Seemingly without effort she invests Vera Stanhope with both endearing and irritating personality tics, and I believe the term you would use for her eyes is "expressive."

The writer of the novels on which this series was based has spoken about the importance of the landscape of Northumberland (the region has the lowest population density in England) to her stories, and there are a great many outdoor and location shots that show the rugged beauty of the region. It's nice to see a program that includes both rural and city settings in a region that is not often highlighted on television.

Main Cast

Brenda Blethyn…Vera Stanhope
David Leon…Joe Ashworth
Kenny Doughty…Aiden Healy
Jon Morrison…Kenny Lockheart

Trivia

In a 2018 interview, Brenda Blethyn shared the fact that the current Chief Constable in Northumberland is a woman, and her name is actually Vera.

What to Binge on Next

The obvious comparison to a show focusing on a unique and driven woman detective is the classic *Prime Suspect*, starring Helen Mirren as detective Jane Tennison, who worked hard to achieve the highest rank she could, despite the police force's long tradition of being a boys' club.

Cleeves is also the author of another popular crime drama in which the landscape plays a large role: *Shetland*, set on the Shetland Islands and starring Douglas Henshall. Another crime drama set in the north of England is *Inspector George Gently*, a police procedural set in the 1960s. That program's lead character, George Gently, is initially frustrated by his sergeant, John Bacchus, until he sees that Bacchus, even with his faults, wants to do the job right. The relationship between Gently and Bacchus is very similar to the one Stanhope forms with her detectives.

You also haven't really lived until you've seen Brenda Blethyn (and Jane Horrocks, and Ewan McGregor, and Michael Caine) star in the British movie *Little Voice*. She plays the role of a woman disappointed in her life who can be oblivious at best and cruel at worst, but she gives the performance her all.

Whitechapel

Run Time

There were four series of this ITV program, and it ran for a total of eighteen episodes between 2009 and 2013. Each episode was forty-five minutes long, making for a total run time of just under fourteen hours.

Creator and Writers

The series was created and written by Ben Court and Caroline Ip, with writing help on two episodes from cast member Steve Pemberton.

What It's About

Detective Inspector Joseph Chandler is set to rise through the ranks of the Metropolitan police when he is assigned to the Whitechapel district and what he hopes will be a quick and straightforward investigation of a woman's murder. It quickly becomes apparent that nothing about the case is what it seems, and soon a "Ripperologist" (an expert on the crimes of Jack the Ripper) demands a meeting with Chandler to explain his theory that a new murderer is seeking to replicate the crimes of the historical one.

Chandler's problems don't end there: in his posting to Whitechapel he is derided for lacking street smarts, and several of the more seasoned detectives there, including his sergeant, have little respect for him or desire to help him. But as Chandler learns to trust his gut, it becomes clear that he is making progress on the case and he begins to earn his subordinates' grudging respect. Likewise, his respect for the Ripperologist Edward Buchan and his idea to utilize his subject expertise to capture their modern-day killer helps the team accept Buchan as a part of their unit.

Why It's Bingeworthy

This show is not only a well-plotted and characterized police procedural, but also adds elements of horror and the supernatural (as well as historical drama) to its formula. That's a lot to do, and *Whitechapel* does it well.

Phil Davis is a veteran character actor and you see him all over British television (here he's one of the police "heroes," in the first episode of *Sherlock*, he played an unnerving villain). His rough edges dovetail nicely with Rupert Penry-Jones's well-tailored ones, and Penry-Jones does a good job of playing the smooth "boys' club" operator who is nonetheless deeply troubled by obsessive compulsiveness and perfectionism. Steve Pemberton, another British television stalwart, also turns in a fine performance as the somewhat bumbling but very dedicated "Ripperologist."

The cinematography is also worth noting here. Sometimes the program is actually hard to see, as it seems set in perpetual darkness, but it also makes it an excellent program to watch when you need a good old-fashioned scare.

Main Cast

Rupert Penry-Jones...Joseph Chandler
Phil Davis...Ray Miles
Steve Pemberton...Edward Buchan
Sam Stockman...Emerson Kent
Claire Rushbrook...Caroline Llewellyn

Trivia

This show took the importance of its setting quite literally. It was actually filmed in the East End of London, and almost always at night.

In the first two series, the story arc played out over each season's three episodes. In the third and fourth seasons, the format changed slightly so that each series contained three different stories.

What to Binge on Next

Jack the Ripper, it seems, will always be a popular subject; another recent crime drama series (albeit one actually set in Jack's nineteenth-century era), *Ripper Street*, follows the action of a group of detectives working in the East End shortly after Jack the Ripper has committed his crimes.

Another crime drama with a unique premise is *Life on Mars*, about a 21st-century police detective who, during the course of a kidnapping and murder investigation, is in a car accident and somehow time travels back to the 1970s (or has he?), where he is also a detective and must re-learn his police craft according to the rules of a different era.

If the horror aspects of *Whitechapel* are what you find fascinating, you might also want to see the historical (and extremely frightening) series *Penny Dreadful*, set in the Victorian era and featuring such fantastic creatures as Dorian Gray (and his portrait), Victor Frankenstein, and the devil.

Jackie on...
Four Crime Dramas You Should Start With

Broadchurch

Set in a small, fictional coastal town, *Broadchurch* began with the murder of an eleven-year-old boy, and the ensuing investigation led neighbours to suspect the worse of one another. Through word-of-mouth, it slowly gained popularity and series three was one of the most watched crime dramas in the UK in recent history. Plot details were kept secret and even the actors didn't know what was going to happen until the last minute, adding extra intrigue to the production.

Happy Valley

Happy Valley isn't that well known, even in the UK, but it deserves to be! It is set in Northern England and follows a no-nonsense police sergeant, Catherine Cawood, who is bringing up her grandson after her daughter's suicide. Catherine is obsessed with policing and tracking the man she feels is responsible for her daughter's death; the show's various storylines are twist-packed and morally ambiguous. It's so gripping you'll be cancelling all your plans to watch the rest of the series!

Inspector Morse

Inspector Morse is a classic British crime drama set in the beautiful city of Oxford. In each episode Morse, a senior police officer, is called to investigate a murder, and viewers love the nostalgia of watching the police at work in simpler times. Also fascinating is Morse's flawed character, as he battles against alcoholism and relationship failure. If you're after a gentler crime drama, without gore and violence, then it is the perfect place to start!

Sherlock

Sherlock is based on the mystery stories of Arthur Conan Doyle, but is set in modern-day London. Sherlock uses his extraordinary observational skills and insight to link clues together, and viewers love the clever plot twists and high-octane drama. Story arcs continue across seasons, so start with season one! This is a programme that British people enjoy watching live, so they can discuss their theories on what will happen next. They're almost always wrong, but that's half the fun!

Historical Crime Dramas

Cadfael

Run Time

Cadfael aired from 1994 to 1998, and consisted of thirteen episodes across four series, and each episode was seventy-five minutes long. The total viewing time is just a bit over sixteen hours.

Creator and Writers

Cadfael is based on the historical mystery novels series written by Edith Pargeter (under the pen name "Ellis Peters"). The writing is also credited to Pargeter, although other screenwriters who worked on the series include Russell Lewis and Christopher Russell.

What It's About

Brother Cadfael is a monk in Wales in the first half of the twelfth century, but in addition to living his life according to the rules of his Benedictine order, he also possesses a keen investigative mind and is on hand to solve several murders and other crimes that happen in and around Shrewsbury (where his abbey is).

Although currently living as a monk, Cadfael is an older man and has broad experience of the world through his earlier travels and work as both a sailor and a soldier (and it transpires that he has plenty of knowledge about other people, too, as is evidenced by the revelation of several of his earlier relationships with women). The series focuses not only on Cadfael's crime-solving skills, but also on his friendships with other monks in his abbey, and his mission to both solidly live his faith, as well as to open the eyes of his fellow religious to the realities of the world around them.

Why It's Bingeworthy

Sometimes it's refreshing to watch something completely different, and *Cadfael* is that. The list of mysteries featuring monks and set in the Middle Ages is a very short one indeed, and that makes this program something special right from the start.

Anything with Derek Jacobi in it is always going to be worth watching, and this show does not disappoint. It offers satisfying conclusions to its mysteries and although it can dwell on the darkness in the human heart, it also proves that community friendships and forgiveness can have a redeeming effect on people.

Main Cast

Derek Jacobi...Brother Cadfael
Michael Culver...Prior Robert
Julian Firth...Brother Jerome

Trivia

The primary location of Shrewsbury Abbey and other "medieval" scenes were constructed and filmed in Budapest, Hungary.

Ian Holm was originally cast as Brother Cadfael but eventually turned down the role when it took ITV too long to develop and produce the program.

A hybrid rose was developed in honor of this program and its lead character: the *Rosa 'Brother Cadfael'* was first shown in 1990 and is still an available hybrid.

What to Binge on Next

If you're open to your mysteries being solved by religious types, you might also consider the period crime dramas *Father Brown*, based on the mystery stories of G.K. Chesterton and set in the 1950s, or *Grantchester*, about an Anglican vicar solving crime in a small village outside of Oxford, and which is also set in the 1950s.

Although it is not a television series, the splendid 1982 movie *Ivanhoe* (co-produced by CBS and ITV), also set in the Middle Ages and based on the novel by Sir Walter Scott, features a lot of medieval jousting and religious prejudice and romance. The 1982 adaptation, starring Anthony Andrews and Olivia Hussey, also features performances by such Brit television mainstays as Sam Neill and John Rhys-Davies.

Foyle's War

Run Time

This program consists of twenty-eight episodes in eight seasons. Most of the episodes were ninety minutes in length and aired on ITV between 2002 and 2015; the total run time is forty-two hours.

Creator and Writers

The series was created and mostly written by Anthony Horowitz; other writers were David Kane, Matthew Hall, and Michael Russell.

What It's About

Tightly plotted police procedural meets World War II nostalgia in this stylish series. Early seasons were set during 1940 and the beginning of the war, and later seasons concentrated more on the crimes and only tangentially on the war's effects on British society.

Detective Chief Superintendent Christopher Foyle is uncertain about his role during the war; although his son is in training as an RAF pilot, he wonders if he himself shouldn't be more personally involved in the war. Eventually it becomes clear to him, however, that someone must remain behind to enforce the rule of law within the country, even as the rest of the world seems to spiral into lawlessness. Scrupulously honest and well-suited to the detective's life of methodical pursuit, Foyle is the perfect man to investigate war profiteering, assaults, and murders. He is assisted in his investigations by his driver Samantha ("Sam") Stewart of the MTC (Mechanised Transport Corps, a wartime homefront division), and Detective Sergeant Paul Milner, a former police officer who was called up and is a war casualty who lost his leg in the conflict.

Why It's Bingeworthy

World War II is a consistently popular subject and time period, and this drama certainly looks the part; its costume department gets the tweedy suits, the uniforms, and the women's 1940s and 1950s fashions spot on.

The character of Christopher Foyle, as played by Michael Kitchen, is an appealing combination of a man with a strong moral code who will not be pushed around by those who are higher in rank, a bit of a lone wolf, yet also a caring father and a good friend and mentor to the people with whom he works.

Main Cast

Michael Kitchen...Christopher Foyle
Honeysuckle Weeks...Sam Stewart
Anthony Howell...Paul Milner
Ellie Haddington...Hilda Pierce
Julian Ovenden...Andrew Foyle

Trivia

The show was cancelled after five seasons and was set to end within the show on VE Day and the end of the war; members of the public demanded that the show be brought back. Eventually three more seasons aired between 2013 and 2015, with more of an emphasis on crime-solving and less of a focus on geopolitics.

The name of Foyle was taken from Foyles Bookstore of Charing Cross Road.

What to Binge on Next

Anthony Horowtiz is also the creator of several more recent television series, including *Collision*, which focused on characters' involvement in a huge traffic accident in which they were all involved, and *New Blood*, another police procedural set in London. He also wrote several episodes of the hugely popular mystery series *Midsomer Murders*.

Another drama set during World War II that you might consider is *My Mother and Other Strangers*, which is set in a small Northern Ireland village in 1943, and which focuses on a local family and their community's response to the many American service officers who are stationed in and around their village during the war.

Grantchester

Run Time

From 2014 to 2018, there were three series of six forty-five minute episodes each, and one Christmas special, making the run time about fifteen hours.

Creator and Writers

The show is based on a book of short stories by James Runcie, titled *The Grantchester Mysteries,* and it was developed for television by Daisy Coulam (who is also listed as one of the main writers, along with James Runcie).

What It's About

Set in the 1950s, just outside of Oxford in the rural village of Grantchester, *Grantchester* focuses on the life of vicar Sidney Chambers, a World War II veteran with traumatic war memories, a taste for jazz, compassion for his parishioners, a brisk but generally good-hearted housekeeper, and a vicious case of unrequited love for his socialite friend Amanda. The last thing he really needs is to get involved with the solving of local crimes, or a complex friendship (a bromance, if you will) with local police detective Geordie Keating. But that's exactly what he does.

And it's a good thing he does, because over the course of the series, his relationship with Amanda gets both closer and rockier; his housekeeper despairs of his ever settling down and paying full attention to his church duties; a sweet but often befuddled curate named Leonard arrives to provide assistance with pastoral work but often needs help himself when he gets in over his head. In the face of all these issues, his friendship with Geordie and his work solving crimes is what often provides stability in Chambers's life.

Why It's Bingeworthy

Sometimes you just need a completely compelling drama to sink into, and *Grantchester* is perfect for that purpose. I first found this series when dealing with some personal issues, and it was comforting to be able to completely disappear into its pastoral setting and intense storylines.

Sidney and Geordie are not always heroic, sympathetic characters; both struggle with fidelity in their relationships and both can be too bound up by expectations of what it means to be a man to be totally likable. But their chemistry with each other gives the show emotional heft, and their shared ability to notice small details and solve the crimes (which can sometimes be disturbing in nature but are not often shown too graphically) makes it a satisfying police procedural and amateur detective mystery combined.

Main Cast

James Norton...Sidney Chambers
Robson Green...Geordie Keating
Tessa Peake-Jones...Mrs. Sylvia Maguire
Morven Christie...Amanda Kendall Hopkins
Al Weaver...Leonard Finch

Trivia

The series is actually filmed in the village of Grantchester, as well as in London and Oxford.

It has been announced that a fourth series will be filmed but James Norton will not reprise his role as Sidney Chambers; instead, a new lead character, Reverend Will Davenport, will be played by Tom Brittney.

During the filming of the show, the village's real vicar retired, and several local residents asked James Norton if he would consider taking over.

What to Binge on Next

Another crime drama in which the bromance between the two lead male characters is central to the story is *Sherlock*, starring Benedict Cumberbatch as Sherlock Holmes and Martin Freeman as Dr. Watson.

If your favorite part of this show is the stellar acting done job the leads James Norton and Robson Green, you might consider watching other shows in which they play main roles. Although he plays a completely reprehensible criminal type in *Happy Valley*, there's no denying that Norton is a powerful actor. Robson Green has had a long acting career and has appeared in numerous British TV productions, but is perhaps best known for his role as a psychologist who helps the police understand the criminals they are tracking in *Wire in the Blood*.

Another ecclesiastical mystery series that might appeal to *Grantchester* fans is *Father Brown*, although that show is much gentler in tone.

Inspector George Gently

Run Time

The series ran for eight seasons and a total of twenty-five ninety-minute episodes, for a total run time of nearly thirty-eight hours. It aired on BBC One from 2007 to 2017.

Creator and Writers

Peter Flannery created the show, which is loosely based on the George Gently novels by Alan Hunter. Flannery was also the main writer, although several other writers contributed single episodes, and the final series was written by Charlotte Wolf and Robert Murphy.

What It's About

It's the 1960s in the gritty industrial Northeast region of England, and Detective Inspector George Gently transfers there after his wife is killed in a mob hit. Once there, he is teamed with Detective Sergeant John Bacchus, who is new to the job but is already well-schooled in how to get ahead in corrupt police business by marrying the boss's daughter and manipulating evidence. These and Bacchus's many other somewhat sloppy policing methods are emphatically not okay with Gently.

As they work together, the two detectives learn to respect one another's specialized skills, and while Bacchus never truly loses his impetuousness, he does find himself inspired by Gently's strong but gentle example to become a better investigator and person. This show can be quite dark in subject, tone, and cinematography; all of the social and economic problems of the sixties are on display, with many of their cases involving racism, corruption, and violence toward children and women. From series six onward, a female police officer joins the team, which serves to highlight the strength of their friendship and trust, and adds new dimensions to their understanding (and hers) of new methods of policing and thinking about individuals and communities.

Why It's Bingeworthy

The relationship between Gently and Bacchus, while similar to the mentor/mentee relationship shown in many police procedurals, offers a fresh viewing experience because both men remain very different from one another, and their partnership is a true one in that Gently (although he is the elder of the two) often looks for ways to be more flexible in his thinking and policing, while the younger Bacchus will always be slightly more rough around the edges and more ready to "rattle the cages" of their suspects.

This show also offers a unique time period and setting—although becoming more popular, set pieces from the 1960s are not frequently seen in the crime drama genre, and northern England, especially on the eastern side (Newcastle upon Tyne, etc.), is also not frequently featured in British dramas or comedies. The period music, fashion, settings, and cars all make this a beautiful series to look at, while its unflinching gaze and more forward-thinking attitudes strip away any tendency toward sentimental nostalgia.

Martin Shaw and Lee Ingleby knock their performances out of the park, and I defy you to find a woman of any age who isn't in love with Shaw's gruff, strong, but still wise elder statesman character (although Lee Ingleby has his devoted fans who love his volatility and emotion). As an added bonus, the dynamic between the three detectives when Rachel Coles joins their team (first as a WPC—woman police constable—and later as a sergeant) only becomes more nuanced and interesting.

Main Cast

Martin Shaw…George Gently
Lee Ingleby…John Bacchus
Lisa McGrillis…Rachel Coles

Trivia

In 2009 actor Martin Shaw was in need of assistance from the police himself: he and his long-time girlfriend were stalked for years by a woman named Sandra Price. Price was eventually convicted for the crime and sentenced with a restraining order and community service.

What to Binge on Next

Other dark police procedurals in which the mentor/mentee relationship is an important one are *DCI Banks*, which is set in a similar north England region to *Gently* (Yorkshire); it stars Stephen Tompkinson as DCI Alan Banks, and he strives to help his detective sergeants use their already strong investigative skills to the best of their abilities.

Martin Shaw is most well-known for starring in the crime/action drama *The Professionals* in the late 1970s and early 1980s; it was more of a spy/action

204

program than a police procedural, but is still seen as a classic and ran for nearly sixty episodes. He also played the lead in the BBC One court and legal drama *Judge John Deed*, that aired from 2001 to 2007.

Lee Ingleby also played a Detective Inspector in the three-part adaptation of Val McDermid's *A Place of Execution* (set in the Midlands) that aired in 2008.

If you're interested in the 1960s time period, and are willing to branch out from police dramas, you might also consider the historical drama *Call the Midwife*, about nurse midwives and nuns helping poor women with obstetric and child care in East London in the 1950s and 1960s.

Marple

Run Time

This version of Agatha Christie's mystery novels featuring Miss Marple aired on ITV between 2004 and 2013, and consisted of twenty-three ninety-minute episodes in six series.

Creator and Writers

The show is based on Christie's novels, but used multiple writers. Screenwriters who worked on four or more episodes were Stephen Churchett, Kevin Elyot, and Stewart Harcourt.

What It's About

Agatha Christie's elderly amateur sleuth Miss Jane Marple is one of the best known detectives in all mystery fiction. Miss Marple as she is shown here is a spinster, but is more of the merry variety than the severe type. When not gardening, she keeps busy becoming involved in the alarmingly frequent murders in and around her small village of St. Mary Mead, as well as those further abroad, when she is consulted by various stumped police detectives who are aware of her expertise.

This is standard "cozy" mystery fare, with the crimes often taking place within one household, or among a small group of suspects, and with Miss Marple drawing upon her village experiences with a wide variety of personalities to help her gain insight into crimes.

Why It's Bingeworthy

The creators of this series had the good fortune to find not one but two wonderful actresses to portray Jane Marple: Geraldine McEwan played her for the first three series, and Julia McKenzie took the role over for the last three series. Both women gave Jane a sparkle and a mischievous smile. The show also included a number of notable cameos from such actors as Joanna Lumley, Timothy Dalton, Dan Stevens, Shirley Henderson, and Toby Stephens.

But it isn't all fun and games. Another hallmark of Miss Marple is her unflinching acceptance of human nature, and her sense of justice, and that is also evident in these stories, even though they are often not the most faithful of adaptations of Christie's novels. I hope Christie wouldn't have minded, because these are still very high quality, quickly plotted, and beautifully filmed movies.

Main Cast

Geraldine McEwan...Miss Marple
Julia McKenzie...Miss Marple

Trivia

Nine of these programs were adapted from Agatha Christie novels that didn't originally include Jane Marple.

After the sixth series of the show aired, it was announced that the BBC had acquired the rights to make Agatha Christie adaptations, meaning that ITV will not be able to make any more of this series.

What to Binge on Next

If you simply can't get enough Miss Marple you're going to want to watch *Miss Marple*, an earlier series starring Joan Hickson as Jane Marple (which many people swear by as *the* adaptation to watch). If you're happy to watch anything by Agatha Christie, you should also check out the *Poirot* series, with David Suchet as Hercule Poirot.

Brits seem fairly open-minded about their sleuths being older; other series featuring more mature detectives include *Mapp & Lucia* (the 1985 series, starring a younger Geraldine McEwan and Prunella Scales), *Hetty Wainthropp Investigates* (starring Patricia Routledge), *The Mrs. Bradley Mysteries*, featuring Diana Rigg as the crime-solving widow Mrs. Bradley, and *New Tricks*, a police procedural in which detectives come out of retirement to solve cold cases (although that one is a bit grittier).

The Mrs. Bradley Mysteries

Run Time

This is an extremely short mystery series, perfect when you've got a lazy weekend afternoon and want some quick, light viewing. There was only one series of the program, comprised of a ninety-minute pilot episode and four one-hour episodes, making for a total run time of slightly under six hours. It first aired on BBC One between 1998 and 2000.

Creator and Writers

The series is based on a character created by British mystery novelist Gladys Mitchell (who originally wrote sixty-six novels featuring the Mrs. Bradley character). The five episodes were written by Simon Booker, Gwyneth Hughes, and Julie Rutterford.

What It's About

Mrs. Bradley is a widow of independent means with a flair for investigating crimes. Luckily for her (and unluckily for the perpetrators) multiple such crimes seem to occur wherever she is, even among her circle of family and friends. At her side to aid her with the more working-class side of detection, like engaging other servants and tradespeople in gossip and doing the more physical snooping around, is her loyal chauffeur George Moody. And if the two flirt outrageously with each other while they solve mysteries together, well, so much the better.

Why It's Bingeworthy

This series is short but it's a lot of fun, and the 1920s scenery and costumes are just lovely to look at. Mrs. Bradley is played by one of the incomparable grande dames of British TV, Diana Rigg (she also played the iconic role of Emma Peel on *The Avengers*), and she looks to be thoroughly enjoying the sly naughtiness of the role, while Neil Dudgeon as George Moody is the perfect somewhat-more-conservative-but-still-has-a-twinkle-in-his-eye companion for her. And if all that's not enough, there's also several appearances in three episodes by the always charming Peter Davison (you may remember him as Tristan in *All Creatures Great and Small*, or even as *Doctor Who*'s fifth doctor).

Main Cast

Diana Rigg…Mrs. Adela Bradley
Neil Dudgeon…George Moody
Peter Davison…Inspector Christmas

Trivia

The author who wrote the Mrs. Bradley mystery novel series, Gladys Mitchell, was a member of the "Detection Club" that also included Agatha Christie, Dorothy L. Sayers, and G.K. Chesterton. She also wrote under the pseudonyms of Stephen Hockaby and Malcolm Torrie.

What to Binge on Next

Mrs. Bradley is a bit risqué for her time period and society, what with the living the life of the merry wealthy widow and solving crimes and all, but an even more risk-taking heroine can be found in the *Miss Fisher's Murder Mysteries*, an Australian program featuring amateur detective Phryne Fisher, who carries a gun and is not afraid to track down illegal abortionists who harm women, smugglers, and murderers.

A more gentle program set in a time period similar to that found in *The Mrs. Bradley Mysteries* is *Campion*, about amateur gentleman sleuth Albert Campion and his rather rougher manservant Lugg (starring Peter Davison, who also has a small but important recurring role as Inspector Christmas in the Mrs. Bradley stories).

Poirot

Run Time

Make sure you leave some time to start watching this series; it's one of the longest-running British mystery series available. It aired from 1989 all the way to 2013, and consisted of seventy episodes in total. Episodes in the first few series, thirty-six in all, had a run time of fifty minutes each, while thirty-four episodes, mostly from the latter series, were roughly ninety to one hundred minutes long. That makes calculating the bingewatching time a bit tricky, but in all you're going to have to set aside about eighty-two hours.

Creator and Writers

The series is, of course, based on Agatha Christie's classic mysteries featuring her infamous Belgian detective Hercule Poirot, but this version of the program was created by Clive Exton (who also wrote more than twenty of its episodes). Other credited writers on the series include Anthony Horowitz, Nick Dear, Guy Andrews, and David Renwick.

What It's About

Infamous Belgian detective with the fabulous mustaches, Hercule Poirot, is always in demand when the authorities are stumped as to who has perpetrated what crime. He is not an action hero, but is rather a sartorially fussy and very particular (especially in regard to his epicurean pursuits of his next fine meal and drink) gentleman detective who prefers to exercise the "little grey cells" of his brain over all the rest of his muscles combined.

Although he begins the series as a working detective, available for consultation, he also solves many cases that seem to drop into his lap as he travels or visits friends. And he really tries to be humble about his many great successes, but he is not as good at that as he is at solving mysteries. He has a good friend in former military captain Arthur Hastings, who often accompanies him on his cases, and whose complete misunderstanding of each case actually helps Poirot find his way to the actual truth of the matter.

Why It's Bingeworthy

This series has a bit of a split personality; in the first eight series, Captain Hastings was a frequent character, there was much more humor, and the art deco settings of the 1920s and 1930s were seen more often. Episodes in the latter series, from series nine onward, are darker in tone and less humorous.

Which personality is more interesting to watch? It's a credit to the screenwriters that they are both extremely watchable adaptations.

David Suchet was actually recommended for the part of Poirot by Agatha Christie's family, and he has said that he prepared for the part by reading every single one of Christie's novels in which the detective appeared. That attention to detail shows in his nuanced performance (which is all the more striking because this series aired over the course of twenty-four years).

Also? The mysteries are interesting without being too difficult to solve, and there is very little gore, making it a nice program to watch with the family.

Main Cast

David Suchet…Hercule Poirot
Hugh Fraser…Captain Arthur Hastings
Philip Jackson…Chief Inspector Japp
Pauline Moran…Miss Lemon

Trivia

The first eight series have a much more lighthearted feel; after original creators Clive Exton and Brian Eastman both left the show after 2001, subsequent series and episodes adopted a much darker and grittier tone.

In an earlier adaptation of the Poirot mystery *Thirteen at Dinner*, Suchet played the role of Chief Inspector Japp (opposite Peter Ustinov's Poirot).

What to Binge on Next

If you like *Poirot* chances are good that you'll want to watch more Agatha Christie adaptations, particularly those starring the elderly amateur sleuth Miss Jane Marple. Multiple adaptations starring various actors as Miss Marple are available, including the *Miss Marple* series from the 1980s and 1990s starring Joan Hickson, as well as the revamped series *Agatha Christie's Marple*, starring first Geraldine McEwan and then Julia McKenzie. Also of interest might be the 2015 adaptation of Christie's Tommy and Tuppence (two other amateur sleuth characters) books, *Partners in Crime*.

You might also consider other classic whodunit adaptations, like the version of Sherlock Holmes starring Jeremy Brett (*The Adventures of Sherlock Holmes*) and *The Inspector Alleyn Mysteries*, an adaptation of Ngaio Marsh's crime novels featuring Chief Inspector Alleyn.

Jackie on...
Two Historical Crime Dramas You Should Start With

Cadfael

Cadfael is one of the most original TV series ever shot. It's part murder mystery, part historical drama and will teach you more about the everyday lives of mediaeval people than just about any other programme. If you're after fast-paced action this isn't for you, but if you're looking for a thoughtful drama with excellent acting you'll find a lot to enjoy in this series.

And Then There Were None

Agatha Christie is one of the most famous British authors of the 20th century. Her books have been converted to the small screen on many occasions and most are well worth watching. I couldn't decide whether to highlight an adaptation featuring Poirot, her famous Belgian detective, or one with the cunning Miss Marple. This indecision led me to the 2015 BBC adaptation of *And Then There Were None*, which is unusual for an Agatha Christie as it features neither. It has a fantastic cast, including the magnificent Charles Dance, and will ensure you'll want to watch many more Agatha Christie adaptations in the future.

Literary Adaptations

Brideshead Revisited

Run Time

This adaptation to end all adaptations aired on ITV in 1981, and was an eleven-part series, with each part lasting for an hour. The total run time is eleven hours.

Creator and Writers

The adaptation is based on the novel of the same name by Evelyn Waugh; the screenplay was written by Derek Granger, who was also the film's producer. Although another writer, John Mortimer, received credit for writing the story, his version of the screenplay was not used.

What It's About

A family epic sprawling across two decades (from the 1920s to the 1940s), this story is told by main character, Charles Ryder, and primarily focuses on his complex relationship with the even-more complex Flyte (Marchmain) family. The Flytes are wealthy and aristocratic members of England's upper class, but they are also an anomaly due to their Roman Catholicism, and their adherence to that faith marks them as staunchly independent individuals (and not always admired ones at that) in the class system of the time.

Charles is largely able to ignore the family's religion in his first experiences with them; he becomes fast friends with the younger son of the house, Sebastian, and their whirlwind friendship in Oxford and while staying holidays at Brideshead Castle is a deep and enduring one (and is also populated with other friends who Charles's humorless father finds to be unacceptable as companions for his son). Charles is also attracted to Julia, Sebastian's sister, but as with many aristocratic young women of the time, she is not always able to freely choose with whom she can fall in love and who she will marry. When she does marry, it is out of defiance and to a Protestant man. The family's fortunes wax and wane as its matriarch and patriarch are already living separately (with Sebastian's and Julia's father living abroad with another woman), Julia's marriage is unhappy, Sebastian spirals ever further into alcoholism, and the family's other children also follow paths that do not always lead to their happiness.

The story ends where it began, in 1944 (most of the episodes reveal the backstory of Charles's life; the first episode began with him as a soldier in

1944, being stationed at military headquarters in Brideshead), and it does end romantically, although perhaps not quite in the way that the viewer will expect.

Why It's Bingeworthy

This is perhaps one of the best-known British television literary adaptations of all time. It has been noted for its faithfulness to Waugh's source material, as well as for the career-making roles it provided for its three leads: Jeremy Irons, Anthony Andrews, and Diana Quick as Julia Flyte (and let's not forget Laurence Olivier as Lord Marchmain and John Gielgud as Edward Ryder).

The costuming and set design is gorgeous, and the episodes feature many different locations, not only Oxford and Brideshead, but also Morocco and Venice and even an ocean liner. The story is complex, the characters even more complex, and if you're in the mood for a good long weepy, this is the program you'll want.

Main Cast

Jeremy Irons...Charles Ryder
Anthony Andrews...Sebastian Flyte
Diana Quick...Julia Flyte
Claire Bloom...Lady Marchmain
Phoebe Nicholls...Cordelia Flyte
Simon Jones...Lord Brideshead ("Bridey")

Trivia

Producer Derek Granger originally wanted Jeremy Irons for the role of Sebastian Flyte and Anthony Andrews for the role of Charles Ryder, but each actor felt he was better suited to the other's role and they swapped.

The location that was used for the setting of Brideshead Castle was Castle Howard, at that time owned by George Howard, then-Chairman of the BBC (and therefore the rival of the network ITV, on which this program first aired).

In 2007, this series was named by *Time* magazine as television's greatest literary adaptation ever (it was number one on their list of "100 Best TV Shows of All Time").

The filming of this production began in the summer of 1979, but a technicians' strike later that year paused filming, as did Jeremy Irons's concurrent work starring in the movie *The French Lieutenant's Woman*. Principal photography was finally completed in January of 1981.

What to Binge on Next

Another sprawling family drama (that is also a literary adaptation) that you might also like is *The Forsyte Saga*, based on novels by John Galsworthy and focusing on an upper-class family in England from the 1870s to the 1920s. Also of interest might be Julian Fellowes's drama *Downton Abbey*, focusing on the lives of both the "upstairs" aristocrats and their families, as well as on the lives of their "downstairs" servants.

Jeremy Irons and Anthony Andrews had previously worked together in the 1974 television adaptation of Anthony Trollope's Palliser novels, *The Pallisers*. You might also like to catch Jeremy Irons in the television series *The Borgias*, or Anthony Andrews in the historical film *Ivanhoe* or as sleuth/husband Tommy Beresford in the episode *By the Pricking of My Thumbs* (part of the 2006 *Marple* series featuring Geraldine McEwan as Miss Marple).

Casanova

Run Time

This 2005 miniseries ran for three hour-long episodes, for a total run time of three hours.

Creator and Writers

The program was created and written by Russell T. Davies, and was based on Giaocomo Casanova's memoirs (which spanned twelve volumes!).

What It's About

Eighteenth-century Italian legend Giaocomo Casanova was famous for many things; adventuring, writing, being a scholar and a librarian, but when we hear the name "Casanova," most of us think about only one thing: sex.

And this adaptation does not disappoint. Now elderly and living in poverty as a minor noble's librarian, Casanova looks back on his glory days in Venice, when he was a man of twenty-one, seeking riches but starting with not even a coin in his pocket. Leveraging his brains, his charm, and a streak of good luck, he eventually makes and loses several fortunes and becomes accepted in snobbish Venetian society, but is eventually exiled from the city when he overreaches and seeks to marry his true love, Henriette, who unfortunately is also the intended of the jealous and controlling nobleman Grimani.

Casanova loses Henriette, and his city, and makes his way in the world, eventually moving through Paris and London, meeting and traveling with his son, and eventually losing his lust for life as the pace of change in the world starts to depress even him. But even when old and living in poverty, he still manages to brighten the world of a young woman he befriends in the castle where he has retired (much as she brightens his as well).

Why It's Bingeworthy

Oh, David Tennant, let me count the ways I love thee. David Tennant stars as Casanova here, and even though he plays Casanova with the most cockney of British accents, you just totally get why men want to be him and women want to be with him. He is charming, and hilarious, and heartbroken, all at once. It is quite the performance.

217

All of the characters in this adaptation are well-served by Davies's lively and naughty screenplay, and he also doesn't shy away from the darker parts of Casanova's life or adventures. It's a wonderful adaptation, with a rollicking soundtrack, sparkling interior court scene, and great performances from every single cast member. It's quite unlike most other period dramas you'll see.

Main Cast

Peter O'Toole…Giacomo Casanova (elderly)
David Tennant…Giacomo Casanova
Laura Fraser…Henriette
Rose Byrne…Edith
Shaun Parkes…Rocco
Tom Burke…Giac Casanova (Casanova's son)
Nina Sosanya…Bellino
Rupert Penry-Jones…Grimani

Trivia

David Tennant has brown eyes, and had to wear blue contact lenses to try and match the famously piercing blue eyes of Peter O'Toole, who played the elderly Casanova.

Tennant would also work for Davies in the reboot of *Doctor Who*, taking over as the tenth Doctor after Christopher Eccleston left the show in 2005.

What to Binge on Next

A large amount of the fun and drama in this program is attributable directly to its star performance by David Tennant; you'll probably like other things in which Tennant stars, including *Doctor Who* (in which he played the tenth Doctor from 2005 to 2010); *Broadchurch*, a crime drama in which Tennant is one of the lead detectives; and *Good Omens*, based on the novel by Neil Gaiman and Terry Pratchett.

It's a very bright and completely different period drama, with exaggerated colors and plotlines (as befit a character as oversized as Casanova). Other series that have a unique look or feel, such as the popular crime drama *Sherlock* (starring Benedict Cumberbatch and Martin Freeman) or the musical/crime drama *Blackpool* (also starring, as a bonus, David Tennant!) might also be fun for you to watch.

218

Cranford

Run Time

This adaptation played out over five one-hour episodes, for a total watch time of five hours. It first aired on BBC One in 2007.

Creator and Writers

The program is based on three novellas by Elizabeth Gaskell: *Cranford*, *My Lady Ludlow*, and *Mr. Harrison's Confessions*. Sue Birtwistle and Susie Conklin are the program's creators, while Heidi Thomas wrote the teleplay.

What It's About

In the small Cheshire village of Cranford, it's the women who are firmly in charge. In the manor house of Hanbury Court the widowed Lady Ludlow rules with a firm hand, while in the town the never-married Jenkyns sisters (Deborah and Matty) preside over their circle of friends and the town's culture and activities with a more genteel (but no less firm) touch.

But it's the dawn of the Industrial Age, the 1840s, and the old order is changing. Lady Ludlow's fortune is dwindling, the railroad is coming to the town, and the town's young people want more freedom over their educations and relationships (and by that I mean the freedom to actually get an education and have relationships).

Above all the women of the town (and the men: there are some) are quite happy with their traditional ways, their insular society, and their social activities—but it is a measure of their kindness that they do eventually show themselves willing to adapt to some of society's and life's changes.

Why It's Bingeworthy

This is very much an ensemble piece and although there are a lot of storylines, none of them are too complex and it's satisfying to watch them all resolve in the end. By and large the boy gets the girl, the too-snobby get their comeuppance, and the young and decent are granted more opportunities than they would have in the past; although there are some sadnesses along the way, this is overall a very light and gentle program.

The cast is full of big names. Judi Dench and Eileen Atkins portray the Jenkyns sisters; Francesca Annis plays Lady Ludlow; Jim Carter (the butler from *Downton Abbey*) plays Captain Brown; even Michael Gambon makes a brief appearance.

The works of novelist Elizabeth Gaskell enjoyed a little boost after the popularity of the adaptation of her work *North and South*, and that boost helped this cheerful and woman-dominated adaptation get made.

Main Cast

Judi Dench…Matty Jenkyns
Eileen Atkins…Deborah Jenkyns
Francesca Annis…Lady Ludlow
Claudie Blakley…Martha (the Jenkyns sisters' maid)
Lisa Dillon…Mary Smith
Jim Carter…Captain Brown
…*and too many more to list.*

Trivia

Two of the actors on the program are married in real life: Jim Carter (the retired Captain Brown) and Imelda Staunton (Miss Pole).

Although the program is set in Cheshire, none of the exterior scenes were filmed there.

What to Binge on Next

The program proved popular with viewers and critics, so a sequel, *Return to Cranford*, was filmed and aired in 2009.

There are several adaptations of Gaskell's work available, including *North and South*, about a minister's daughter who falls in love (against her own inclination) with a northern mill owner, and *Wives and Daughters*, about a widower doctor and his adult daughter whose lives are upended when he remarries a woman with an adult daughter of her own. Another long-running drama series that focused on a community and the relationships between its residents is *Lark Rise to Candleford*.

Writer Heidi Thomas is also the creator and writer of the historical drama *Call the Midwife*, about nurse midwives and nuns working in the poor East End of London in the 1960s.

The Forsyte Saga

Run Time

Although the number of episodes and run time is listed differently in different sources, the format of the series released on DVD by Acorn TV for the United States references eight fifty-four-minute episodes for the first series and five fifty-three-minute episodes for the second series, making for a total run time (if you watch both) of nearly twelve hours. It originally aired in 2002.

Creator and Writers

The program is based on novelist John Galsworthy's massive "Forsyte Chronicles" series; most notably the two novels and a story in his "Forsyte Saga": *The Man of Property*, "Indian Summer of a Forsyte," and *In Chancery*. Writing credits are given to Stephen Mallatratt and Jan McVerry.

What It's About

What isn't it about? Love and hate, poverty and riches, kindnesses and cruelties, parents and children, life and death.

But if you want me to narrow it down, here goes. The Forsyte family has influence, riches, and each other, but what one of their sons, Soames, eventually wants more than anything is the beautiful and elusive (and poor) Irene Heron. She emphatically does not want him but is pressured by her widowed stepmother to marry well or to try and make her own living, and decides in the end to marry him.

Big mistake.

There's more to it than that, but the difficult relationship between Soames and Irene forms the backbone of the (often heartbreaking) story. He continues to be obsessed with her, while she soon realizes that she can never love him or his mercenary lifestyle. Other relatives of the Forsyte family also get storylines of their own: Soames's sister also marries for love and chooses a man who eventually gambles away whatever money he can get his hands on; their cousin Jolyon falls in love with his daughter's nanny and leaves his family (and inheritance) behind; their respective parents don't understand what has gotten into the younger generation.

Eventually Irene takes steps to free herself from her abusive marriage, and Soames is also able to step back from his obsessive need for her in order to find another partner for himself, but in the second series their respective children repeat the pattern all over again, this time by falling in love with each other despite their parents' forbidding of their match.

Why It's Bingeworthy

Anyone with a penchant for stories in which the path of true love never runs smooth will find a lot to enjoy here. The story is a wide-ranging one about complex family relationships and dynamics, and also has a lot to say about the difficulty of romantic affairs: either partners truly do love each other but simply cannot overcome their own personal shortcomings and addictions, or partners loathe one another but find it difficult to leave (as does Irene, particularly in this time period, when it was much more difficult for a single woman to pay her own way in the world).

This 2002 miniseries had to be especially good, as the BBC had originally made an adaptation of the books in 1967 that became one of the most-watched and most-loved TV miniseries ever. The casting here is strong (Amanda Root as Winifred Forsyte and Ben Miles as her roguish gambling husband Montague Dartie are particular standouts), the costumes and interior and exterior settings are opulent, and there are more than enough plotlines to keep you engaged throughout.

Main Cast

Gina McKee...Irene Heron Forsyte
Damian Lewis...Soames Forsyte
Rupert Graves...Jolyon Forsyte ("Young Jolyon")
Gillian Kearney...June Forsyte
Corin Redgrave...Jolyon Forsyte
Amanda Root...Winifred Forsyte Dartie
Ben Miles...Montague Dartie
Ioan Gruffudd...Philip Bosinney

Trivia

The format of the original novels and this series differ significantly. Many of the stories in the novels were told through the gossip and memories of other characters, so the writers who adapted these stories had to rearrange events and timing to make the adaptation a more straightforward linear story.

The 1967 adaptation of *The Forsyte Saga* originally aired on BBC Two in 1967, but was rerun the following year on BBC One and garnered a huge audience, collecting more than eighteen million viewers for its final episode.

What to Binge on Next

Anglophile purists may also want to track down the 1967 version of the show; although it is in black and white, it is still considered a must-see BBC production. It consists of twenty-six hour-long episodes.

Another literary adaptation that is similar to *The Forsyte Saga* is *Daniel Deronda*, based on the novel by George Eliot. It stars Romola Garai as Gwendolen Harleth and Hugh Dancy as Daniel Deronda, and is definitely of the melodramatic school: Gwendolen and Daniel share friendship and a strong connection, but Gwendolen marries a different man for his money (after her family's fortunes disappear), who turns out to be abusive. Daniel, meanwhile, is struggling to help another friend of his, a woman singer who is also Jewish, to make a living as a singer, when he learns a secret about his own past that will change everything.

The classic drama *Berkeley Square*, a ten-part series that first aired in 1998, follows the exploits of three nannies who work for wealthy Berkeley Square families, and might also be a similar watch to *The Forsyte Saga*.

Jackie on…
Kids' Programs in the UK (Part One)

Blue Peter is the longest running children's programme in the world. It was first broadcast in 1958 and has entertained generations of children with its magazine-style content. The presenters perform a range of tasks - from challenges like skydiving, to craft projects and cookery. They also interview celebrities and engage in the cultural issues of the day. Over the years *Blue Peter* has also become famous for its pets. The dogs, cats and tortoises on the show are all household names. It's a classic of British television!

Peppa Pig is an animated series for the under-5's, but many adults enjoy watching it as much as their children. The lovable family of pigs charm audiences with their honest portrayal of family life. Accident-prone Daddy Pig is always breaking things; Peppa Pig has arguments with her little brother, George; and Mummy Pig is constantly juggling tasks to keep the family afloat. Despite the problems, each episode ends on a positive note. It's a charming series for everyone!

223

Hornblower

Run Time

There are eight two-hour movies in this literary adaptation of three of C.S. Forester's historical novels featuring the character Horatio Hornblower. The first four movies aired from 1998 to 1999; the latter four ("the new adventures") aired from 2002 to 2003. The total run time is sixteen hours.

Creator and Writers

These eight episodes were based upon three of C.S. Forester's Hornblower novels: *Mr. Midshipman Hornblower*, *Lieutenant Hornblower*, and *Hornblower and the Hotspur*. Each program was written by a different writer, the first four of whom were Russell Lewis, Mike Cullen, Patrick Harbinson, and Chris Ould.

What It's About

Horatio Hornblower joins the Royal Navy during the French Revolutionary and Napoleonic Wars of the late nineteenth century. He is not wealthy enough to purchase a commission outright, and therefore must make his way up the naval ranks, starting as a midshipman. Wars rank among the least of his problems; most often he finds himself between the rock of demanding and cruel senior officers and the hard place of the paid sailors who do the actual work and have little respect for most of the officers.

From the beginning of his tenure Hornblower begins to make his mark, showing himself a leader by first volunteering without complaint for many of the duties he will expect his inferiors to perform, and by virtue of his sharp intellect, which he uses to concoct plans that help everyone on the ship stay alive and uncaptured (as well as capturing some ships of their own), which steadily gains him the loyalty of all on board. Accordingly, he rises through the ranks, but the life of a Naval officer of any rank is a dangerous and unpredictable one, and Hornblower and his crew face a variety of challenges in many different locations, including imprisonment in Spain and having to escape from behind enemy lines in France.

Why It's Bingeworthy

Okay, Hornblower as star Ioan Gruffudd plays him (and probably as Forester wrote him; I don't know, I've never read the books) doesn't have a real advanced sense of humor, but he's a stand-up guy who looks after his friends and dependents alike, and that's comforting to watch (and let's not

224

forget that Mr. Gruffudd is just *so* good-looking). The supporting cast in this program is also strong; Robert Lindsay is the perfect mentor for Hornblower, and Jamie Bamber as his friend Lieutenant Kennedy and Paul McGann as his colleague Lieutenant Bush are all perfectly cast.

The production values for this program were high, making each episode feel more like a standalone feature film. In addition to storylines about the friendships and difficulties among the officers, there is also plenty of action in this series, with multiple battles both on land and at sea.

Main Cast

Ioan Gruffudd…Horatio Hornblower
Robert Lindsay…Captain Pellew
Paul McGann…William Bush
Jamie Bamber…Archie Kennedy

Trivia

The ship used for filming many on-board scenes was built especially for the production, and its expense and the time it took to build nearly halted filming (which was already costing ten million pounds). In later series the real historical ship *HMS Victory* was refurbished to be used in the shooting.

The seventh installment of this series, *Hornblower: Loyalty*, was written by Niall Leonard, who is perhaps better known as Mr. E.L. James and the screenwriter of the movie adaptations of her bestsellers *Fifty Shades Darker* and *Fifty Shades Freed*.

What to Binge on Next

If you like adventure and men who look after their compatriots, you're definitely going to want to watch the Sharpe television dramas, a series of sixteen standalone films (all with different names, but starting with *Sharpe's Rifles*), based on Bernard Cornwell's novels. They focus on the exploits of soldier Richard Sharpe in the early 1800s, fighting in any number of Great Britain's military skirmishes and wars, and they star Sean Bean.

Another costume drama you might enjoy is *Poldark*, set in 1700s Cornwall and based on the novels of Winston Graham. Its main character is Ross Poldark, who is no stranger himself to adventure and taking responsibility for the soldiers and workers in his care.

Little Dorrit

Run Time

This adaptation first aired in 2008 with a sixty-minute premiere episode, twelve half-hour episodes, and another sixty-minute finale, so however you watch it, the total run time will be about eight hours.

Creator and Writers

The program is adapted from Charles Dickens's novel *Little Dorrit*. The screenplay was written by Andrew Davies.

What It's About

Amy Dorrit has only ever known one home: the Marshalsea Debtors' Prison, where her father has been imprisoned, and she along with him, for more than twenty years. Ironically, her father's long tenure in the prison means he has a kind of seniority there; he has a good relationship with the prison's staff and Amy is allowed out to attend her job as a seamstress for a rich elderly woman, Mrs. Clennam. Mrs. Clennam won't spend the money to maintain her house and it's falling down around her, but she seems determined not to notice, even more so when her long-estranged son Arthur returns from he and his father's work in India to mend their rift.

When Amy meets Arthur, she falls in love with him, and for much of the story Arthur is completely unaware of Amy's love. When she and her family abruptly experience a change of fortune and she must learn to behave as a lady of property, she becomes even more desperately unhappy.

But, again, this being Dickens, it all comes right in the end (although I won't tell you how), with the wicked getting their just deserts and the righteous finding their own happy endings.

Why It's Bingeworthy

Well, I hate to play the Dickens card again, but it IS Dickens. What's more, it's very approachable, watchable, and not way-too-long Dickens (which is always a worry with Dickens). I know the Brits love him and he's got a fair number of fans stateside, too, but he was never particularly my cuppa: I had to read *Great Expectations* in high school and all I remember from the story is that it gave me the strong desire to slap Pip around a little bit for being so clueless.

But I digress. This is not a story that is adapted as often as *Great Expectations*, or even *Oliver Twist*, so it's well worth a watch. The two leads (Claire Foy and Matthew Macfadyen) are both delightfully understated actors and they put a lot of feeling into their characters. Likewise, the son of the jailer who falls in love with Amy Dorrit, only to have his love go unrequited (John Chivery), is an absolute charmer, as played by actor Russell Tovey.

Main Cast

Claire Foy…Amy Dorrit
Matthew Macfadyen…Arthur Clennam
Tom Courtenay…Mr. Dorrit
Judy Parfitt…Mrs. Clennam
Russell Tovey…John Chivery
…*and too many more to list.*

Trivia

Besides brief appearances on the programs *Being Human* and *The Doctors*, this was 22-year-old Claire Foy's first big starring role.

What to Binge on Next

This is not the first Dickens story to be adapted by Andrew Davies; he also wrote the 2005 version of *Bleak House*, starring Gillian Anderson. The 1998 adaptation of Dickens's *Our Mutual Friend* might also strongly appeal to fans of *Little Dorrit*; it's got a lovely love story as well, and Anna Friel and Steven Mackintosh are pretty much the cutest couple ever.

Another Victorian-era literary adaptation you might consider is *Wives and Daughters*, in which another man is too clueless to realize when the best woman in the entire neighborhood is in love with him.

Claire Foy is also rapidly becoming the queen of historical dramas; you might also want to see her as Anne Boleyn in *Wolf Hall* or as Queen Elizabeth II herself in *The Crown*.

Middlemarch

Run Time

This 1994 adaptation of George Eliot's 1871 novel of the same name aired on BBC Two in six episodes. One episode was seventy-five minutes long and the rest were an hour long, making for a total run time of six hours and fifteen minutes.

Creator and Writers

The program is based on George Eliot's classic novel, and the screenplay is by Andrew Davies (it's one of his earlier adaptations).

What It's About

The town of Middlemarch is full to bursting with a variety of personality types. There's the sincere Dorothea Brooke who seeks to better herself with a marriage to the intellectual but much older Reverend Edward Casaubon, who turns out to be not so much an intellectual as a fussy and demanding elderly tyrant. Complicating matters for Dorothea is the appearance of the charming and young Will Ladislaw, who actually does engage her in intellectual conversation and who is much kinder than her husband, but it's not really in Dorothea's character to engage in an affair.

Also in town is the dashing young physician Dr. Lydgate, who also has high ideals and wants to bring the highest quality of medical care to his community, but whose unsuccessful marriage to a beautiful socialite (Rosamond Vincy) quickly lands him in financial trouble. Rosamond's brother Fred has financial troubles of his own, and these are stopping him from gaining the heart and the hand of the woman he loves.

There's a lot going on, and it's all very Victorian, what with people being in love and trying to act like they're not, and complicated wills and financial shenanigans dictating the courses of people's lives galore. And yet? There's happy endings to be had, if you just stick with it.

Why It's Bingeworthy

This early Davies adaptation garnered great reviews and has given this series a reputation it is still enjoying as one of the more faithful and enjoyable Victorian literature adaptations around. It is also an adaptation of a George

Eliot novel, which means it is a little something different from the countless Austen, Brontë, and Hardy adaptations currently available.

Other reviewers have noted that Davies's dialogue (as always) is lively, and that the popularity of this adaptation in Great Britain actually kicked off a small Eliot craze (the book was even re-issued in paperback to capitalize on the show's success). All that and a young and dashing Rufus Sewell playing the part of Will Ladislaw? Count me in!

Main Cast

Juliet Aubrey...Dorothea Brooke
Patrick Malahide... Edward Casaubon
Rufus Sewell...Will Ladislaw
Douglas Hodge... Dr. Tertius Lydgate
Trevyn McDowell...Rosamond Vincy
Jonathan Firth...Fred Vincy

Trivia

This miniseries cost $10 million to make.

Jonathan Firth, who plays Fred Vincy, is the younger brother of Colin Firth.

What to Binge on Next

George Eliot was also the author of *The Mill on the Floss* and *Daniel Deronda* (among other novels); the former was adapted into a 1997 television movie starring Emily Watson, the latter was adapted as a four-part miniseries in 2002 (and was also adapted by Andrew Davies).

This program has a lot to say about social class and money; another adaptation that you might enjoy if you like it is Elizabeth Gaskell's *North and South*, about a young woman's growing understanding of the advantages and disadvantages of mill work (and her love for a mill owner who she fears is too mercenary).

Rufus Sewell stole the show in this program; he also did a fair bit of show-stealing in the historical drama series *Victoria*, about the early days of Queen Victoria's long reign, in which he played (with questionable historical accuracy) the dreamy Lord Melbourne.

The Moonstone

Run Time

The 2016 adaptation that aired on BBC One ran for five forty-five minute episodes, for a total run time of nearly four hours.

Creator and Writers

This adaptation is based on the novel *The Moonstone* by Wilkie Collins. It was adapted for the screen by Rachel Flowerday and Sasha Hails.

What It's About

Nothing could go wrong if you inherited a big diamond from your uncle on your eighteenth birthday, could it?

Well, it could, if that huge diamond is known as the Moonstone and was originally carried away from India by your corrupt military uncle. When Rachel Verinder inherits the diamond on her birthday, it is stolen later that night, and the suspects are many: family members? Servants? Three traveling entertainers who may or may not be Hindu priests whose sworn mission is to recover the jewel? At the same time Rachel learns that the man she loves, her cousin Franklin Blake, has been lying to her about the amount of debt he is in. It's not, all things considered, a great birthday.

When Rachel refuses to see him, Franklin decides he must solve the unsolved mystery of who took the jewel, and engages the help of Rachel's servant Gabriel Betteredge, and the formerly retired detective Sergeant Cuff to help him discover the truth. Eventually they will—but only after the requisite number of surprises, plot twists, and cliffhangers.

Why It's Bingeworthy

Author Wilkie Collins is often considered a precursor to such mystery writing greats as Agatha Christie, and he certainly knew how to write a convoluted (it appeared in serial form, or several installments, when first published, a format which helped develop the importance of the cliffhanger) but satisfying story. He's also an author that has not had as many adaptations as have many other Victorian authors, so it's nice to see something different.

Although none of the actors in this adaptation are really household names, they do a great job with their roles (Leo Wringer as the servant Gabriel Betteredge is a particular joy to watch), and the cinematography and music in this program is everything brooding and foreboding that you could want.

Main Cast

Terenia Edwards…Rachel Verinder
Joshua Silver…Franklin Blake
Leo Wringer…Gabriel Betteredge
Rosanna Spearman…Jane McGrath
John Thomson…Sergeant Cuff
Stewart Clarke…Godfrey Ablewhite

Trivia

The novel, *The Moonstone*, was written in an epistolary format, with the story being told through different characters' letters and writings. The screenwriters of this production, Flowerday and Hails, wrote their story in a non-linear fashion to reflect the novel's format.

This adaptation was commissioned for BBC One Daytime, a service which offers a "diverse array of programming in daytime from challenging quiz shows to documentary series, consumer programmes, factual-entertainment and drama."

What to Binge on Next

You may have had enough of this story after this adaptation, but if you want to see it told in another way you might try another popular adaptation, the 1996 television movie *The Moonstone*, starring dashing Greg Wise (also known as Mr. Emma Thompson) and a very young Keeley Hawes.

Another new adaptation of *The Woman in White*, another novel by Wilkie Collins, aired in 2018, and is also enjoyably dark and gothic.

Any number of other dark Victorian-era twisty-and-turny stories might appeal to you if you liked this program, among them: *Dark Angel*, a dramatization of the life of Victorian serial killer Mary Ann Cotton; Charles Dickens's *Bleak House* (starring Gillian Anderson); and *Affinity*, an adaptation of a Sarah Waters novel about a woman in Victorian-era England who visits and tries to support women in prison, becoming particularly fascinated by one of the inmates, who is also a spiritual medium.

North and South

Run Time

Four one-hour episodes make this a mere four-hour bingewatch. It first aired on BBC One in 2004.

Creator and Writers

This drama is an adaptation of Elizabeth Gaskell's novel *North and South*; the television scripts were written by Sandy Welch.

What It's About

Margaret Hale is living a comfortable life with her family in the more agrarian and temperate south of England when her Anglican pastor father has a crisis of faith, leaves his parish living, and moves his wife and daughter to the more industrial north of England.

More specifically, they move to the cotton mill town of Milton (based on the city of Manchester), where her father attempts to start a new life as a tutor-for-hire, and Margaret is thrown into two very different classes of people: mill owners, and their laborers. The former are shown to be mostly miserly types intent on getting the most work that they can out of their employees, but mill owner John Thornton, who signs on to receive tutoring from Margaret's father, seems to be cut from slightly different cloth: he needs to turn a profit to keep his mill running, but he believes that helping his workers keep healthy and adequately compensated will be the best for his bottom line. Although Margaret finds more friendship and fellowship among the mill laborers than among her new society's upper class, she also finds herself drawn to Mr. Thornton, who falls in love with her despite himself and makes her the most painful offer of marriage since Mr. Darcy muffed it up in *Pride and Prejudice*.

Although Margaret learns to appreciate the charms of Milton and its people, her family struggles to find its place, and a series of truly unfortunate events heap hardship upon hardship on Margaret and her mother. They return to the south to live with relatives, but Margaret finds that it is not so easy to leave Milton—or the earnest and magnetic John Thornton—behind her.

Why It's Bingeworthy

Don't start watching this one at ten p.m., honestly. I made that mistake and didn't go to bed until after I'd watched the last installment, at 2 a.m. Although, frankly? It was so worth it.

This series gives you a great feel for the history of the beginning of the Industrial Age, and for the entrenched nature of the class system in Great Britain. It's one of your shorter adaptations, so it's easy to watch anytime, and the romance here is absolutely top-notch. Daniela Denby-Ashe and Richard Armitage as Margaret and John respectively display a truly smokin' chemistry in a program that is very low on actual physical contact; and the supporting players are excellent as well, particularly Sinéad Cusack as Thornton's devoted mother who doesn't take kindly to anyone who doesn't recognize his potential the way she does.

The romance is not the only aspect of the story that this program does well. Margaret also develops a friendship with a woman who works in one of the cotton mills (as well as with her family), which helps her understand the workers' struggles.

Knowledge of this program also gives you the perfect question for finding fellow Anglophiles. If you ask someone if they've seen *North and South*, and they say, "The miniseries with Patrick Swayze?" you can move on (although I'm not throwing shade at Patrick, I'm a total Swayze Fangirl). If they say, "Oh my god, Richard Armitage," then you know you've found a kindred spirit.

Main Cast

Daniela Denby-Ashe…Margaret Hale
Richard Armitage…John Thornton
Tim Pigott-Smith..Richard Hale
Lesley Manville…Maria Hale
Sinéad Cusack…Hannah Thornton
Pauline Quirke…Dixon

Trivia

After the program first aired, so many fans of the show logged onto the BBC message boards that they crashed the BBC website.

Daniela Denby-Ashe originally auditioned for the role of Fanny Thornton (John Thornton's sister), but the producers decided they wanted her to play the role of Margaret Hale instead.

Although the story is set in Milton, a city based on Manchester, much of the production was filmed in Edinburgh.

What to Binge on Next

Although less interested in issues of social class and industrialization, the 2009 adaptation of Jane Austen's *Emma* starring Romola Garai and Jonny Lee Miller also offers a wonderful (and wonderfully romantic) relationship between the main characters. It was also written by *North and South*'s screenwriter Sandy Welch. Welch also wrote the screenplay for the 2009 adaptation of Charlotte Brontë's *Jane Eyre*.

Although considerably darker, Thomas Hardy's story *Tess of the D'urbervilles* shows more of the stratification between the rich and poor characters (similar to *North and South*). The 2008 adaptation starring Gemma Arterton is more recent, but I confess to preferring the 1998 edition starring Justine Waddell and Jason Flemyng, who somehow manages to be both repellant and appealing as Alec D'urberville.

Fans of Richard Armitage might want to check out two subsequent television series in which he appeared: *Robin Hood* (as the villain Guy of Gisborne) and *MI-5* (as spy Lucas North), or even his guest-starring role on the last series of *The Vicar of Dibley*.

Pride and Prejudice

Run Time

The run time of the 1995 version that first aired on BBC One and the American A&E network was five and a half hours; it aired in six fifty-five minute episodes.

Creator and Writers

The program is based on Jane Austen's novel *Pride and Prejudice* and for this version the screenplay was written by Andrew Davies.

What It's About

Is there an Anglophile alive who doesn't know the basic plot points of Jane Austen's novel *Pride and Prejudice*, or who hasn't seen the BBC/A&E adaptation starring Colin Firth?

I didn't think so. But we'll cover it anyway, for the sake of consistency. It is a truth universally acknowledged that a young man with a fortune must be in want of a wife (so begins the book), and so begins the movie, with the wealthy and eligible Mr. Bingley renting a house in the neighborhood where a genteel but decidedly down-market family named the Bennets live. The Bennets, mind you, are a household that consists of a wry father, an overdramatic mother, and five eligible daughters in need of very good matches just to maintain their position in society (as their father's estate and their home will be "entailed" away from them, to go instead to their father's nearest male relative, a practice that survived until 1925).

Things get really interesting when Mr. Bingley brings along his even wealthier and even more eligible friend Mr. Darcy, and they are both introduced to all of the Bennet girls. Mr. Bingley falls for the most beautiful, Jane (the eldest), and although their love affair faces challenges of its own, it is not the focus of the story. The real story is the spark that flies between Mr. Darcy and the next eldest Bennet, Elizabeth. First they are sparks of anger as Mr. Darcy suggests that Elizabeth is not good-looking enough to "tempt him" and Elizabeth responds with indignation; later, as the pair get to know one another better, Elizabeth finds that she must get over her initial aversion to him (the prejudice) and recognize that he has many good and caring qualities, and Darcy must get over his aversion to her low position and uncouth family (the pride) to see her lively and intelligent true nature.

Why It's Bingeworthy

The shirt that launched a thousand other movies: well, not quite. But the sight of Colin Firth as Mr. Darcy taking an impromptu swim in a pool on his estate, and thereafter striding back to his estate, all handsome and dripping, has been extensively explored in pop culture and in chat rooms on the Internet ever since it happened. The scene was even re-imagined to great effect in the fun modern take on the story titled *Lost in Austen*.

Austen's work here, and the high-quality adaptation of her work to a film lengthy and sumptuously produced enough to really bring it alive, is representative of all her work: romantic, but also remarkably clear-eyed and timeless. People are, of course, still considering prospective dates and mates based at least partially on their prospects and finances, and other people are rejecting other dates and mates based at least partially on unsavory family and class and personality qualities. Although there have been numerous film adaptations of this story, this is recognized to be the gold standard against which all the others are measured. Its writer (literary screenwriter extraordinaire Andrew Davies) did a fine job of capturing character quirks as well as Austen's underappreciated (to my mind) humor, which is present in nearly every scene.

Main Cast

Jennifer Ehle...Lizzie Bennet
Colin Firth...Mr. Darcy
Susannah Harker...Jane Bennet
Crispin Bonham-Carter...Mr. Bingley
Alison Steadman...Mrs. Bennet
Benjamin Whitrow...Mr. Bennet

Trivia

Actress Anna Chancellor, who played Mr. Bingley's snobbish sister, is actually a direct descendant of Jane Austen's brother Edward.

For a short while after filming, stars Jennifer Ehle and Colin Firth (Elizabeth and Darcy) had a romantic relationship in real life.

Susannah Harker, who played the role of Jane Bennet, is the daughter of actor Polly Adams...who played Jane Bennet in a 1967 adaptation of *Pride and Prejudice*.

The program is credited with creating a wave of "Austen mania": in 1996, after the program had aired, membership in the North American chapter of the Jane Austen Society increased by more than fifty percent.

What to Binge on Next

If you feel like following this program up with some more Austen adaptations, you'll find an embarrassment of riches; all of Austen's novels have been adapted numerous times. In my opinion, the adaptations that match both the skill and the fun of this one are 2009's *Emma*, starring Romola Garai and Jonny Lee Miller; the 1995 feature film *Persuasion*, starring Amanda Root and Ciarán Hinds; and the 2007 version of *Northanger Abbey*, starring Felicity Jones and J.J. Feild.

You will of course also want to see the film adaptation of Helen Fielding's chick lit novel *Bridget Jones's Diary*, a modern revamp of *Pride and Prejudice*, starring (who else?) Colin Firth as Mark Darcy and Renee Zellweger as Bridget Jones. If you don't mind having a zombie-filled horror story mixed in with your Jane Austen classic, you might also enjoy the 2016 film *Pride and Prejudice and Zombies* (based on Seth Grahame-Smith's novel of the same title).

Oh, and if you like screenwriter Andrew Davies? He is listed in Wikipedia as writing no fewer than forty-two adaptation and television screenplays; that should keep you busy for a while.

Sense and Sensibility

Run Time

This 2008 adaptation consisted of three hour-long episodes, for a total run time of three hours.

Creator and Writers

This is another Jane Austen adaptation (of her novel of the same name), and the screenplay was written by Andrew Davies.

What It's About

The Dashwood family (mom and three daughters) are cast into financial woe when their patriarch dies, leaving their father's son by his first wife as the sole heir to his fortune and estate. They might still have been okay had the son of the family, John Dashwood, been married to anyone but Fanny (formerly Ferrars) Dashwood, but by the time she's done convincing John how much money their family needs it's lucky the Dashwood women get to keep anything their father bought them while alive.

Although the family (Mrs. Dashwood, Elinor, Marianne, and Margaret) eventually decides they must leave Norland Park, life at which has become a misery, there is one bright spot in their time there: a visit from Fanny's brother, Edward Ferrars, with whom Elinor falls in love. Fanny makes it clear, however, that her brother must marry a rich woman, so when the Dashwoods hear that Mrs. Dashwood's cousin, Sir John Middleton, has a cottage for them, they leave to make a new life in Devonshire.

Here the family crosses paths not only with the Middletons, but also with their neighbor, Colonel Brandon, and a dashing young rake named Willoughby, with whom Marianne falls in love. Nothing seems to go right for the sisters; Willoughby leaves Marianne to marry a rich woman and Elinor's love for Edward is crushed when it becomes clear they can't be together, but don't worry: it's Austen. It'll all come right in the end.

Why It's Bingeworthy

Some fans will swear by the 1995 film version, starring Emma Thompson as Elinor and Kate Winslet as Marianne, and more power to them; it's a good film, and Emma Thompson is worth watching in whatever she does. But I love this more recent adaptation, and not just because the casting director had the sense to cast David Morrissey as the smokin'-hot (and don't forget kind) "older" Colonel Brandon.

The story is Austen, and therefore is awesome. But this production brings with it more bingeworthy facets: beautiful locations and shots of the ocean filmed on location in Berkshire, Surrey, Buckinghamshire, and Devon; a wonderful soundtrack by the talented Martin Phipps; wonderful costumes that seem less fussy but are somehow richer-looking than costumes in earlier productions; and of course the joy of seeing Austen's humor come alive when properly handled by a good screenwriter and a talented cast.

Main Cast

Hattie Morahan...Elinor Dashwood
Charity Wakefield...Marianne Dashwood
Janet McTeer...Mrs. Dashwood
Dan Stevens...Edward Ferrars
Dominic Cooper...John Willoughby
David Morrissey...Colonel Brandon

Trivia

The opening scene of this adaptation was a bit sexier than you usually see in Austen adaptations; the Jane Austen Society described it as "too raunchy."

In Austen's novel, the difference in the ages between Colonel Brandon and Marianne is somewhere between fifteen and twenty years; in this production, David Morrissey is about sixteen years older than Charity Wakefield (who play Brandon and Marianne, respectively).

What to Binge on Next

This adaptation was aired along with several others produced in the same time period, which were shown on PBS's Masterpiece Theatre in the U.S., as part of "The Complete Jane Austen." Other new Austen adaptations created for that series included *Emma* (starring Romola Garai and Jonny Lee Miller, 2009), *Mansfield Park* (starring Billie Piper and Blake Ritson, 2007), *Persuasion* (starring Sally Hawkins and Rupert Penry-Jones, 2007), and *Northanger Abbey* (starring Felicity Jones and J.J. Feild, 2007). They were all excellent. Another film shown as part of the "Complete Jane Austen" was the biopic *Miss Austen Regrets*, which was based on Austen's letters and diaries and which starred the impeccable Olivia Williams and Greta Scacchi.

The Tenant of Wildfell Hall

Run Time

This adaptation consists of three fifty-five-minute episodes, for a total run time of nearly three hours. It first aired in 1996 on BBC One.

Creator and Writers

The program is based on the novel of the same name by Anne Brontë. It was adapted for the screen by David Nokes.

What It's About

When a woman, her young son, and their domestic servant arrive one night at Wildfell Hall, all of the established families in the area are consumed with curiosity to know who she is and why she's there. Perhaps the most curious about the young woman, Helen, is her smallholder neighbor Gilbert Markham; he visits her frequently and they form a friendship, although neither her few friends in the area nor his family approve of their meetings.

Eventually Gilbert pressures Helen to tell him why she and her son live in seclusion at Wildfell; she writes him a letter, and the rest of the story is told in flashbacks: how she married a rakish young man, had a baby, and then discovered her husband was wasting her money on drunken debauches, and that he was also unfaithful to her. When she could see him starting to teach their son his cruel ways, she left him and hid to escape his wrath.

It doesn't look like there is any way for Helen to be free of her husband, raise her son in peace, or for she and Gilbert to pursue their growing feelings for another. But you'll simply have to watch the whole thing to learn if there's a happy ending for any of the characters involved.

Why It's Bingeworthy

Ah, the Brontës. Patron saints of young girls ready to sigh over every tragic love affair that they possibly can. This is a refreshing adaptation simply because it is by Anne, and not by Charlotte or Emily (whose books *Jane Eyre* and *Wuthering Heights* have been adapted with much more frequency than has this one), and the story, although dark and sometimes a bit moralizing in tone, still shows humor where the hypocrisies of "polite society" are concerned. It's a quick watch, the scenery is hauntingly beautiful, and the soundtrack is lovely as well.

Tara Fitzgerald is one of the most underrated Brit actors around, and she puts in a star turn here, by turns naïve, angry, and forgiving. Ditto for Toby Stephens; he's dashing in all the right places and although his character is quite unlikable at times, his teasing smile never fails to charm.

Main Cast

Tara Fitzgerald...Helen Graham
Toby Stephens...Gilbert Markham
Rupert Graves...Arthur Huntington
Sarah Badel...Rachel
Jackson Leach...Arthur Huntington, Jr.

Trivia

Toby Stephens and Tara Fitzgerald would go on to star together in another Brontë adaptation; the 2006 version of *Jane Eyre*. They were not love interests in that production, however: Fitzgerald played Eyre's evil aunt Mrs. Reed and Stephens played Edward Rochester (Jane Eyre's employer).

Toby Stephens is the son of British acting legend Maggie Smith.

What to Binge on Next

You're of course going to want to watch some more Brontë adaptations; my personal favorites are the 2009 version of *Wuthering Heights* (starring real-life couple Charlotte Riley and Tom Hardy) and the 2006 *Jane Eyre* (starring Ruth Wilson and Toby Stephens).

Tara Fitzgerald has appeared in many other television series and films that you might enjoy, among them *Requiem* (a mix of thriller and family drama) and the film *Brassed Off!*, in which she and Ewan McGregor play residents of a coal-mining town that is about to have its mine closed. You might also like Toby Stephens in the swashbuckling pirate series *Black Sails*.

In this adaptation the delectable Rupert Graves (nobody else makes being evil look so good) plays the playboy husband; in the adaptation *The Forsyte Saga* he plays "young" Jolyon Forsyte, who at first glance is also not a very good husband (he leaves his first wife for their nanny), but when married to the right woman, he proves himself to be a kind and loving spouse.

Tipping the Velvet

Run Time

Tipping the Velvet consists of three sixty-minute episodes, for a total run time of three hours. It was produced by the BBC and aired in 2002.

Creator and Writers

The story is based on (and quite faithfully follows) Sarah Waters's 1998 novel *Tipping the Velvet*. The screenplay was written by Andrew Davies.

What It's About

Eighteen-year-old Nancy Astley lives and works with her family in their oyster restaurant in Whitstable. Although her family is working-class, they enjoy a comfortable standard of living and Nan's family is loving, Nan can't help but feel that something is missing, particularly in her relationship with her young man, Freddie. When the family goes to see a show in the local theater and one of the acts is a "masher" (a popular type of female entertainer in Victorian times who dressed and performed songs as a male impersonator) named Miss Kitty Butler, Nan feels moved in a new way and begins to perceive what she has been missing in her relationships.

Nan and Kitty become friends and eventually leave Whitstable to perform in London. Soon they engage in a fully emotional and physical relationship, although Kitty wants to keep it a secret. After Nan takes a short visit home to see her family, she returns to find Kitty engaged to their male manager. She is heartbroken and leaves Kitty and show business.

Tumultuous years follow, including a stint where Nan dresses as a man and provides various sexual favors for men (although never allowing them to learn she is a woman) for money, and an interlude where she serves as a kept lover for an older woman, but eventually Nan finds a way to be truer to herself and to openly pursue the true love she needs. When she meets Kitty again (with Kitty wanting to resume their prior secret relationship), she has the strength to decide that that is no longer what she wants.

Why It's Bingeworthy

Waters's 1998 novel was well-received and won many awards, and many critics praised this adaptation for its faithfulness to the original book, as well

242

as for its portrayal of both the emotional and physical aspects of lesbian love affairs.

The program is acted wonderfully, with a strong cast in Rachael Stirling (as Nan), the incomparable Keeley Hawes (as Kitty), and Anna Chancellor (as Diana Lethaby). While the soundtrack is dated both the interior and exterior locations look very authentically Victorian, and the costumes are wonderful.

Main Cast

Rachael Stirling…Nan Astley
Keeley Hawes…Kitty Butler
Anna Chancellor…Diana Lethaby
Jodhi May…Florence Banner
John Bowe…Walter Bliss
Hugh Bonneville…Ralph Banner

Trivia

Author Sarah Waters appears as an extra in the film (as a member of the audience in one of the characters' performances).

In 2015 the novel was also adapted as a stage play and received rave reviews when it ran in London.

What to Binge on Next

In 2005 the BBC filmed another Sarah Waters adaptation; this time of her book *Fingersmith*, a complicated tale of female love and deception. Sally Hawkins, who had a small role in *Tipping the Velvet*, plays one of the main characters in this production. Another BBC drama, *The Secret Diaries of Miss Anne Lister*, features a main character who lived openly as a lesbian in nineteenth-century Yorkshire (and is based on actual diaries).

Screenwriter Andrew Davies is a one-man historical drama machine; his other projects include the adaptations *Pride and Prejudice* (the 1995 version, starring Jennifer Ehle and Colin Firth), *Wives and Daughters* (from the novel by Elizabeth Gaskell), and *Little Dorrit* (by Charles Dickens), among many, many others.

Under the Greenwood Tree

Run Time

This adaptation is more of a feature-length movie than it is a series; there are no separate episodes, and it is only ninety minutes long.

Creator and Writers

This film is adapted from the Thomas Hardy novel of the same name; it first aired on ITV in 2005. Ashley Pharaoh wrote the screenplay.

What It's About

The alternate title for this story could be "Local Girl Makes Good"—the local girl being Fancy Day, who is the daughter of the lowly local estate's groundskeeper, but who has been educated in the (relatively speaking) bright lights and big city of Exeter. When she returns to her hometown of Milwood, ready to fulfill her destiny of a good marriage, travel, and success, she finds herself being wooed by three very different men: the prosperous farmer/landowner Mr. Shinar, the erudite and cultured new vicar Parson Maybold, and the earthy and charming carrier (a Victorian version of a delivery person) Dick Dewy. Who will she choose?

Her father thinks she should marry for money. The pastor thinks she will be his partner in travel and church service. And Dick Dewy? He is determined to make her forget everything except their overwhelming chemistry, and the fact that since he has met her he has found the ambition to make something of himself and his family's business.

Why It's Bingeworthy

As if the names weren't enough to win you over to this program (Dick Dewy? Fancy Day? Subtlety, thy name is Thomas Hardy) its romance should be. Because it is much, much more romantic than it sounds. Sure, it's romance at the end of the nineteenth century, so you know it's going to end in a wedding, and the more prosaic women among you may be pulling for Fancy to choose either the vicar and world travel or the wealthy older man and a powerful position in the social order of the day, but everyone who's either young or young at heart is going to take one look at Dick Dewy as James Murray plays him and know, immediately and forever, who Fancy Day should really pick.

Over the course of the story the year turns from Christmas to spring to high summer to the autumn, and it's all photographed beautifully (which is fitting, considering that one of Thomas Hardy's recurring themes was nature and its beauty and power). This story also has something to say about change and the difficulties people faced adjusting to the new order of the coming Industrial Revolution over the more agrarian and slower-paced earlier world. And the music is great.

Main Cast

Keeley Hawes…Fancy Day
James Murray…Dick Dewy
Steve Pemberton…Farmer Shinar
Ben Miles…Parson Maybold

Trivia

Under the Greenwood Tree is one of the lesser known of Thomas Hardy's novels, but this is the third cinematic adaptation of it: earlier movies based on the story were produced in 1918 and 1929!

What to Binge on Next

This adaptation and story is actually not representative of most of Thomas Hardy's novels and adaptations; it's much, much lighter. Most of his stories are dark and are quite clear-eyed about the specific challenges facing women in his nineteenth-century era. Although much darker in tone, two other of his adaptations that examine the ascendance of industrial society over an agrarian one and the divisions between social classes are *The Mayor of Casterbridge* (check out the 2003 adaptation starring Ciarán Hinds and Juliet Aubrey) and *Far from the Madding Crowd* (I like the 1998 version with Nathaniel Parker and Paloma Baeza, but if you're looking for something more recent there's also a 2015 feature film starring Carey Mulligan and Matthias Schoenaerts).

At its heart *Under the Greenwood Tree* is just pure romance; another adaptation that will have you swept up in the love story between its principal characters is *North and South*, starring Richard Armitage and Daniela Denby-Ashe, about the love between a minister's daughter from the agrarian south of England and a cotton mill owner from the industrial north.

Vanity Fair

Run Time

There have been many, many adaptations of this story, but this 2018 version produced by ITV consists of seven episodes, each nearly an hour in length, making its total run time just a touch under seven hours.

Creator and Writers

Adapted from the popular novel by William Makepeace Thackeray, the program was executive-produced and the screenplay written by Gwyneth Hughes.

What It's About

Heirs and soldiers and women who want to marry them, oh my!

The heroine of this tale, if she can be called such, is Rebecca ("Becky") Sharp, a poor young woman who knows she will need to marry well if she is to have any comfort at all. To this end, she befriends a kind woman who also happens to be wealthy: Amelia ("Emmy") Sedley. The two get along just fine until a number of soldiers make their lives more complicated.

Emmy falls in love with an (unscrupulous) officer named George Osborne, while Becky sets out to marry Emmy's brother Joseph ("Jos"), a civil servant who has done well in the East India Company (and is therefore one of the richest men she has met). Becky is not successful in that marriage plan, but Emmy marries Osborne, even though another (better) military officer, William Dobbin, has fallen in love with her.

Battles and wars intervene, time passes, Becky makes an ill-advised marriage to a younger son in a rich household, Captain Rawdon Crawley (who ends up cut off from the family fortune because his aunt dislikes Becky), and both Emmy and Becky have sons, but their paths increasingly diverge. Eventually Becky ends up, destitute, in Germany, where she is discovered again by Emmy, Emmy's brother Jos, and William Dobbin (Emmy's husband George having died in battle many years before). Becky joins their group and is able to return home to England, where, very much against type, she helps Amelia recognize that her husband George did not really deserve Amelia's lifelong devotion, and that Amelia should consider accepting Dobbin's love.

Why It's Bingeworthy

First of all, there's about enough story material here for three movies, not just the one. And Olivia Cooke as Becky Sharp! Just when you think you've got her all figured out...she looks right at you (and she does; the character often breaks the "fourth wall" to directly address you) and you feel yourself having to re-evaluate her all over again.

It's always been a popular story, and it's been adapted many times (most recently in a 2004 film starring Reese Witherspoon, as well as in television adaptations in 1998, 1987, and 1967), so many people already know the story and will enjoy seeing it acted out with a more modern sensibility and with such lush costumes and settings.

Main Cast

Olivia Cooke...Becky Sharp
Claudia Jessie...Amelia Sedley
Charlie Rowe...George Osborne
Tom Bateman...Rawdon Crawley
Johnny Flynn...William Dobbin
Michael Palin...William Makepeace Thackeray

Trivia

Actor Olivia Cooke has admitted that when she was cast in the role of Becky Sharp, she didn't actually know that *Vanity Fair* was based on a novel. (When she learned that she did get a copy of the novel and read it!)

What to Binge on Next

This is a period drama, but it doesn't really feel like one. If you like its bold heroine and its modern sensibility, you might also consider other recent literary adaptations like *A Discovery of Witches* (based on the novel by Deborah Harkness), new Agatha Christie adaptations like *And Then There Were None* (2015) and *Ordeal by Innocence* (2018), and *A Very English Scandal* (2018), adapted from the novel by John Preston and starring Hugh Grant.

If you like your female protagonists as sharp as this Becky Sharp, you might also enjoy the Australian mystery series *Miss Fisher's Murder Mysteries*, featuring the thoroughly modern Phryne Fisher as an intrepid female detective in 1920s Melbourne.

The Way We Live Now

Run Time

The 2001 adaptation consists of four one-hour episodes for a total watch time of four hours.

Creator and Writers

The story is based on the novel of the same title by Anthony Trollope, and the screenplay was written by (who else?) Andrew Davies.

What It's About

Illustrious banker and financier Augustus Melmotte arrives in London with his daughter Marie and to much fanfare: he is seen as THE man to invest with, and all of London society moves to place their money in his care, while Sir Felix Carbury, a gambler and a wastrel (although a very charming one) makes plans to marry Marie.

One of Melmotte's many investment schemes is that of a railroad; he is aided in this venture by engineer Paul Montague, who seeks to help plan the railroad. Sir Felix also has a sister, Henrietta, whom Paul meets and with whom he falls in love, an attachment that is complicated by the fact that an American widow he had previously courted, Mrs. Hurtle, is in London and attempting to force him to marry her.

When it becomes clear that the railroad plan is no more than a scheme on paper designed to bilk investors out of their fortunes, the shares plummet and many tragic events are put into motion, although Paul Montague's decision to tell the truth about the railroad plan pays off with karma and allows him to find a happy ending.

Why It's Bingeworthy

Business is corrupt. Money rules. Society is hypocritical about interpersonal relationships, and pretty much everything else.

Sounds like today, doesn't it? Except it's not. It's how Anthony Trollope satirized the society he lived in when he first wrote his novel back in 1875.

Although concerned with issues of social class and marriage, this is a unique adaptation in its focus on nineteenth-century financial and business

248

shenanigans, which are all more interesting than you might think they could be. It's a lively program, full of greedy (and completely over-dramatic) characters, and with an undertone of Trollope's sly humor and clear-sighted view of society's less savory qualities running underneath.

The cast here is full of big stars: David Suchet stars as Melmotte, while Matthew Macfadyen turns in a thoroughly cad-like performance as Sir Felix Carbury, and always-energetic actor Shirley Henderson absolutely dominates the action as the naïve (but later the furious and merciless) Marie Melmotte.

Main Cast

David Suchet...Augustus Melmotte
Shirley Henderson...Marie Melmotte
Cheryl Campbell...Lady Carbury
Matthew Macfadyen...Sir Felix Carbury
Paloma Baeza...Henrietta Carbury
Cillian Murphy...Paul Montague
Miranda Otto...Mrs. Hurtle

Trivia

The diminutive Shirley Henderson, who plays the vengeful Marie Melmotte here, became more famous later for playing the school-age girl ghost Moaning Myrtle in the Harry Potter movies.

The director of this program, David Yates, would go on to direct several of the Harry Potter movie adaptations (including *Harry Potter and the Half-Blood Prince*).

This program won the 2002 BAFTA award for Best Drama Serial.

What to Binge on Next

Trollope is not adapted as often as some of his other Victorian contemporaries, but if you like this program you might also enjoy the program *He Knew He Was Right*, also by Trollope, and also something different, as its storyline is about a husband whose growing (and unfounded) mistrust of his wife leads to the failure of their marriage. Older miniseries also based on his works include *The Barchester Chronicles* (1982) and *The Pallisers* (1974).

One of the primary appeals of this program is watching David Suchet steal every scene he's in throughout it; to see Suchet in his signature role, as Agatha Christie's Belgian detective Hercule Poirot, you might also want to check out the long-running mystery series *Poirot*.

Another literary adaptation in which money plays a large part in the storyline is Charles Dickens's *Little Dorrit*, set primarily in the Marshalsea Debtors' Prison.

Jackie on...
Kids' Programs in the UK (Part Two)

The Magic Roundabout is a classic children's television programme that originally began in 1965, but has had several relaunches since. Many of the characters from this series have entered popular British culture - including Dylan the dopey rabbit, Ermintrude the motherly cow, and Zebedee, who bounces everywhere on a spring. The series gained cult status, with many people saying the characters were taking psychedelic drugs. Despite this, the series has been loved by generations of children who are unaware of these claims.

David Walliams is a British comedian who has written many books for children. Every Christmas one of his books is adapted for television and these have become an annual treat for the whole family. They are not festively themed, so can be enjoyed at any time of year. The most famous one is probably *The Boy in the Dress* which is about a boy exploring gender themes; but *Gangsta Granny*, *Billionaire Boy*, and *Mr. Stink* are also well loved.

Wives and Daughters

Run Time

This 1999 adaptation aired on BBC One and consisted of four seventy-five minute episodes, for a total run time of five hours.

Creator and Writers

The adaptation is based on the 1866 novel *Wives and Daughters* by Elizabeth Gaskell; the screenplay was written by Andrew Davies.

What It's About

Although Molly Gibson is widely considered around town to be a "poor motherless girl," she actually grows into a young woman who enjoys her life of relative independence (for a woman of the time) and keeping house for her father, the town's physician. Her cozy existence is upset, however, when her father meets a widow in distressed circumstances, thinks himself in love with her gentility and flattery, and marries her.

Suddenly Molly must conform to her stepmother Hyacinth's ideas of behavior befitting a lady, and her father slowly learns that a marriage made in haste is often repented of at leisure, as she is a woman demanding of both attention and resources. Thankfully Molly has a place of refuge: the local manor house and landed gentry family the Hamleys, who are wealthy but down-to-earth in their habits and attitudes (and most importantly, the unaffected love for Molly). While visiting them, Molly falls a bit in love with both of their sons: the elder, a poet who flunks out of Oxford, and eventually (and more lastingly) the younger, a naturalist.

The bright spot in Molly's new family arrangement is the arrival of her stepsister Cynthia, a high-spirited and lively companion for her, who nonetheless entangles herself in several both wise and unwise flirtations from which she often depends upon Molly to disentangle her.

Why It's Bingeworthy

This adaptation is vintage Gaskell: so sweet, so innocent, and yet with an understanding of the sometimes petty nature of the human heart as clear as crystal. Molly Gibson is every woman who's ever had a powerful crush, only to see the object of her affection lavishing all his attention on a lesser woman who doesn't even really return his devotion. You want to smack her male protagonists upside the head, you really do, but at some point you just roll your eyes and get over it and go back to loving them, even though they're idiots.

In my opinion Justine Waddell has never really achieved the recognition she deserves; she puts in a star turn here as Molly Gibson; sweet, but never so sweet that you don't like her. Likewise, this movie showcases a very young Keeley Hawes, who is great in everything she does but who is particularly charming here as the manipulative Cynthia.

Main Cast

Justine Waddell...Molly Gibson
Bill Paterson...Dr. Gibson
Francesca Annis...Mrs. Kirkpatrick
Keeley Hawes...Cynthia Kirkpatrick
Anthony Howell...Roger Hamley
Tom Hollander...Osborne Hamley
Michael Gambon...Squire Hamley

Trivia

More than 1,000 costumes were required during the filming of this series.

The novel on which this story is based was first published as a serial, and is Gaskell's final book: she died shortly before its completion in 1865, and the story was finished by Frederick Greenwood.

What to Binge on Next

The first adaptations you're going to want to track down after watching *Wives and Daughters* are the excellent recent versions of Elizabeth Gaskell's novels, including *North and South* and *Cranford*.

Another literary adaptation in which a man does not realize that the woman right under his nose is the best woman for him is *Little Dorrit*, based on Charles Dickens's novel.

Justine Waddell has appeared in several well-regarded literary adaptations; she is also the tragic central figure of Tess in the 1998 adaptation of *Tess of the D'urbervilles*, and plays Estella in the 1999 adaptation of Charles Dickens's *Great Expectations*.

Wolf Hall

Run Time

This program first ran on BBC Two in 2015 and aired for six hour-long episodes, for a total run time of six hours.

Creator and Writers

This adaptation is based on the historical novels *Wolf Hall* and *Bring Up the Bodies* by Hilary Mantel. The screenplay was written by Peter Straughan.

What It's About

Basically, the books and the movie detail the rise to power of Thomas Cromwell, minister to King Henry VIII, whose perhaps most infamous achievements are helping the king enter into his marriage to Anne Boleyn, and then, later, helping him exit it as well (which was accomplished, of course, by Anne's exiting the world by the king's order of execution).

In between those two events there are many hours' worth of Cromwell's recollections of how he first met Cardinal Wolsey (an earlier advisor to the king), won favor for himself after Wolsey's downfall, his engineering of the king's marriage to Anne Boleyn and his machinations to encourage Sir Thomas More to accept the match, and many other political and interpersonal twists and turns at the court and with Henry himself.

Why It's Bingeworthy

If you see *Wolf Hall*, the novel, you might be wondering how anyone could adapt it into a mere six-hour story (the books are what they call "doorstoppers"—they're big!). One very nice thing about this excellent adaptation is that now you can act like you've read two very well-regarded books, and save yourself the time of actually doing so.

This series was also hugely critically popular (and did well in the ratings, too), gaining particularly strong reviews for its faithful adaptation of the novels, its period detail, and the high-quality costuming, sets, and acting.

Main Cast

Mark Rylance...Thomas Cromwell
Damian Lewis...King Henry VIII

Claire Foy…Anne Boleyn
Bernard Hill…Duke of Norfolk

Trivia

The program was nominated for three Golden Globe awards and won the 2015 Golden Globe for Best Miniseries or Television Film.

This is not the first time actor Mark Rylance has played a role in a Tudor drama. In the feature film *The Other Boleyn Girl* he played Anne Boleyn's father.

This adaptation is reported to have cost £7 million to produce.

What to Binge on Next

There are any number of television series and movies that also focus on the Tudor era in history. If you liked *Wolf Hall*, you might also consider the excellent miniseries about his daughter, Queen Elizabeth I, from her youth to her death: *The Virgin Queen*, starring Anne-Marie Duff and (a very young and pre-huge-Hollywood-stardom) Tom Hardy. Also of interest might be the sexy (and perhaps not very historically accurate, starting with the slim physique of Jonathan Rhys-Meyers as Henry VIII) series *The Tudors*. The documentary series *Six Wives with Lucy Worsley*, presented by historian Lucy Worsley, is also a great overview of the King's six wives and the history of the period.

In this program Damian Lewis plays Henry VIII, not really the kindest or most loving of husbands. In the miniseries *The Forsyte Saga*, based on the novels by John Galsworthy, he also plays a controlling and unpleasant husband in Victorian-era England.

If you're fascinated by the political machinations in this program, you might also consider the more modern-day and still very complex political thriller *House of Cards* (the British 1990 program, starring Ian Richardson, not the 2013 Kevin Spacey version). Never watch an American program when there's a British alternative to be had.

Jackie on...
Three Literary Adaptations
You Should Start With

Pride and Prejudice

Nothing is more British than a Jane Austen novel, so if you're looking to watch your first British literary adaptation you have to start with *Pride and Prejudice*. Portrayals of Mr Darcy don't get better than the one by Colin Firth in this classic—especially the lake scene! You can't fault the acting or sets either. This is literary adaptation gold!

Tipping the Velvet

Sarah Waters is one of my favourite authors so it's no surprise that I love this literary adaptation. This tale of a Victorian lesbian love affair is sensitively portrayed, with beautiful costumes and fantastic acting. The sexual content might be too much for some, but I was impressed by the tenderness of those scenes. The plot was compelling and, as with most of Sarah Waters's stories, you never quite know what will happen next.

Wolf Hall

Hilary Mantel's *Wolf Hall* won the Booker Prize in 2009. This beautifully crafted adaption brings the book to life. The costumes are amazing and the acting superb. Everything's shot atmospherically, giving an imposing mood to the series that works well. It's perfect for anyone looking for a more nuanced take on the well-known and often-portrayed Tudor period of history.

Appendix 1
Appendix 2
Lists
Index

Appendix I: A Word about Doctor Who

There is perhaps no British television show that is more famous or has been seen by more viewers, domestically and internationally, than the science fiction program *Doctor Who*.

So why doesn't it have its own chapter here?

Well, for one thing, and you might consider this highly ironic, as I just wrote an entire book about British television and how much I love it, I've never really been a very big *Doctor Who* fan.

Which is not to say that the program doesn't have a place in my heart. When I was just a young farm girl, stuck in the Midwest and with only three network channels and PBS to watch, every now and then on Saturday afternoons I could catch glimpses of the 1985 series of *Doctor Who*, starring none other than Peter Davison. I was only eleven or so at the time, but all the same, dapper Peter Davison with his cricket sweater and celery stalk boutonniere awakened a monster-sized crush within my pre-pubescent self. I really should go back and watch that series in its entirety.

Because there is so much great British television to watch, I quite simply have just not had the time to view all or most of the *Doctor Who* series. In addition to those few Peter Davison episodes, I did watch the entire 2005 rebooted series, featuring Christopher Eccleston as the Doctor, and I watched at least two of the series in which David Tennant appeared as the tenth doctor. And then? I just kind of ran out of interest, although given world enough and time, I'd like to polish off all of the "new" series, up to and including the latest one, starring Jodie Whittaker as the first female Doctor.

Below you will find information on the "new" series of *Doctor Who*, starting with the Christopher Eccleston season and working forward. For older series, there are any number of other books (also listed below) and websites that can help you decide which classic series you want to watch, who people consider the "best" Doctor, and all sorts of other information and trivia. Getting involved with *Doctor Who*, you'll find, is kind of a lifetime job. But it's good work if you can get it.

Doctor Who Series Since the 2005 Reboot

Ninth Doctor: Christopher Eccleston was the first new Doctor in the "Revival Era" (according to Wikipedia), and appeared in one series of thirteen episodes in 2005.

Tenth Doctor: David Tennant took over the role from Eccleston starting in 2006, and appeared in three series of thirteen episodes each, along with five slightly longer Christmas specials.

Eleventh Doctor: In 2010 Matt Smith started his run as the Doctor, and he also appeared in three series of thirteen episodes each, along with two Christmas specials.

Twelfth Doctor: Peter Capaldi became the twelfth Doctor Who in 2014, and appeared in three series of twelve episodes each.

Thirteenth Doctor: *Doctor Who* finally joined the modern age when its Doctor regenerated as a woman, played by Jodie Whittaker, for the series that began airing in 2018.

Books about *Doctor Who*

Burk, Graeme, and Robert Smith. *The Doctors Are In: The Essential and Unofficial Guide to Doctor Who's Greatest Time Lord*. ECW Press, 2015.

Campbell, Mark. *Doctor Who: The Episode Guide*. Pocket Essentials, 2007.

Doctor Who: Essential Guide to Fifty Years of Doctor Who. Penguin Books, 2013.

Farrow, Joanna. *Doctor Who: The Official Cookbook*. Harper Design, 2016.

Gibson, Annabel. *Doctor Who: Character Encyclopedia*. DK Publishing, 2013.

Hearn, Marcus: *Doctor Who, the Vault: Treasures from the First Fifty Years*. Harper Design, 2013.

Kistler, Alan. *Doctor Who: A History*. Lyons Press, 2013.

Loborik, Jason. *Doctor Who: The Visual Dictionary*. DK Publishing, 2014.

Appendix 2:

Jackie on Five TV Shows Every Brit Knows

Broadchurch is a crime drama set in a small, fictional coastal town. Through word-of-mouth, it slowly gained popularity and series three was one of the most watched crime dramas in the UK in recent history. *Broadchurch* began with the murder of an eleven-year-old boy and the investigations led people to suspect many of their neighbours of involvement in the crime. The combination of this suspicion with the continual barrage of media coverage gave a realistic insight into how a crime impacts a typical British community.

The series was widely discussed in the media, with people coming up with variety of theories about what might have happened. There was complete secrecy around the plot and even the cast were kept in the dark until the last minute.

West Bay in Dorset, where parts of the series were filmed, has become a tourist attraction, with people travelling miles just to photograph themselves next to the famous cliffs. *Broadchurch* is worth watching for the beautiful scenery alone, but it also has one of the most gripping plots you're likely to come across. You'll want to watch it with a few friends, as some of the plot twists are so clever you'll need to talk about them!

Cold Feet is a comedy drama which follows the lives of three couples from Manchester as they negotiate a range of difficulties - including affairs, work problems, and parenthood. The programme first aired for five series, from 1997 to 2003. After a break of thirteen years, it returned to show how the couples were coping with their teenaged kids and life in the digital age.

The longevity of this series means that it has a special place in the heart of the British TV audience. Many people have seen these characters develop over the decades and feel a deep emotional connection with them. Over the years, *Cold Feet* has tackled difficult subjects, including male depression, teen pregnancy, and the challenge of caring for elderly relatives. This makes it sound like a depressing show, but it also has many funny moments.

Doctor Who is a television classic. It first aired in 1963 and since then has evolved through 26 seasons, with thirteen different actors playing "the Doctor". It is a science fiction drama in which the characters travel through time to prevent terrible things from happening in the future, whilst also protecting Earth from alien creatures.

Doctor Who plays an important role in British culture. Whilst it could be said to have a cult following, the themes of Doctor Who are familiar to every British person, whether they watch the programme or not; references to the dustbin-shaped daleks or the Doctor's sonic screwdriver pop-up in many other areas. You might not want to watch all 800+ episodes, but it's worth seeing enough to understand the themes that every British person has grown to know and love.

The Great British Bake Off is a reality show in which a group of amateur bakers gather in a tent and compete to produce the best cakes, breads and pies. It is now in its ninth series and remains one of the most watched programmes on British TV.

The wonderful thing about *Bake Off* is the camaraderie between the contestants. Despite the fact that the worst baker leaves at the end of each episode, there is no animosity between them. They laugh at their mistakes, but also show pride when they achieve a spectacular bake, and each week viewers learn a little bit more about the bakers. It is a feel-good show which will inspire any viewer to attempt a bit of baking. It's also the perfect programme for anyone wanting to learn more about British innuendo

The Vicar of Dibley is a sitcom set in a small English village - where the arrival of a new woman vicar challenges the community to do things differently. The eccentric locals soon come to love their new vicar's style, and her genuine care for everyone is heart-warming. One of the greatest appeals of the show is that the entire family can sit down and watch it together - a factor which made its Christmas specials particularly popular.

The gentle humour is typically British, with much of it focusing on the differences between the classes of society. The series ran from 1994 to 1998, and although parts of it feel slightly dated now, it is still well worth watching today.

Lists

Comedies You Can Watch in Under Twelve Hours
Black Books
Detectorists
Fawlty Towers
Gavin & Stacey
The Inbetweeners
The IT Crowd
Moone Boy
The Office
Reggie Perrin
Spaced
Spy

Comedies Featuring Romance
As Times Goes By
Coupling
Gavin & Stacey
Him & Her
Lovesick
May to December
Miranda
To the Manor Born
Vicious

Comedies Featuring Jobs and the Working World
Are You Being Served?
Black Books
The IT Crowd
Miranda
The Office
Reggie Perrin
Spy
Toast of London
The Vicar of Dibley

Comedies Featuring Physical Humor
Blackadder
Black Books
Dad's Army
Father Ted
Fawlty Towers
Keeping Up Appearances

Miranda
Mr. Bean
The Vicar of Dibley

Sketch Comedy Programs
A Bit of Fry and Laurie
The Catherine Tate Show
French & Saunders
Little Britain
Man Stroke Woman
The Mighty Boosh
That Mitchell and Webb Look
Monty Python's Flying Circus

Dramas Featuring Romance
Ballykissangel
Bob & Rose
Call the Midwife
Casanova
Cold Feet
The Crown
Cucumber
Daniel Deronda
Doc Martin
Downton Abbey
The Durrells in Corfu
Emma
The Forsyte Saga
Jane Eyre
Last Tango in Halifax
Mansfield Park
Middlemarch
Monarch of the Glen
North and South
Northanger Abbey
Outlander
Persuasion
Poldark
Pride and Prejudice
Robin Hood
Sense and Sensibility
Sparkhouse
Stella
The Tenant of Wildfell Hall

The Tudors
Tipping the Velvet
Under the Greenwood Tree
Victoria
William and Mary
Wives and Daughters
Wuthering Heights

Dramas Featuring Jobs and the Working World
All Creatures Great and Small
The Bletchley Circle
Call the Midwife
Cucumber
Doc Martin
Hornblower
Hotel Babylon
Hustle
Kavanagh QC
Lark Rise to Candleford
MI-5
Miss Austen Regrets
The Paradise
The Secret Diary of a Call Girl
Mr. Selfridge
Silk
Trust Me
The Way We Live Now

"Coming of Age" Programs
Brideshead Revisited
Derry Girls
The Inbetweeners
The Misfits
Moone Boy
Outnumbered
Shameless
Skins
Tipping the Velvet
Wives and Daughters
The Young Offenders

Programs Featuring Friendships
Absolutely Fabulous
All Creatures Great and Small

Ballykissangel
Being Human
Black Books
Brideshead Revisited
Call the Midwife
Cold Feet
Coupling
Dad's Army
Death in Paradise
Detectorists
Extras
Father Ted
Fresh Meat
Gavin & Stacey
The Good Life
Hornblower
Hustle
Inspector Lewis
The I.T. Crowd
Jeeves & Wooster
Lark Rise to Candleford
Men Behaving Badly
Miranda
Moone Boy
Murder in Suburbia
New Tricks
Our Friends in the North
Peep Show
Robin Hood
Scott & Bailey
Sherlock
Spaced
Waiting for God
The Wrong Mans

Horror/Supernatural
Being Human
Black Mirror
Dead Set
Good Omens
In the Flesh
Jekyll
The Living and the Dead
The Misfits

Penny Dreadful
Primeval
The Secret of Crickley Hall

Programs Featuring Communities/Ensemble Casts
All Creatures Great and Small
Ballykissangel
Blackpool
Broadchurch
Call the Midwife
Cranford
Cucumber
Doc Martin
Father Brown
Grantchester
Lark Rise to Candleford
Midsomer Murders
Monarch of the Glen
Mr. Selfridge
Robin Hood
Shameless

Programs Featuring "Underdogs"
Being Human
Black Books
Case Histories
Dad's Army
Death in Paradise
Detectorists
Extras
Father Ted
Hetty Wainthropp Investigates
The I.T. Crowd
Keeping Up Appearances
Miranda
Moone Boy
New Tricks
The Office
One Foot in the Grave
Only Fools and Horses
Red Dwarf
Reggie Perrin
Robin Hood
Shameless

Spaced
Spy
Toast of London
Vera
The Vicar of Dibley
Waiting for God
The Wrong Mans

Programs with Political Themes
The Amazing Mrs. Pritchard
Bodyguard
House of Cards
MI-5
The New Statesman
State of Play
Yes, Minister
Yes, Prime Minister

Lone Wolf Police Procedurals
Case Histories
Endeavour
The Fall
Inspector Morse
Jack Taylor
Luther
Marcella
Prime Suspect
Prime Suspect: Tennison
Rebus
A Touch of Frost
Vera

Literary Adaptations You Can Watch in Under Four Hours
Casanova
The Moonstone
North and South
Sense and Sensibility
The Tenant of Wildfell Hall
Tipping the Velvet
Under the Greenwood Tree
The Way We Live Now

Index

271

272

273

Sarah Cords has worked as a farm market vendor, waitress, barista, librarian, book indexer, brand blogger, and fact-checker. She is the author of *The Real Story: A Guide to Nonfiction Reading Interests* (2006) and *Now Read This III: A Guide to Mainstream Fiction* (with Nancy Pearl, 2010). She lives in Wisconsin and her main goal in life is to teach her kids to appreciate the humor in *Keeping Up Appearances*.

Jackie Bailey worked as an analytical chemist for several major pharmaceutical companies before having children. Whilst they were young she became an online bookseller and reviewer (farmlanebooks.co.uk). She recently founded a company (umami-chef.co.uk) producing koji, the starter material for miso and a range of other Japanese fermented foods. She lives in Worcestershire, England, and loves TV comedy dramas like *Cold Feet*.

CPSIA information can be obtained
at www.ICGtesting.com
Printed in the USA
LVHW041530010320
648616LV00010B/597